Idioms of Inquiry

SUNY Series in Political Theory:
Contemporary Issues

John G. Gunnell, Editor

Idioms of Inquiry

Critique and Renewal
in Political Science

Edited by TERENCE BALL

State University of New York Press

Published by
State University of New York Press, Albany

© 1987 State University of New York

For information, address State University of New York
Press, State University Plaza, Albany, N.Y., 12246

Library of Congress Cataloging in Publication Data

Idioms of inquiry

(SUNY series in political theory. Contemporary issues)

Includes index.
1. Political science—Philosophy.   I. Ball, Terence.
II. Series.
JA71.135   1987   320′01   86-23033
ISBN 0-88706-457-4
ISBN 0-88706-458-2 (pbk.)

10 9 8 7 6 5 4 3 2

Contents

Preface

My aim in commissioning these essays has been twofold. It is first of all critical: despite our other differences, we are agreed that former modes of political inquiry have yielded less than was once hoped for and are now largely exhausted. My second and more important aim is ultimately constructive: We want to suggest several alternative ways to talk and therefore to think about and practice political inquiry. By introducing and exploring these alternative idioms of inquiry, we hope to contribute something of value to the continuing conversation regarding not only how politics is to be understood but also how it is to be practiced. That is, we want to emphasize that the questions raised here, far from being of an abstractly academic character, have a bearing not only on our practices as political inquirers but as political agents and citizens as well.

I would like to express my special thanks to the editor of this series, John G. Gunnell, for his early encouragement and subsequent patience. My thanks also to Michele Martin of State University of New York Press for her uncommon tact and editorial expertise and to Judith Block for her help in seeing this project through its final phase. My most heartfelt thanks must be reserved for the contributors, who agreed to join, and then steadfastly stayed with, this slow and sometimes balky enterprise.

Introduction

I

Political scientists exhibit a recurrent and almost obsessive interest in the state of their discipline (Finifter 1983; Nelson 1983). And when the patient's temperature and pulse are taken, its condition is almost always revealed to be even worse than was originally expected. Political science, it is said, suffers from a variety of ailments. It is afflicted with wild mood swings ranging from euphoria to listlessness, depression, and a lack of direction; it has failed to become a genuine science; it is compartmentalized into hermetically sealed subfields and further bifurcated into those that are normative and those that are empirical. The poor patient is, in short, in mortal peril. Having been thus diagnosed, however, the patient is periodically pumped up with shots in the arm, kicks in the pants, or — more recently — the miracle cure afforded by this or that new paradigm. The realization that yesterday's miracle drugs look suspiciously like snake oil only adds to the widely shared sense of malaise.

To this already extensive list of ills, I would like to add two others: hypochondria and amnesia. We political scientists have an unhealthy obsession with the health of our discipline and a misplaced faith in fixes and cures. Our amnesia arises from our foreshortened sense of history. We cut ourselves off from our own history in any number of ways, one of them being our penchant for dividing our past into two periods. The first, and by far the longest, is the Dark Age before behavioralism, in which superstition reigned, statistics had not yet been invented, empirical questions were entangled in normative ones, and the state rewarded political inquirers by giving them hemlock instead of research grants. That benighted past being happily behind us, we need not ponder its possible relevance to our present enlightened age. The recent history of our discipline is all the history we need to know.

1

That foreshortened history is revealing, less for the methodological breakthroughs it yielded than for the militaristic metaphors once used to describe it. Before the "Behavioral Revolution" of the late 1950s and early 1960s could be consolidated into a legitimate regime, there occurred, not a counterrevolution launched by disgruntled traditionalists, but a revolution within the revolution. In the epistemological and methodological battles fought during the 1960s and 1970s between behavioralists and their post-behavioral critics, no one was killed (although there were rumors that some had been bored to death), but many were wounded. Wounds were inflicted upon some people's pride or, more often, their patience. Behavioralists who, as revolutionaries, had been eager to debate philosophical issues wanted to get on with their research, unburdened by philosophical disputes; their critics insisted on debating and berating them in the idiom of philosophy.

Theirs was not, however, the empiricist-*cum*-positivist philosophical idiom on which most behavioralists had been weaned, but the newer post-positivist philosophy of science and the philosophy of language, action, and meaning as well. Nagel and Hempel were out of favor; Toulmin, Kuhn, Feyerabend, Lakatos, and Laudan were in. Later still, in the late 1970s and early 1980s, behavioralists were bewildered or bored (or both) by their critics' repeated references to Gadamer's hermeneutics, Habermas's Critical Theory, and to French deconstructionists, post-structuralists, and other similarly suspicious continental characters with farfetched ideas and unpronounceable names. Faced with foreign competitors speaking in strange and incomprehensible tongues that they did not know or care to learn, many mainstream political scientists were content to adopt a protectionist policy of intellectual isolationism.

That they should have done so is not altogether surprising. Much the same sort of thing happened earlier when behavioralist revolutionaires dismissed their elders' old-fashioned historical and institutional approach to the study of politics. To take but one example among many, consider what happened to the concept of the state. During the 1950s and 1960s, those who were wont to speak in the traditional idiom of the politics of the state were told that their language was outmoded. The state, it was said, is out of date and should therefore be supplanted by the more scientific idiom of structural-functionalism and General Systems Theory, in which the political system appeared only as one among several sub-systems (Easton 1953, 1965). By the early 1980s, however, the state was back with a vengeance born of two decades of contempt (Carnoy 1984), leaving older behavioralists to lament the theoretical heresies of the young (Easton 1981).

This and many other small incidents are part of a larger story. The history of political thought — in which the behavioral revolution and its aftermath comprises only one of the more recent episodes — is the story of older orthodoxies being criticized and replaced by revolutionary challengers. The revolutionaries, in their turn, come to be the guardians of a new orthodoxy, which is, in its turn, challenged by critics. What Isaiah Berlin says of the history of human thought is perhaps particularly apposite in the history of political inquiry: "The history of thought and culture is a changing pattern of great liberating ideas which inevitably turn into suffocating straitjackets" (1979, 159). And yet, despite the brief but incandescent appearance of post-behavioralism and subsequent challengers, the behavioral strait jacket still seems to be quite firmly in place. No one — not even latter-day behavioralists — seems to be especially enthusiastic about this turn of events. How then are we to account for this apparent lack of progress?

A number of explanations can be offered, one of which has to do with institutional inertia. Once ensconced in large bureaucratic institutions like the modern multiversity, old orthodoxies are hard to challenge, much less replace. In addition, graduate education today tends to be in the hands of yesterday's revolutionaries. Still concerned to keep the faith pure and to guard the memory of the revolution, they create the young in their own image. And the young, in their turn, become the guardians of a once bright but now ossified vision. More mundanely, though no less significantly, research funds allocated today are apt to go for the same types of projects which were supported yesterday. Each of these factors acts as a drag upon change, and, viewed as explanations, each is doubtless valid, if only in part. Various other explanations are also available (Ball 1987). But I would like to suggest one possible explanation to which scant attention has so far been paid.

II

I mentioned earlier the policy of intellectual isolationism and protectionism adopted by guardians of the older behavioralist orthodoxy. It is, no doubt, easy enough to blame them for their narrow-mindedness, their short-sightedness, their parochialism, and much else besides. I want to suggest, however, that the fault may not be theirs alone, for their critics' voices were often strident, their tone often hectoring, and their attitude too often contemptuous. On this I can speak with some authority, for I was, and remain, one of these critics. Although a bit mellower with advancing age, I remain convinced that political science is not immune to — and its practitioners cannot escape from — philosophical, methodological, and moral questions about their science's presuppositions, practices, and implications. I am no less convinced that we failed

4

to communicate this message to skeptical or suspicious colleagues. And at least one of the reasons for our failure was that we did not heed what I take to be the main message of modern hermeneutics and of classical politics. Communities, including the communities of inquiry that we presumably inhabit, are communicatively constituted; they exist only insofar as their members continue to converse, in a civilized manner, within a context of differences (Gadamer 1975, 1976). The proper attitude is less one of live and let live than of talking and listening. Mutual understanding is a matter of translating from one idiom into another. This we largely failed to do. Instead of attempting to be reasonably civilized conversational partners, we proceeded like debaters eager to score points. The points were scored easily enough; but that should never have been our aim in the first place.

For better or worse, we teach and write within, and for fellow members of, a particular discipline. We therefore cannot afford to be ignorant or intolerant of any of the voices in what, presumably, is a common conversation. Yet it remains true that civilized conversation, far from precluding criticism, actually invites it. Indeed, criticism — not imitation — is the sincerest form of flattery. To take someone seriously enough to engage them in conversation is a compliment and to trouble to criticize their views an even higher compliment — a Socratic compliment, so to speak. There are at least two ways in which the conversation can be joined. The first consists of exposing contradictions and incoherencies in idioms heretofore unexamined and presumed to be coherent (Ball 1983). The second is to demonstrate what it might mean to speak in other, alternative idioms (White 1985). Since Socrates, both strategies have been definitive of the domain and intent of political theory. Both are amply evident in the following essays.

Far from speaking with a single voice, the contributors to the present volume speak in their own voices and in distinctly different idioms. These contrasting idioms of inquiry — rational-choice, realist, hermeneutical, critical-theoretical, Popperian, feminist, and Foucauldian — should not obscure our most important point of agreement. The old orthodoxy is no longer viable (if, indeed, it ever was) and should, we believe, be criticized and, if possible, supplanted — though not by any new orthodoxies. Despite our differences, we are united in our conviction that political inquiry is irreducibly heterodox. It is, indeed, more like a conversation than a monologue.

Each of us attempts to take a particular idiom of inquiry in its own terms, testing its plausbility and tracing its internal limitations. We attempt to show what older problems and issues might look like if they are recast and redescribed in alternative idioms or vocabularies. We want, in Richard Rorty's words, to suggest that "scientific breakthroughs are not so much a matter of deciding which of various alternative hypotheses are true, but of finding the right jargon in which to frame hypotheses in the first place . . ." (1982, 193). And, not least, we want to show how political inquiry and analysis is implicated in and contributes to political life. The complexities and contradictions of the latter are, inevitably, mirrored in the former. Although it is true that theorizing necessarily involves a certain amount of simplifying, it is no less true that an oversimplified, abstract, and ahistorical social science does violence to the richly textured reality with which we must deal, not only as scientists but also as agents and citizens. If we are to play these roles well, we will need the knowledge, the insight, and perhaps the chastening of a less orthodox, more open, less complacent, and more critical science of politics. These, then, are the convictions that motivate our common conversation in this volume.

III

Our conversation proceeds in the following way. If we are to speak of progress (or the lack thereof) in political science, we need to employ an idiom which includes criteria for determining what is to count as progressive. In the opening essay, I attempt to show how the search for such criteria led post-positivist philosophers of science to become historians and sociologists of science from whom social scientists, and political scientists in particular, might gain some insight into the historical dimension of their own discipline. Not the least of the lessons to be learned is that the older positivist distinction between empirical and normative theory is impossible to sustain and that a rapprochement between political science and political philosophy is not only possible but necessary.

Because political science has yet to enter its own post-positivist phase, the essay by James Farr begins by questioning the remaining vestiges of the older positivist orthodoxy. For Farr, the alternative idiom of situational analysis, as adapted from the work of Sir Karl Popper, promises to supply satisfactory explanations of at least some political phenomena. These explanations are especially satisfying insofar as they succeed in exhibiting puzzling or problematic actions as rational acts, given specific circumstances as understood by the agent or actor herself. Farr's focus on the self-understandings of political agents is the touchstone to which all of our contributors repeatedly return, albeit in different ways and in quite different idioms.

Following up on the theme of rationality, Russell Hardin shows how rational choice theories conceive of "rationality" in radically different ways. Indeed, these theories offer not a single unified idiom of inquiry but competing and possibly incompatible dialects. Depending upon which rationality assumptions are adopted, agents whose behavior is held to be wholly rational and explicable from one theoretical perspective might not be so considered from another. In the rational choice idiom, anomalies arise when we attempt to advance explanations that are both formally coherent and empirically well-corroborated. Thus, the once highly touted hope that the rational choice idiom might result in formalized mathematical models which are at once elegant and realistic is shown to be rather implausible at present.

The situations in which political agents act are, of course, often difficult ones for the inquirer to characterize. More often than not, finding the correct (or most appropriate) characterization is not only a matter of discovering agents' aims and intentions but of grasping the meaning that an act or situation holds for the actor. As I attempt to show in my second essay, political agents are self-interpreting animals whose actions must be explained in light of their own self-understandings. Any social science which attempts this must therefore begin (if not end) by being an interpretive or hermeneutical one whose methods are more closely akin to textual interpretation and criticism than to chemistry or physics.

The preceding idioms are alike in presupposing a particular conception of rationality — namely, a means/end or instrumental view involving conscious agents, meaningful alternatives among ends, and viable choices among means to those ends. Yet, if political science is to be genuinely critical social science, Stephen White argues, it cannot be content to presuppose such a simple strategic view of rationality and human agency. Building upon the work of Jürgen Habermas and the tradition of Critical Theory, White sketches and illustrates the core of an alternative research program in which the concept of communicative rationality is central. Given this research program, it then becomes possible to construct the concepts constitutive of political discourse and inquiry — power, for example, and modernization — in ways that enable the theory's audience or addressees to see through and to emancipate themselves from the forces that oppress them. Thus, the kind of understanding that a critical social science makes possible is a critical understanding of agency, situation, and self.

Critical Theory has not been without its critics, one of the most formidable of whom was, as Michael Gibbons notes, the late Michel Foucault. According to Foucault, hermeneutics and Critical Theory are alike in helping to create the sort of self-scrutinizing, transparent subject required by the disciplinary or carceral society. Gibbons argues, against Foucault, that the capacity for social and self-criticism is deeply constitutive of any conception of political action and moral agency. Hence, any social science that fails to recognize these constituent elements of human action can hardly hope to describe, much less explain, it. To this degree, at least, a hermeneutical conception of political inquiry is vindicated.

Yet, as various structuralists and their post-structuralist successors remind us, human agents act in a world constituted by large-scale social structures that are not the products of anyone's plan or intention. Political decisions are taken, and power exercised, within the restricted spaces delineated by these structures. Human agents are reduced to role-bearers, whose aims and intentions are shaped by the structures within which they are socialized and in whose terms they interpret the meanings of their own and others' actions. If this is so, several things logically seem to follow. First, agents are the creations of structures, not the other way around. Thus, agents' intentions, far from being primary, are actually artifacts of larger-scale structures beyond the agent's ken or control. Third, the social meanings on which interpretive inquiry focuses are, at the very least, less central than the structures within which they are spawned and whose purposes they may serve.

For all their criticisms of positivism and empiricism, the structuralist and post-structuralist perspectives share with their *bêtes noires* a suspicion of the interpretive or hermeneutical idiom. The political inquirer appears to be impaled on the horns of a dilemma. On the one horn, we have the subject-centered idiom of hermeneutics, and, on the other, some sort of (ostensibly objective) inquirer-centered idiom. Must one then choose between them? Not at all, argues Fred Dallmayr. What is needed, he maintains, is to move beyond the equally cloying idioms of "empiricism" and "hermeneutics" to a third, more genuinely synthetic idiom which he (following Anthony Giddens) calls "structuration." Avoiding antinomies of all sorts, structuration attempts to reconcile agency and structure, in part by focusing on human beings as language-using communicators. Just as there can be no human society without language and no language without speakers, neither can there be structures without agents (and vice versa). Thus, structures not only constrain agents, but they make meaningful action possible as well. Agents, in their turn, reproduce — and, on occasion, criticize and change — these structures. From this synthetic perspective, agency and structure are seen to be not so much causally related (in one direction or the other) as they are mutually constitutive of social practices and political possibilities.

Although not often viewed as allies, one contemporary school of metascience, "realism," shares several things in common with structuralist and post-structuralist perspectives on political inquiry. Both are critical of classical "atomistic" empiricism; both are critical of interpretivism; and both place primary emphasis on the ways in which relations between social subjects are systematically structured. As Jeffrey Isaac notes, it is simplistic at best and false at worst to conceptualize political relations in terms of observable relations between individuals. It is misleading, for example, to view power as a relation between individual agents (or, as Hobbes would have it, between an active "agent" and a passive "patient"). They do not meet as individuals but as actors located within a web of larger, relatively stable and enduring social structures which they did not create and over which they have little, if any, control. It is by virtue of their location within larger structures of relations that political agents have and exercise power. Metascientific realists resolve the agency/structure problem by maintaining that agents and agencies, natural and social alike, have certain inherent causal capacities or "powers" operating through structurally embedded "mechanisms" that the social sciences must discover and describe. In the modern world, says Isaac, not the least of these relatively enduring structures is the state, which thereby returns yet again, this time under the rubric of realism. A realist perspective also allows us to view the study of political ideas and ideologies in a newer and more illuminating light. Political ideas are seen to be neither disembodied irrelevancies nor expressions of individual intention, but are an ineliminable feature of the legitimation and critique of linguistically structured social practices.

Like Foucault and other post-structuralists, realists are wont to view power relations in situational terms, where the situations are (*pace* Popper) linguistically constrained and structurally specified. And both, along with Critical Theory, are interested in the ways in which these appear in historically specific settings and are addressed to particular audiences.

One such setting and audience, as Kathy Ferguson notes, is the tightly structured and relatively enduring setting in which women (and men) have had their "place." Taking her cue from Foucault, Ferguson attempts to show how particular conceptions of political inquiry have helped to legitimate and reinforce certain conceptions of political life. For Foucault, social science, as previously practiced, has been a form of carceral or disciplinary discourse through which the world that we know and inhabit has been constituted, codified, and legitimated. It is an idiom in which science and expertise, knowledge and power, discipline and control, are fused. Following up on this Foucauldian theme, Ferguson shows how political science has heretofore constituted its object via an unexamined "male-ordered" idiom. The picture of political inquiry, and of political life, emerging from this idiom or discourse is distorted in subtle and systematic ways. An alternative feminist discourse, she suggests, would disclose another world with distinctly different possibilities for human communication and cooperation. Like White and Gibbons,

Ferguson holds out the hope that our capacity for critical reflection may yet transform not only political inquiry but political life as well.

It is tempting to suppose that we might one day meet, not as socially constructed men and women or, indeed, as role-bearers of any kind, but as mutually transparent truth-tellers. The vision of a society, in which human communication is undistorted and cooperation is enhanced by social subjects who are as transparent to others as to themselves, is not altogether novel. In one version or another, the vision of mutual transparency is as old as Rousseau and Marx and as recent as Habermas and G.A. Cohen. If our actions and relations were transparent, there would then be no need for a social science, because nothing would be hidden and we would already know everything we need to know in order to live a life free from oppression of all sorts. In the concluding essay, Donald Moon argues that the hope of attaining such transparency is both incoherent and unrealizable, thereby defending the claims of a suitably critical social science, deflating Habermas's more utopian hopes, and allaying Foucault's worst fears in one fell swoop.

On this chastening note our conversation comes not to an end, exactly, but to a pause. It might be worth pausing to consider a number of questions, among them the following. How do the different idioms of inquiry conceive of explanation or of understanding? How do they construct agents, agency, rationality, intentionality, and meaning? How do they conceive of the relation between agency and structure? What relation, if any, do they envision between political inquiry and political life? On what grounds might their respective visions be assessed and criticized? The list is not exhaustive, nor is it meant to be. Like the essays that follow, it is intended to be suggestive of idioms and possibilities as yet unarticulated and unthought.

References

Ball, Terence. 1983. "Contradiction and Critique in Political Theory." In Nelson (1983).

————. 1987. "The Politics of Social Science in Post-War America." In *Promise and Peril: Politics and Culture in Post-War America*, edited by Lary May. Chicago: University of Chicago Press.

Berlin, Isaiah. 1979. *Concepts and Categories*. New York: Viking.

Carnoy, Martin. 1984. *The State and Political Theory*. Princeton: Princeton University Press.

Easton, David. 1965. *A Systems Analysis of Political Life*. New York: Wiley.

————. 1981. "The Political System Beseiged by the State." *Political Theory*. 9:303–25.

Finifter, Ada W. 1983. *Political Science: The State of the Discipline*. Washington, D.C.: American Political Science Association.

Gadamer, Hans-Georg. 1975. *Truth and Method*. New York: Seabury.

————. 1976. *Philosophical Hermeneutics*. Berkeley and Los Angeles: University of California Press.

Nelson, John S., ed. 1983. *What Should Political Theory Be Now?* Albany: State University of New York Press.

Rorty, Richard. 1982. "Social Science and Social Hope." In *Consequences of Pragmatism*. Minneapolis: University of Minnesota Press.

White, James Boyd. 1985. *When Words Lose Their Meaning: Constitutions and Reconstitutions of Language, Character, and Community*. Chicago: University of Chicago Press.

Part I

Rationality and Progress In Political Inquiry

Terence Ball

1

Is There Progress in Political Science?

T he idea that progress in human affairs is possible, and perhaps even inevitable, has been badly battered in the twentieth century. Two world wars, the Holocaust, and the threat of nuclear annihilation appear to testify against any notion that things are bound to improve with the passage of time. Only one area of human endeavor appears to have escaped unscathed. The natural sciences can surely serve as a paragon of progress. There is, after all, widespread agreement that Aristotle's physics is inferior to Newton's and that the latter's has, in turn, been superseded by Einstein's. Progress in the natural sciences is said by realist philosophers of science to be possible because successive theories represent ever closer approximations to the truth. And even anti-realists agree that the natural sciences are progressive.

But what of the social sciences and of political science in particular? It is by no means clear that B.F. Skinner's psychology surpasses and improves upon Freud's, or that Levi-Strauss is a better anthropologist than Malinowski, or that Milton Friedman is a better economist than Keynes. Nor, for that matter, is it easy to decide whether David Easton is a better political scientist than Charles Merriam (much less Aristotle). If we are to gauge the progress of political science, we will need criteria by which we can judge whether one theory represents an advance over another. This will permit us to construct a narrative that is a story of progress or, failing that, of decline and decay.

Until quite recently, the story of political science's progress proceeded along the following lines. The history of political science is a story of struggle between idealism and empiricism. Idealists, or "normative" theorists, are interested in criticizing the real world and/or constructing ideal ones; they are concerned with the world as it ought to be, not with

13

the world as it really is. Empiricists are interested in describing what is and in explaining how the socio-political world actually works. Armed with a distinction between normative and empirical thinkers, we can now retell the story of political science as a progressive discipline. Plato, accordingly, becomes the first normative theorist and Aristotle "the first great political scientist." (Berelson and Steiner 1964, 13). Plato's "brilliant flights of philosophical fancy" can be contrasted with the "solid good sense" of Aristotle (Dahl 1963, 24). Just as the natural sciences have progressed by freeing themselves from theology and philosophy, so must the social sciences be shorn of the prescientific encumbrances of normative political philosophy. While the former is concerned with facts, the latter is interested in values. This, then, is the rationale for distinguishing between empirical political science and normative political philosophy.

The distinction between empirical and normative (or, fact and value, is and ought) is derived not from science but, ironically, from philosophy — specifically, from the philosophical perspective variously referred to as logical empiricism, positivism, or naturalism. This is not the place to repeat positivism's central tenets or to rehearse the numerous and arguably decisive objections that have been levelled against its view of science and explanation, its is/ought distinction, and the like (Gunnell 1986, ch. 2). Instead, I propose to look to post-positivist philosophy of science in order to formulate criteria by which we may reassess the progress, or lack thereof, of political science.

I will do this by reconstructing an ongoing conversation among several philosophers of science and political scientists. I begin by reconsidering the seminal work of Thomas Kuhn, Imre Lakatos, and Larry Laudan. I will retrace attempts by behavioral political scientists and their critics to adapt Kuhn's framework to their own purposes, including that of exhibiting the progressive character of their respective disciplines. The failure of those attempts has led some political scientists to fall back on comfortable, but discredited, positivist verities. I want to argue that no such retreat is required or even possible. The framework constructed by Lakatos (and later modified by Laudan) permits us to gauge the progress of the sciences, both natural and social, in a way that avoids the snares and pitfalls of Kuhn's earlier approach. The irony is that this approach requires a rapprochement between empirical political science and normative political theory. I will conclude by suggesting that ours is a conversation consisting of many voices, each speaking in different idioms. If I am right, political science progresses in much the same manner that a conversation progresses, and this conversation extends over time and includes not only our contemporaries but our ancestors as well.

I. Kuhn and His Critics

The influence of Thomas Kuhn's *Structure of Scientific Revolutions* on the thinking of political scientists has been both checkered and curious. Kuhn's reception by political scientists went through three more-or-less distinct phases. At first he was hailed by proponents of "scientific" or "behavioral" political science for having provided (among other things) an explanation for the persistent tendency of political scientists to talk past each other: They have been operating within different paradigms of political inquiry; so long as no authoritative single paradigm emerges, they will continue to do so, and political science will remain in its present "backward" ("underdeveloped," "immature," or "revolutionary") condition. But then, as Kuhn argued, the natural sciences themselves have, at times, been similarly unsettled. This was taken by some political scientists as a sign of hope. Political science had, they believed, undergone its own revolutionary phase (lasting two decades, three centuries, or 2,500 years, depending on how one measures it) but was now about to become a "normal" or "mature" science in Kuhn's sense. This, at least, was the hope expressed in two A.P.S.A. presidential perorations (Truman 1965; Almond 1966). One, indeed, went so far as to suggest that "a new more surely scientific (*sic*) paradigm" was emerging in political science (Almond 1966, 869). Others expressed similar hopes (Wahlke 1979). The only trouble was that no one agreed as to whether the emerging paradigm was to be interest-group analysis, structural functionalism, mathematical game theory, biopolitics, or even behavioralism as a whole.[1] Kuhn's own warning to the contrary notwithstanding (1962, 15), political scientists — along with other social scientists[2] — joined in searching for paradigms in their respective fields.

The season of hope proved to be remarkably short-lived. The opponents of a scientific or, more precisely, a behavioralist political science soon found in *their* Kuhn an able ally. Focusing first on Kuhn's account of "normal" science and the sociology of settled scientific communities, these critics emphasized the narrowness and dogmatism of normal science. If that is what a normal or mature science looks like, they argued, then political scientists should want no part of it. Paradigms do not (on their reading of Kuhn) merely dominate, they tyrannize; and so, political scientists committed to free inquiry should resist all blandishments to make theirs a "normal" science (Euben 1969; Wolin 1968, 1969; Ryan 1972; Beardsley 1974). Political science should rather strive, as one commentator put it, to "attain a multiparadigmatic condition" (Beardsley 1974, 60). Or, to put it in Kuhn's terms: Political science should remain in its present "immature" state.

The second part of the anti-behavioralist critique consisted of drawing out the nonrational and relativistic implications of Kuhn's account of scientific change. In *The Structure of Scientific Revolutions*, Kuhn averred that the decision to abandon one paradigm in favor of another is not a rational affair at all, but is rather more closely akin to a conversion experience (1962, 150, 157). This claim and its implications did not go unheeded by opponents of behavioral political science. For Kuhn had (as they believed) shown the natural sciences to be quite as subjective and normative as the behavioralists' caricature of traditional political theory held that enterprise to be. And so, these new relativists maintained, the acceptance of one paradigm and the rejection of another is not a rational process but a matter of personal "values" and even "existential" choice (Gunnell 1968, 1969; Miller 1972). A further and rather more ominous implication (to which I shall return shortly) is that meaningful communication, and indeed truth itself, is necessarily *intra*paradigmatic; that is, between adherents of different paradigms, no rational communication would be possible. Thus, a permanent failure to communicate would inevitably characterize a multiparadigmatic political science.

The third phase of Kuhn's reception by political scientists can best be characterized as outright repudiation (Landau 1972a, ch. 2, 1972b; Stephens 1973). Frightened by the specter of epistemological relativism, some political scientists were understandably tempted to retreat to pre–Kuhnian verities about objectivity, testability and falsification, and the like. Fortunately, the choice need not be between retreat and surrender. For we can — to extend the military metaphor — advance to new and more defensible ground. As we shall see, Lakatos has suggested one way of getting there; but, before explicating his strategy, I want to set the stage by reexamining several features of Kuhn's account of scientific change.

In *The Structure of Scientific Revolutions* Kuhn disputed the "cumulative" or "text book" conception of scientific change, namely that the growth of scientific knowledge results from applying the neutral instrument of scientific method to independently existing reality; that this method requires, among other things, that theories be tested against reality and, should they fail, be discarded as falsified; and that scientific advance consists in the gradual accumulation of ever truer hypotheses and theories. This vision of scientific development is plausible, Kuhn argues, only if one ignores the actual (as distinguished from the textbook) history of science. Close and careful study of the history of science reveals significant conceptual and methodological discontinuities, sometimes of revolutionary proportions. Revolutions are, however, relatively infrequent. The greater part of the history of science is the story of "normal science," that is, the enterprise of resolving the "puzzles" which arise, as a matter of course, in attempting to force recalcitrant nature into the conceptual pigeonholes of an exemplary theory or "paradigm". More often than not, natural phenomena can be conceptualized, interpreted — and, if need be, reinterpreted — to square with the expectations generated by the dominant paradigm. Sometimes, however, would-be puzzles turn into "anomalies," that is, phenomena for which the master-theory affords no plausible explanation. The presence, and indeed the proliferation, of anomalies does not, of itself, suffice to falsify the theory. Instead, the members of the scientific community devote their energies and attention to solving the soluble. During such periods, scientific advance conforms to the textbook picture: It is steady, continuous, and cumulative. This idyll can, nevertheless, be interrupted by the appearance of a rival paradigm which, Athena-like, springs fully formed from the head of a master-theoretician and purports to account for the anomalies of the old even as it indicates new directions for research. The appearance of a rival paradigm signals the onset of a crisis and even, quite possibly, a thoroughgoing revolution. In science, as in politics, a revolution succeeds when scientists' loyalties and allegiances are transferred from the old to the new paradigm. And this victory, in its turn, inaugurates a new era of normalcy.

My purpose in briefly recounting the original (1962) Kuhnian conception of scientific change is to suggest that, contrary to a widely held misconception, it is not the role assigned to paradigms that distinguishes Kuhn's account. Indeed, the concept of theoretical paradigms is, in the history of philosophy, rather old-hat.[3] It is, rather, Kuhn's distinction between normal and revolutionary science that distinguishes, and must carry the weight of, his account of scientific change. Two questions immediately arise. The first is conceptual: Is the distinction between normal and revolutionary science a coherent one? The second question is empirical: Does the history of science support the distinction between normal and revolutionary science?

Whether Kuhn's theory of scientific change is internally consistent or inconsistent depends upon which of two theses he subscribes to. The first I call the "thesis of perfect (or strict) incommensurability," which holds that the phenomena of scientific investigation count as (relevant) facts solely by virtue of their being statable in a theoretical language. All meaningful observation-reports are, on this view, theory-laden. Furthermore, there being no neutral observation-language common to any two theories, the observation-reports of the one are not translatable into (or recognizable as meaningful) observation-reports in the other. The second thesis, "the thesis of imperfect (or partial) commensurability," holds that scientific theories are, in a way roughly analogous to natural languages, mutually intertranslatable.[4] That is, at least some phenomena-reporting sentences of the theory T will have roughly corresponding meaning-equivalents in another theory T'. However partial and unsatisfactory, communication between theories in a given domain (for example, microphysics) is at least possible.

Although Kuhn at first appeared to subscribe to the thesis of strict incommensurability (1962, 4, 19, 102, 111, 147), he later denied it explicitly (1970a, 1970b). The denial is important. For if Kuhn were to subscribe to the strict thesis, his theory of scientific change would be internally inconsistent. After all, according to Kuhn, any master-theory or paradigm permits one not only to explain certain phenomena but also to recognize other phenomena as (presently) inexplicable or anomalous. The solving of puzzles and the unearthing of anomalies are part of normal science. Just as any number of compatible facts do not suffice to confirm a theory, neither can any number of recalcitrant phenomena (anomalies) serve to disconfirm it. Even so, as Kuhn acknowledges, the accumulation of anomalies may eventually undermine the scientists' confidence in the paradigm. This paves the way for the appearance of a rival paradigm which, in a successful revolution, replaces the older anomaly-ridden master-theory.

The question immediately arises, however, as to how — given the thesis of strict incommensurability — the second theory (T') could possibly be adjudged better than the first (T). Surely, it is not better in that it fits the facts more closely, because the (theory-laden) facts that T' explains cannot be (the same as) those that T explains and, further, the phenomena that T fails to explain cannot be the same as those T' does explain (Shapere 1964, 1966). In other words, if facts are recognized as such only in the light of a theory, and if theories are strictly incommensurable, then T and T' necessarily explain quite different phenomena. Therefore, Kuhn cannot, without contradiction, subscribe to the strict incommensurability thesis while maintaining that theory T' explains phenomena that are anomalous with respect to theory T. Wholly incommensurable theories cannot, logically, recognize, much less explain, the same phenomena. It follows from this that one theory or paradigm cannot, strictly speaking, rival or be better than another.

In later clarifications of his position, Kuhn denied that he ever subscribed to the thesis of strict incommensurability (1970a, 1970b, 1974). He now insists that he accepts the thesis of partial commensurability, and so his theory of scientific change is at least internally consistent. Internal coherence, however, is not everything. We may still ask whether the history of science supports the distinction between normal and revolutionary science, and whether the distinction is accurate and useful. Initially, Kuhn maintained that the history of science is, for the most part, the story of normal science, interrupted infrequently by scientific revolutions, which he characterized as thoroughgoing "changes of world view" or "gestalt switches" (1962, ch. 10). But, as Kuhn's critics hastened to note, the history of science does not conform to this scheme. For example, changes of theory — paradigm shifts — are not the sudden all-or-nothing changes that Kuhn pictures them to be; they are more likely to take many years. Scientific change is also rather more piecemeal and continuous than Kuhn originally suggested. A paradigm does not fall, all at once, in a great cataclysmic crash; it is more likely to erode over time (Toulmin 1970). For example, the Newtonian paradigm was not a monolith until Einstein utterly demolished it; rather, it was a ravaged shell of a theory, cracked in many places, and scarcely able to support the ever-increasing weight of the evidence against it. Kuhn's "big bang" or revolutionary account of scientific change does not fit the facts, even here.

Kuhn soon conceded as much. Small-scale minirevolutions, he acknowledged, occur frequently in the history of science (1970b, 249–50). Kuhn's concession to his critics, however, undercut the distinction between normal and revolutionary science which had been the linchpin of his theory of scientific change. For them, all normal science would be revolutionary to some unspecified degree. Kuhn's account of scientific change was thereby transformed into a theory of permanent revolution. Having rendered otiose the distinction between normal and revolutionary science, Kuhn emptied it of much of its supposed heuristic and explanatory value. Ironically, Kuhn's attempted revolutionizing of normal science lends support not to a revolutionary theory of scientific change but to an evolutionary one.[5] Thus, the boldest and most original aspects of Kuhn's account of scientific change were either considerably watered-down or entirely abandoned.

In the face of these and other apparently decisive objections to Kuhn's account, some political scientists lamented that "We are back where we started before the Kuhnian paradigm (*sic*) was adopted by political science" (Stephens 1973, 488). Such despair was hardly warranted, however, for even Kuhn's most ardent critics readily acknowledged the value and importance of his contribution to the history and philosophy of science. One of his achievements was an all but definitive destruction of the textbook picture of scientific progress as a steady growth-by-accumulation of ever-truer hypotheses and theories. For all its rhetorical exaggeration, Kuhn's conception of scientific change-through-revolution has had the signal merit of reminding us that the scientific enterprise is, above all, a dynamic, discontinuous, and not wholly cumulative one. As a result, no political scientist nowadays would maintain that "A science of politics which deserves its name must build from the bottom up . . . An empirical discipline is built by the slow,

modest, and piecemeal accumulation of relevant theories and data"
(Eulau 1964, 9). Whatever their view of scientific development, Kuhn
and his critics are agreed in repudiating this vision of growth-through-
accumulation; facts, hypotheses, and theories are not building blocks
which can be stacked on top of each other. Disciplines do not grow and
develop by simple accretion.

Another of Kuhn's important contributions was his recognition of
the inseparability of history and philosophy of science; neither can proceed successfully without the other. More important still was Kuhn's
undermining of naive falsificationism (that is, the doctrine that facts can
falsify theories). Just as Popper showed that the "test of experience"
cannot prove or verify the truth of a theory, so Kuhn has shown that
such tests never suffice to refute a theory. Theories are never falsified
simpliciter, not even by rank anomalies. Thus falsifiability cannot serve
as the "demarcation criterion" for distinguishing science from non-
science (or pseudo-science). On this point, Kuhn and his critics agreed.
They disagreed, however, over Kuhn's contention that there can be no
methodological demarcation criterion, but only, as it were, a political
one, in that only the powers-that-be in a given scientific community can
decide what is science and what is not, and that their extra-scientific and
historically variable standards of judgment are a matter of taste and
fashion only and are therefore beyond rational criticism (1962, chs. 3,
10–12). Although Kuhn and his defenders (Doppelt 1982; Bernstein
1983) deny the charges of relativism and irrationalism levelled by
Lakatos and others, these accusations have stuck. And in Lakatos's case,
they have led to the formulation and elaboration of different — and
arguably more defensible — demarcation criteria.

II. Lakatos's Alternative Account

Lakatos and Kuhn agreed that the history of science does not support the view that an elegant theory can be killed (or falsified) by an ugly
fact. Theories are made of sterner stuff, and facts, being theory-laden,
are not so hard and unyielding as classical empiricists had supposed. The
mistake of the older empiricists was to assume that facts and theories are
wholly separable in all cases, and that the truth-content of the latter can
be ascertained simply by comparing it with the former. This view,
Lakatos contends, is mistaken.

Lakatos begins by distinguishing three species of falsificationism,
which he terms "dogmatic," "methodological," and "sophisticated
methodological" falsificationism, respectively. Dogmatic falsificationism
holds that while facts never suffice to prove theories, they do suffice to
disprove them. "Falsifiability" thus serves as the demarcation criterion

between science and non-science, for, in order to qualify as scientific, a proposition or a theory must be potentially falsifiable: criteria of refutation must be specified and one or more crucial experiments conducted; if the theory or proposition fails in its direct encounters or confrontations with Nature, it must be given up (Lakatos 1970, 95–97).

Dogmatic falsificationism rests, however, upon two mistaken assumptions. The first is that there is some clear-cut dividing line between observational and theoretical propositions.[6] The second assumption is that if a proposition qualifies as a basic or observational one, then it is either incorrigibly true or incorrigibly false; that is, "one may say that it was *proved* [or disproved] from facts." Lakatos (1970, 97–98) calls this "the doctrine of observational (or experimental) proof."

Both of these assumptions however, are, mistaken — the first mistaken in fact, the second in logic. The first is mistaken inasmuch as there is in fact no clear-cut borderline between observational and theoretical propositions. "For there are and can be no sensations unimpregnated by expectations and therefore there is no natural (i.e., psychological) demarcation between observational and theoretical propositions" (Lakatos 1970, 98). By way of example, Lakatos cites the case of Galileo's supposed refutation of the Aristotelian theory of flawless celestial spheres:

> Galileo claimed that he could 'observe' mountains on the moon and spots on the sun and that these 'observations' refuted the time-honoured theory that celestial bodies are faultless crystal balls. But his 'observations' were not 'observational' in the sense of being observed by the — unaided — senses: their reliability depended on the reliability of his telescope — and of the optical theory of the telescope — which was violently questioned by his contemporaries. It was not Galileo's — pure, untheoretical — *observations* that confronted Aristotelian *theory* but rather Galileo's 'observations' in the light of his optical theory that confronted the Aristotelians' 'observations' in the light of *their* theory of the heavens. This leaves us with two inconsistent theories, *prima facia* on a par (Lakatos 1970, 98).

Because even our most direct observations are impregnated with expectations, there is no natural dividing line between "basic" or observational propositions and theoretical ones.[7] All observation involves interpretation.

The second assumption upon which dogmatic falsificationism rests — its doctrine of experimental (dis)proof — is also mistaken, but for a different reason. It is mistaken, Lakatos says, because of "a basic point in elementary logic," namely: "Propositions can only be derived from [and be consistent or inconsistent with] other propositions." Therefore "no factual proposition can ever be proved [or disapproved] from an experiment" (1970, 99). Dogmatic falsificationism mistakenly posits a world of hard facts that is both independent of and comparable with our systems of propositions, that is, theories. But it is not independent, inasmuch as no natural line of demarcation separates observation from theory; nor is it comparable, inasmuch as propositions can be compared only with other propositions. Dogmatic falsificationism is therefore untenable.

A second and less objectionable kind of falsificationism Lakatos calls "methodological" falsificationism. As against dogmatic falsificationism, it holds that the division between observational and theoretical propositions is not natural but conventional; that is, where to draw the line is a methodological decision. For example, the sorts of basic observational propositions against which we test the predictions of a theory T' are not the pure and unsullied "*protocol sentences*" envisioned by earlier positivists; rather, they are propositions drawn from another "touchstone" theory. Thus, in testing the Aristotelian theory of celestial bodies, Galileo admitted as basic or observational propositions the theoretical propositions of another theory — in this case, his (still-unrefined) optical theory. For purposes of testing, and falsifying, one theory, we use another. "The methodological falsificationist," says Lakatos, "uses our most successful theories as extensions of our senses ..." (1970, 107). In other words, a proposition which is a "theoretical" one in T may be accorded "observational" status in T'.[8]

Methodological falsificationism adopts a demarcation criterion which is, to say the least, more liberal than that proposed by dogmatic falsificationism: It admits as "scientific" any theory which has "potential falsifiers," even if they derive from some other, as-yet-unfalsified, theory. Consequently, many more theories may now be regarded as scientific ones. Both kinds of falsificationism hold, however, that a theory enjoys scientific status by continually "sticking its neck out." The scientist puts his theory's head on the block by "specifying, in advance, an experiment such, that if the result contradicts the theory, the theory has to be given up" (Lakatos 1970, pp. 96, 112). The difference is that the latter's conception of observation and testing, and hence falsification, is more liberal than the former's.

Even so, Lakatos argues that methodological falsificationism is not liberal enough. Its standards of falsification are still too strict to square with, or do justice to, the history of science. If we apply its standards, many of the most respected theories of yesteryear would be accounted prescientific, unscientific, or even pseudo-scientific. Theorists are almost never inclined to bet their theories on a crucial experiment (in which the theory is not confirmed once and for all, but merely not falsified *this* time). Such an all-or-nothing, go-for-broke attitude is, Lakatos says, "reckless" and "daredevil" (1970, 112). In fact, he says, scientists tend to be bold in their conjectures but cautious in their refutations; good theories being hard to come by, they hold fast to what they have already.[9] And yet, theories do get falsified; one theory is rejected in favor of another, and the scope and explanatory power of successive theories increases. But how is this sort of progress possible? If we are to answer that question we must first ask: How—by what standards or on what grounds — is one theory to be rejected as inferior to another? Any satisfactory answer to that question, Lakatos avers, cannot be given in isolation from, or in ignorance of, the actual history of science. But then, he says (1970, 114), "If we look at the history of science, if we try to see how some of the most celebrated falsifications happened, we have to come to the conclusion that either some of them are plainly irrational, *or* that they rest on rationality principles different from those [espoused by dogmatic and/or methodological falsificationists]." Faced with this choice, Kuhn opts for the former: choosing between rival theories or paradigms is not a wholly rational matter. Lakatos, by contrast, opts for the latter: there are principles of scientific rationality, criticism, and falsifiability — only they are not the ones advanced by dogmatic and/or methodological falsificationists.

Against Kuhn and earlier falsificationists alike, Lakatos advanced his own methodology of scientific research programs. The linchpin of his theory of criticism and scientific change is to be found in his doctrine of "sophisticated methodological" falsificationism (or "sophisticated" falsificationism, for short). On this account a theory qualifies as scientific by virtue of its being falsifiable in a new and methodologically more sophisticated sense:

> The sophisticated falsificationist regards a scientific theory T as falsified if and only if another theory T' has been proposed with the following characteristics: (1) T' has excess empirical content of T: that is, it predicts *novel* facts, that is, facts improbable in the light of, or even forbidden by, T; (2) T' explains the previous success of T, that is, all the unrefuted content of T is contained (within the limits of observational error) in the content of T'; and (3) some of the excess content of T' is corroborated (Lakatos 1970, 116).

Sophisticated falsificationism has two key merits. First, it squares with the history of science;[10] and second, it avoids the sort of irrationalism implied by Kuhn's earlier (1962) account of scientific choice and change.[11]

For the sophisticated falsificationist, the problem is no longer how to distinguish between science and pseudo-science *simpliciter*, but, rather, "how to demarcate between scientific and pseudoscientific *adjustments*, between rational and irrational changes of theory" (Lakatos 1970, 117). What Lakatos proposes, then, is to provide not merely a descriptive account of scientific change, but a *theory of scientific progress* — and progress, moreover, of an eminently critical and rational sort.

Scientific progress, according to Lakatos, can only be gauged by looking at the successes and failures, not of single theories but of successive series of theories, each sharing common core assumptions. Such a series he calls a "research program." A research program consists of a "hard core" of not-directly-criticizable assumptions.[12] The hardness of this hard core is assured by the program's *negative heuristic*; that is, the methodological rule that criticism be directed away from the hard core of the program.[13] The program's *positive heuristic*, by contrast, prescribes the construction of a "protective belt" of auxiliary assumptions and hypotheses which serves to protect the program's hard core. "It is this protective belt," Lakatos says, "which has to bear the brunt of tests and get adjusted and readjusted, or even completely replaced, to defend the [hard] core. A research program is successful if all this leads to a progressive problem-shift; unsuccessful if it leads to a degenerating problem-shift" (1970, 133).[14] We gauge the progressiveness of a research program by looking at the character of the adjustments made in its protective belt:

> Let us take a series of theories T_1, T_2, T_3, ... where each subsequent theory results from adding auxiliary clauses to (or from semantical reinterpretations of) the previous theory in order to accommodate some anomaly, each theory having at least as much content as the unrefuted content of its predecessor . . . . [A] Series of theories is *theoretically* progressive (or 'constitutes a theoretically progressive problem-shift') if each new theory has some excess empirical content over its predecessor, that is, if it predicts some novel, hitherto unexpected fact . . . . [A] theoretically progressive series of theories is also *empirically progressive* (or 'constitutes an empirically progressive problem-shift') if some of this excess empirical content is also corroborated, that is, if each new theory leads us to the actual discovery of some *new* fact. Finally, . . . a problem-shift [is] *progressive* if it is both theoretically and empirically progressive, and *degenerating* if it is not. We 'accept' problem-shifts as 'scientific' only if they are at least theoretically progressive; if they are not, we 'reject' them as 'pseudoscientific'. Progress is measured by the degree to which a problem-shift is progressive, [i.e.] by the degree to which the series of theories leads us to the discovery of novel facts. We regard a theory in the series 'falsified' when it is superseded by a theory with higher corroborated content (Lakatos 1970, 118).

Theories are, then, never falsified absolutely but only relatively; that is, they are superseded by better theories. As Lakatos put it: "There is no falsification before the emergence of a better theory" (1970, 119).

By way of illustration, Lakatos cites "the most successful research programme ever" — Newton's gravitational theory. "In Newton's programme the negative heuristic bids us to divert the *modus tollens* from Newton's three laws of dynamics and his law of gravitation. This 'core' is 'irrefutable' by the methodological decision of its protagonists: anomalies must lead to changes only in the protective belt . . . " Newton and the Newtonians did just that. From the beginning Newton's gravitational theory

> was submerged in an ocean of 'anomalies' (or, if you wish, 'counterexamples'), and opposed by the observational theories supporting these anomalies. But Newtonians turned, with brilliant tenacity and ingenuity, one counter-instance after another into corroborating instances, primarily by overthrowing the original observational theories in the light of which this 'contrary evidence' was established. In the process they themselves produced new counter-examples which they again resolved. They 'turned [as Laplace said] each new difficulty into a new victory of their programme' (Lakatos, 1970, 133).

The lesson to be learned from this and many other historical examples is twofold. It is first a lesson in tenacity: the task of keeping a theory (or series of theories) afloat in the ocean of anomalies requires dogged persistence and ingenuity on the part of its defenders. The second lesson is one of tolerance: critics should be tolerant of attempts to save theories from refutation. Neither lesson is taught by dogmatic and/or methodological falsificationists; quite the contrary, both are alike in holding that tenacity in defending a theory is very nearly a crime against science. Against this view, Lakatos argues that the history of science is the story of bold conjectures boldly and tenaciously defended against apparently decisive counter-evidence.

This does not mean that theories cannot be criticized and even, eventually, falsified. Rather, it means, that criticism must be directed against successive adjustments in the protective belt surrounding the hard core of that series of theories which constitutes a research program. The critic must ask: Are these adjustments progressive or degenerating ones *within the context of this particular research program*? That is, are these adjustments content-increasing or content-decreasing ones? Do these adjustments enable us to predict novel facts even as they explain old anomalies?

A good research program is a good swimmer, mainly because its "protective belt" serves as a life belt, keeping the hard core afloat on an ocean of anomalies. So long as this belt can be adjusted in progressive, (that is, content-increasing) ways, the research program is in no danger of sinking. But, by the same token, a research program begins to list and take on water when its protective belt can no longer be adjusted in progressive ways, that is, when adjustments amount to no more than content-decreasing semantical ones and/or when they fail to anticipate new facts. Only then is the research program itself, hard core and all, in any danger of sinking. But, no matter how waterlogged it becomes, a research program will not sink and have to be abandoned until a better, more buoyant one comes along to replace it. In any case, the decision to abandon one research program in favor of another is not taken lightly (*contra* earlier falsificationists), nor is it nonrational (*contra* Kuhn); it is at every step a critical, considered decision in light of available alternative theories against which the progressiveness (or degeneration) of successive problem-shifts is gauged. Science is, then, both rational and progressive.

But is political science such a science? Is it, or can it be, rational and progressive? Are there, or might there one day be, research programs in political science? Before turning to these questions, however, we need to look critically at the strengths and the shortcomings of Lakatos's approach.

III. From Research Programs to Research Traditions

Up to this point, my discussion has focused on a number of interrelated problems in the history and philosophy of the natural sciences — in particular, problems of commensurability and criticism, falsification and scientific progress. Because the practicing political scientist might well wonder what all this has to do with her inquiries, let us consider some of the advantages to be gained by viewing political inquiry through Lakatosian lenses.

The first advantage, already alluded to is that political science can now dispense with its pseudo–Popperian, or dogmatic, conception of falsifiability.[15] That is, we can abandon the outmoded and untenable view that a theory can be tested directly against the facts which are wholly independent of the theory under test, and which, if they do not correspond, require us to abandon the theory as falsified. With Lakatos's aid, immediately we can see what is wrong with such claims as these: "Whether [an empirical] proposition is true or false depends on the degree to which the proposition and the real world correspond" (Dahl, 1963, 8). "If no evidence about the real world can possibly disprove a

proposition, it can hardly be called scientific or empirical in character"
(Polsby 1980, 5). These claims exhibit both of the mistakes made by
dogmatic falsificationists, namely, the mistake of supposing that there is
a "real world" completely independent of, yet comparable with, our
theories, and the logical mistake of believing that facts can "disprove"
propositions.

A Lakatosian perspective also throws a kinder light on attempts to
save a research program from criticism by means of various adjustments
to its protective belt. Indeed, a scientist operating within the assumptions
of a research program will, quite rightly, spend much of her time and effort in strengthening this protective belt, so as to better protect the program's hard core. That is not to say that the hard core is not itself
falsifiable, or that it is to be protected at all costs by making just any sort
of theoretical adjustments in the protective belt. Not all adjustments are
acceptable; some represent the progress, others the degeneration, of a
research program. If an adjustment is content-increasing, it is progressive. But if an adjustment is merely ad hoc—consisting, for example, of a redefinition of terms or the addition of some hypothesis which
explains an old anomaly but fails to lead to the discovery of new facts —
then that adjustment represents a content-decreasing or degenerating
problem-shift.

Although Lakatos's conception of research programs marks a major advance beyond both positivist objectivism and anti-positivist
relativism (Bernstein, 1983, Part II), it has not been without its critics.
Chief among these is Larry Laudan, who argues that despite its many virtues, Lakatos's liberalized Popperian program is still too strict to square
with the history of science. For one thing, Lakatos accepts as evidence of
progress only empirical discoveries, thereby ruling out conceptual in-
novations that may allow for the interpretive recasting of existing empirical evidence. For another, "Lakatos' claim that the accumulation of
anomalies has no bearing on the appraisal of a research programme is
massively refuted by the history of science" (Laudan 1977, 78). Lakatos
attempts to get around this difficulty by averring that stories of scientific
progress and degeneration must be couched in terms of "rational
reconstructions," in which "one tells history *as it ought* to have happened," not as it really did. What we need, then, are not idealized
reconstructions featuring ideally rational researchers but actual histories featuring real researchers facing real problems (Laudan 1977,
pp. 168–70). Like Kuhn, Laudan insists that the history of science (and
any accompanying assessments of rationality and progress) is an inescapably interpretive or hermeneutical activity. Scientific theories are
sets of historically and culturally specific concepts and ideas whose
meaning must be interpreted by the historian of science. From this it

follows that the historian of science must be a historian of ideas whose task is to reconstruct the past by constructing an interpretation that is intelligible without being anachronistic (Laudan 1977, ch. 6; compare Kuhn 1977, pp. xii–xiv).

Laudan recommends replacing Lakatos's "research programs," with their rigid and unchanging cores and cumbersome "protective belts," with what he calls "research traditions." Very briefly, "a research tradition provides a set of guidelines for the development of specific theories" belonging to that tradition. Laudan cites as examples of research traditions Cartesian physics, Newtonian physics, Freudian psychology, psychological behaviorism, and Marxism. The core of a research tradition consists of "an ontology which specifies, in a general way, the types of fundamental entities which exist in the domain or domains within which the research tradition is to explain all the empirical problems in the domain by 'reducing' them to the ontology of the research tradition." (Laudan 1977, 79). This reduction is really a matter of translation and interpretation via the vocabulary of any given tradition. The concepts and ontological categories constituting the Marxian research tradition, for example, include class struggle, the materialist interpretation of history (featuring the forces and relations of production, ideological superstructure, and so forth); those of Cartesian physics include mind and matter; those of Freudian psychology include the unconscious, the id, ego, and superego, sublimation and transference, and so on. A research tradition has, so to speak, a conceptual core — a common language allowing researchers within that tradition to communicate with and to criticize each other. It is an ongoing conversation, conducted in a distinctive and readily identifiable idiom or "lexicon" (Kuhn 1984). It also specifies the ways in which the entities describable in this lexicon can, and cannot, interact. In the Marxian tradition, for example, moral and political ideas cannot have an existence wholly independent of social or material-productive circumstances. And, not least, a research tradition specifies the sorts of methods and instrumentation appropriate to the study and understanding of the relevant entities. Thus, for example, behaviorists may use mazes, electrical shocks, and aversion therapy, but not the "talking cure" favored by Freudians. In short, says Laudan, "a research tradition is a set of general assumptions about the entities and processes in a domain of study, and about the appropriate methods to be used for investigating the problems and constructing the theories in that domain (1977, 81).

How then is scientific progress or growth to be gauged, given Laudan's liberalized modification of Lakatos's scheme? Research traditions, unlike the theories belonging to them, "are neither explanatory, nor predictive, nor directly testable." Although not falsifiable, a research tradition — depending on the types of theories is spawns — may be more or less fruitful. In turn, its fruitfulness is to be assessed in terms of those theories' ability to allow for the posing and solving of puzzles and problems arising within that tradition. In other words, "a successful research tradition is one which leads, via its component theories, to the adequate solution of an increasing range of empirical and conceptual problems" (Laudan 1977, pp. 81–82). To see how this might work in practice, let us consider the case of a well-known research tradition in political science.

IV. The Rational Choice Research Tradition in Political Science

Although often regarded as a recent research program, the "rational choice" genre is in fact old enough to count as a research tradition in Laudan's sense and to have incurred its share of anomalies (see Hardin, this volume). The progenitor of that tradition is Hobbes, and his progeny include Condorcet, Bentham, James Mill, and F.Y. Edgeworth, not to mention more modern thinkers like Downs, Tullock, and Riker. The rational choice research tradition has at its core certain ontological presuppositions. Chief among these—and characteristic of any research tradition in the social sciences—is a particular "model of man" (Moon 1975), or, if you prefer, a paradigm of personhood. (The latter expression, though nonsexist, has the distinct disadvantage of being considerably more cumbersome than the former.) This model consists of a "fundamental conceptualization of what it is to be a person, including not only an account of human needs and capacities, but also a view of how a person is related to others" (Moon, 1983, 183). The rational choice program's model of man views human beings as rational self-interested calculators. People are assumed to be rational, and rationality, in turn, is defined in instrumental terms: to be rational is to choose that course of action (policy, state of the world, and so forth) which will be most efficient in satisfying one's own ordered preferences. The objection that these basic assumptions are themselves unrealistic or are refuted by the facts of human behavior in the real world, carry little weight with contemporary positive theorists (Friedman 1953, ch. 1; Riker and Ordeshook 1973, ch. 2). This is because (to speak again in Lakatos's idiom) to admit as relevant any direct criticism of the hard core would violate the negative heuristic, that is, the methodological rule that criticism is to be directed away from the hard core and toward the program's protective belt.

The idea of progressive and degenerating problem-shifts in the rational choice tradition is especially well illustrated in the various recent attempts to resolve the "paradox of voting."[16] Although ahistorically minded game theorists appear not to know it, the paradox is a venerable one, having been formulated by Hegel in *The Philosophy of Right* (1821). Hegel notes that the paradox arises for the first time in a particular period, and then only in connection with the mass participatory politics of the modern age. The paradox is therefore not only an interesting theoretical anomaly but a pressing *political* problem badly in need of solution. "Popular suffrage, . . . especially in large states," says Hegel, "leads inevitably to electoral indifference, since the casting of a single vote is of no significance where there is a multitude of electors. Even if a voting qualification is highly valued and esteemed by those who are entitled to it, they still do not enter the polling booth. Thus the result of [popular suffrage] is more likely to be the opposite of what was intended" (Hegel 1967, pp. 202–203).

In a sense, then, the paradox of voting was already old-hat when Anthony Downs encountered it in attempting to explain political participation in terms of a utility-maximizing model of rational choice and behavior. Downs' theory predicts that an agent would not vote, inasmuch as his single vote would not appreciably alter the probability of his getting what he wants (in this case, his preferred candidate's winning); hence, he will not "spend" the time and effort to "buy" what he can get for "free." The paradox stems not from the fact that people do, nevertheless, vote (theories are not confuted by facts *simpliciter*) but from several internal or theoretical anomalies. Consider: a rational agent will "pay the cost" of voting only if, as a result he stands a better chance of getting what he wants for himself. Now, in a two-candidate race in which many votes are cast, one voter's chance of affecting the outcome is insignificant; therefore, it will not "pay" for him to vote. But then (each rational calculator will reason), other rational agents will reach the same conclusion, and no one will vote. In that case he should vote, because the election will end in a 1–0 victory for his candidate. Presumably, however, each rational agent will reach a similar conclusion about the value of his single vote, and so everyone will vote. In that case, however, each voter's chance of affecting the outcome of the election will be neligible and so, again, no one will vote. This circle, if not vicious, is at least dizzying. At the very least, it poses a problem for Downs' theory. But, more than that, if it cannot be resolved by means of one or more theoretical adjustments, the hard core of the rational choice program itself may be in jeopardy. Such "adjustments" were proposed, first by Downs and later by Riker and Ordeshook.

Downs attempts to resolve the paradox of voting by means of the following adjustment. A rational citizen, he argues, will pay the cost of voting, even if he thereby gains nothing, because he derives satisfaction from "do[ing] his share in providing long-run benefits" for himself and others, through helping to maintain the democratic system (Downs 1957, 270). But then, as Barry notes:

> 'Doing his share' is a concept foreign to the kind of 'economic' rationality with which Downs is working. It requires our citizen to reason that since the benefits he gets depends on the efforts of others, he should contribute too. This may be good ethics, but it is not consistent with the assumptions of the model, which require the citizen to compute the advantage that accrues to him from his doing *x* rather than *y*; not the advantage that would accrue to him from *himself and others* doing *x* rather than *y*, unless, of course his doing it is a necessary and sufficient condition of others doing it (Barry 1970, 20).

Or, to say the same thing in Lakatosian language: Downs' proposed adjustment violates the negative heuristic of the rational choice program, inasmuch as it calls into question the hard core assumption that a rational agent will not "pay" for something if he can get it for nothing. That, after all, is why he will not vote: given that he prefers *A* to *B*, and that many people prefer either *A* or *B* and will vote accordingly, then the probability that *his* voting for *A* will result in *A*'s winning, is very small indeed; and, so long as there are *any* "costs" accruing to him from voting, he will not vote. If his candidate wins, he can enjoy the fruits of victory without having to pay for them. But then, extending this logic to the long-term rewards accruing to himself and others from maintaining the democratic system, one has to admit, as Downs does, that "he will actually get this reward [too], even if he himself does not vote" (Downs 1957, 270). Therefore, it is still irrational for him to vote. To argue otherwise, as Downs insists upon doing, is to reject the rational choice program's hard core tenets of self-interestedness and instrumental rationality. Downs's proposed adjustment is therefore impermissible, representing as it does a degenerating problem-shift in the rational choice program.

Another sort of adjustment is proposed by Riker and Ordeshook (1968). Rejecting Downs' introduction of other-regarding (or even altruistic) motives into the calculus of voting, they attempt to resolve the paradox of voting in terms consistent with the program's assumption of self-interestedness. A rational person does stand to gain from voting, they argue, even if those gains be such non-material psychological "satisfactions" as those stemming from "affirming allegiance to the political system," "affirming a partisan preference," and even "compliance with the ethic of voting" (Riker and Ordeshook 1968, 28). This adjustment is, however, sadly ad hoc. As Barry remarks:

> Now it may well be true that much voting can be accounted for in this way, and one can of course formally fit it into an 'economic' framework by saying that people get certain 'rewards' from voting. But this *is* purely formal. And it forces us to ask what really is the point and value of the whole 'economic' approach. It is no trick to restate all behavior in terms of 'rewards' and 'costs'; it may for some purposes be a useful conceptual device, but it does not in itself provide anything more than a set of empty boxes waiting to be filled. . . . Insofar as it includes voting as a purely expressive act, not undertaken with any expectation of changing the state of the world, it fails to fit the minimum requirements of the means-end model of rational behavior (Barry 1970, 15).

Riker and Ordeshook's adjustment consists of redefining the concept of "reward" to include all sorts of "satisfactions." But their broadening the concept of reward in this way and in this direction represents a degenerating problem-shift inasmuch as it resolves a theoretical anomaly by means of a verbal or terminological adjustment.

If these were the only sorts of adjustments to be made in the protective belt of the rational choice program, we might well wonder whether that program itself — hard core and all — is salvageable or even worth saving. However, Ferejohn and Fiorina (1974) proposed a solution to the paradox of voting which may well have constituted a genuinely progressive problem-shift in the rational choice program. Their proposed adjustment is easily summarized. Rational choice theorists took a wrong turn, they argued, in "equating the notion of rational behavior with the rule of maximizing expected utility" (1974, 535). Their solution is to assume not that voters are expected-utility maximizers but that they are instead maximum-regret minimizers; that is, instead of maximizing gains, they minimize their maximum loss, interpreted as "regret." Their "minimax regretter" votes, not because he expects to increase significantly the probability of his candidate's winning, but because he wishes to avoid the most regretful possible outcome, namely, his candidate's losing by one vote. In contrast, with the expected-utility maximizer,

> The minimax regret decision maker uses a simpler rule. He imagines himself in each possible future state of the world and looks at how much in error each of his available actions could be, given that state. Then he chooses that action whose maximum error over the states of nature is least. If asked why he voted, a minimax regret decision maker might reply, 'My God, what if I didn't vote and my preferred candidate lost by one vote? I'd feel like killing myself.' Notice that for the expected-utility maximizer the probability of such an event is very important, whereas for the minimax regret decision maker the mere logical possibility of such an event is enough (Ferejohn and Fiorina 1974, 535).

Assuming, then, that voters are indeed minimax regretters rather than expected-utility maximizers, it *is* rational for them to vote. Given this assumption, we can now predict higher levels of voter turnout. Thus, the paradox of voting is solved or, rather, dissolved. Or is it?

The "adjustment" proposed by Ferejohn and Fiorina at first sight seems to be quite consistent with the rational choice tradition's ontological and conceptual core (unlike Downs'); and it is not merely an ad hoc verbal stratagem designed to rid that tradition of a persistent anomaly (unlike that of Riker and Ordeshook). Their adjustment appears, moreover, to be a content-increasing or progressive one, in that it leads to the prediction of new and unforeseen facts. For example, it predicts that in a three-candidate race a minimax regretter will not vote for his second-choice, even when his most-preferred candidate is likely to lose and his least-preferred one likely to win. And this, in turn, suggests some promising lines of research into voter choice in multiparty systems.

Despite its initial promise, however, Ferejohn and Fiorina's adjustment soon led to troubling anomalies requiring further adjustments of an arguably degenerate sort. Although limitations on space prevent me from reconstructing the conversation occasioned by Ferejohn and Fiorina's attempt to resolve the paradox of voting, it may be worth noting the many idioms in which it was conducted. Some critics claimed that their adjustment fails to predict significantly different outcomes (Strom 1975). Others maintained that the minimax-regret solution was a pseudo-solution (Stephens 1975) and that it is not applicable to voting decisions (Mayer and Good 1975), at least by "ethical voters" (Goodin and Roberts 1975). Still other critics suggested that the minimax-regret solution gives rise to paradoxes of its own (Beck 1975). Others brought empirical evidence to bear against Ferejohn and Fiorina's attempted solution of the nonvoting paradox (for example, Aldrich 1976). Their reply (Ferejohn and Fiorina 1975) failed to satisfy their critics, however, and the conversation continues even now (for example, Aldrich and Simon 1986).

My purpose in briefly recounting the broad contours of this conversation within the rational choice tradition is to suggest that its direction is inherently unpredictable, save that every solution to old anomalies will more often than not yield new problems calling for further adjustments. Just what these anomalies and adjustments might be — and whether they would in their turn represent progressive or degenerating problem-shifts — could not have been predicted but could only be seen retrospectively (Lakatos 1971; Laudan 1977; Kuhn 1984). Minerva's owl, as Hegel reminded us, takes flight only at dusk.

V. How to be a Good Political Scientist: A Plea
For Tolerance in Matters Theoretical[17]

In dwelling at some length on the rational choice tradition, I have not meant to imply that political science has only one genuine research tradition at present. Quite the contrary: I should rather say that political science has now, or has had, a number of promising research programs or traditions. I am thinking particularly of two prominent and late-lamented programs: Marxism and functional analysis. In concluding, I want to suggest, perhaps a bit tendentiously, that these programs might have been killed off prematurely. Their protagonists lacked the necessary tenacity, their critics the necessary tolerance, required to give these programs a fighting chance. Of course, their demise may, upon examination, be shown to be no more than just; nevertheless, they have been rather harshly treated. Never having been adequately protected, they became (in Lakatos's phase) sitting ducks for the dogmatic falsificationists. These (and perhaps other) downed ducks should be retrieved and their life histories reconstructed and examined with care. We should ask ourselves: Were they given a fighting chance? Were their respective cores given adequate protection? Which (if any) of the adjustments in their protective belts were progressive, and which were not? And how successful were they in posing and solving problems arising within their respective traditions?

Of course critics can, and should, criticize. But how much credence should be given to criticisms of budding research programs? While defending the criticizability of all research programs, Lakatos remarks:

> ...criticism does not — and must not — kill as fast as Popper [and other falsificationists] imagined. Purely negative, destructive criticism, like 'refutation' or demonstration of an inconsistency, does not eliminate a programme. Criticism of a programme is a long and often frustrating process, and one must treat budding research programmes leniently.

Lakatos adds (with a sympathy for the social sciences rare among philosophers of science) a further warning about "the destructive effect of naive falsificationism upon budding research programs [in the social sciences]" (1970, 179). And Laudan, likewise, defends the so-called "immature" sciences (Laudan 1977, pp. 150–151).

We political scientists have not, I fear, treated our budding research programs (or traditions) very leniently. On the contrary, we have made them into sitting ducks; and, in a discipline which includes many accomplished duck hunters, this has often proved fatal.[18] If we are to be good sportsmen we need to take Lakatos's and Laudan's schemes seriously. This involves a number of moves. It requires, first of all, that we give up our long-held dogmatic falsificationist views; second, that we be tenacious in defending and tolerant in criticizing research programs; third, that we distinguish between core and auxiliary assumptions, directing our defenses and/or criticisms accordingly; fourth, that our criticisms be retrospective and directed against adjustments in the protective belt of the program in question; and, finally, that we judge the success-to-date of a research tradition and the theories composing it in terms of the progressiveness or degeneration of successive adjustments and attempts at problem-solving.

Consider, for example, the case for "scientific" Marxism. Is Marxism, as one of its defenders (Ollman 1979, ch. 4) has claimed, the best (and perhaps the only) basis for a genuinely scientific social science? To answer that question, we must begin by demarcating between science and non-science (or pseudo-science). This requires that we be able "to demarcate between scientific and pseudo-scientific adjustments, between rational and irrational changes of theory" (Lakatos 1970, 117). We need, in other words, to rationally reconstruct the history of Marxism, then to determine whether successive adjustments have not only taken care of old anomalies but have, at the same time, predicted new facts; that is, we need to know whether successive adjustments in the Marxian research program represent content-increasing problem-shifts or content- decreasing ones. For example: Does Lenin's theory of imperialism represent a progressive or degenerating problem-shift within the Marxian research program? One may also ask the same question of Trotsky's theory of permanent revolution, Lukacs's account of reification, Althusser's "structuralizing" of Marx's theory, and Roemer's and Elster's attempt to marry Marxism and game theory, among others.

Despite their differences, the accounts of scientific progress advanced by Kuhn, Lakatos, and Laudan have wide-ranging implications for the social sciences and for political science in particular. Perhaps one of the most striking of these implications is that the putative gap between traditional or normative political theory and empirical political science is now narrowed if not obliterated. Indeed, the so-called normative theories of the past may now be viewed as methodological prescriptions, because what they prescribe is that we view man and society in certain ways and not in others.[19] Thus Hobbes, for example, commended to us the model of man as a rational self-interested calculator; and modern positive theorists follow in his footsteps. And Rousseau, arguing against Hobbes, commended to us the view that human beings are other-regarding social beings, their wants and aspirations being a product of their education and upbringing, and students of "political socialization" and "civic culture" follow in his footsteps, as do some feminist theorists. Thus, the relationship between "normative" political theory and "empirical" political science is very nearly symbiotic. The "oughts" of "normative" theory are as much methodological as they are moral. Hence, the history of political thought is central to the enterprise of political science. It is only with the wisdom of hindsight that we rationally reconstruct, examine, and criticize our research traditions. To date, there is no better way of gauging the progress of political science.

Notes

This is a revised and expanded version of Ball (1976). Many of the themes and arguments in that earlier essay grew out of conversations with Donald Moon, Stephen Toulmin, and the late Imre Lakatos. I should also like to thank Moon for criticizing an earlier version of this essay and John Aldrich for subsequent bibliographic guidance.

1. For a survey of would-be paradigms of political science, see Holt and Richardson (1970). On the role of paradigms in the history of political theory, see Wolin (1968).

2. Here I include sociology (Friedrichs 1971; Smolicz 1970; Lebowitz 1971), psychology (Palermo 1971; Welmes 1973; Boneau 1974), and economics (Coats 1969; Stanfield 1974).

3. Although Kuhn popularized the term "paradigm," he did not coin it. Our word "paradigm" is derived from the Greek *paradeigma*, meaning model, pattern, or exemplar. In the *Republic*, for example, Plato speaks of his ideal polity as a "paradigm (*paradeigma*) laid up in heaven" (592b). The first to speak of paradigms in the natural sciences was the eighteenth-century philosopher Georg Christoph Lichtenberg, for whom a paradigm was an accepted standard model or pattern into which we attempt to fit unfamiliar phenomena; when we have done so, we say we have "explained" or "understood" them. It is in this sense also that Wittgenstein (1969) spoke of paradigms and Austin (1970, 202) of "thought-models." This earlier use of the term is rather more precise and restricted that Kuhn's original (1962) use of "paradigm" as a portmanteau concept enclosing exemplary scientific achievements, theories, successful experiments, *Gestalten*, and world views, among other notions (Masterman 1970). Attempting to control such terminological inflation, Kuhn later (1970a, 1974, 1985) preferred to speak instead of exemplary theories, or "exemplars," for short.

4. The analogy between paradigms and natural languages was drawn by Popper (1970) and accepted, with amendments, by Kuhn (1970a. pp. 200-204; 170b, pp. 267-271). More recently, Kuhn (1984) has extended the linguistic model, construing theoretical languages as "lexicons." See further, Davidson (1982) and Rorty (1979).

5. Kuhn subsequently said that his "view of scientific development is fundamentally evolutionary" (1970b, 264). For two rather different evolutionary theories of scientific change, see Popper (1972, ch. 7) and Toulmin (1967, 1972).

6. Popper terms this "the naturalistic doctrine of observation"; Nietzsche called it, rather more colorfully, "the dogma of immaculate perception."

7. On this much, at least, Kuhn and Lakatos agreed. For extended discussions of the theory-laden character of observation, see Hanson (1968), Spector (1966), Feyerabend (1970), and Machamer (1971, 1973).

8. Lest one think that such observational propositions are somehow suspect, if not indeed inferior to direct "eyeball observation," Lakatos reminds us that "calling the reports of our human eye 'observational' only indicates that we 'rely' on some vague physiological theory of human vision" (1970, 107).

9. Up to this point, Lakatos agrees with Kuhn. But, as we shall see, Kuhn differs from Lakatos in viewing this as a social-psychological fact about the behavior of scientists, rather than as a methodological maxim or principle implicit in scientific practice.

10. Consistent, that is, with a "rational reconstruction" of the history of science; see Lakatos (1971). As we shall see, this soon proved to be a troublesome sticking point.

11. Lakatos does not supply us with a wholly rational method for choosing a research program; rather, he provides a means of "keeping score" in the contest between rival research programs (1971, 101).

12. The idea that such assumptions subtend all scientific inquiry is not entirely novel. Burtt (1954) speaks of "metaphysical foundations," Collingwood (1940) of "absolute presuppositions," Popper (1962, ch. 4) of "myths," Toulmin (1961, chs. 3–4) of "ideals of natural order," and Laudan (1977, pp. 99–81) of a research tradition's "ontology" and its accompanying "metaphysical and methodological commitments," in much the same way that Lakatos talks about the hard core of a research program.

13. Lakatos's point—despite the forbidding jargon in which it is expressed — is essentially a simple and commonsensical one. It is that we can never get anywhere if we always dwell on the "fundamental assumptions" of a theory (or a series of theories), instead of its "payoff." The "hands-off" policy prescribed by the negative heuristic allows the scientist to get on with her work without having to constantly defend her core assumptions.

14. Although never explicitly defined, a problem-shift is a change in directions (or directives) for research. A change is fruitful, promising — "progressive" — if it permits the prediction of new facts even as it accounts for old anomalies, and is "degenerating" if it resolves old difficulties by means of verbal and/or ad hoc stratagems which do not point out new directions for research.

15. I say pseudo-Popperian because Popper never was — despite many social scientists' misreading of him — a dogmatic faslificationist; he is, rather, a methodological falsificationist, though not a "sophisticated" one (Lakatos, 1970).

16. The following Lakatosian analysis of the paradox of voting was first suggested to me by Donald Moon. I have followed fairly closely the account of it given in Moon (1975, pp. 196–204).

17. This title is borrowed, with amendment and apologies, from Feyerabend (1963).

18. Among those who have hunted — and presumably killed — structural-functional ducks are Gregor (1968) and Flanigan and Fogelman (1967). Prominent among those who have stalked Marxian ducks are Acton (1957), Plamenatz (1963, vol. II, chs. 5–6), Popper (1963, vol. II, chs. 18–21), and Gregor (1965, chs. 4–5). All are superb critics but poor sportsmen: they went duck hunting with antiaircraft guns. Their sort of falsificationism virtually guarantees success in hunting. Is it then any wonder that we look, usually in vain, for new paradigms in our discipline? No duck in its right mind would fly into our sights.

19. Of course that is not what they intended to recommend, nor is that all they did. For a lucid and suggestive discussion of these matters, see Wolin (1968) and Moon (1975, pp. 209–216).

References

Acton, H.B. 1957. *The Illusion of the Epoch*. Boston: Beacon Press.

Aldrich, John. 1976. "Some Problems in Testing Two Rational Models of Participation." *American Journal of Political Science*, vol. 20 (November): 713–33.

—— and Dennis M. Simon. 1986. "Turnout in American National Elections." *Research in Micropolitics*, vol. 1: 271–301.

Almond, Gabriel A. 1966. "Political Theory and Political Science." *American Political Science Review* (December): 869–79.

Austin, J.L. 1970. *Philosophical Papers*. 2d ed. Oxford: Clarendon Press.

Ball, Terence. 1976. "From Paradigms to Research Programs: Toward a Post-Kuhnian Political Science." *American Journal of Political Science*, 20 (February): 151–177.

Barry, Brian. 1970. *Sociologists, Economists and Democracy*. London: Collier-Macmillan.

Beardsley, Philip. 1974. "Political Science: The Case of the Missing Paradigm." *Political Theory* (February): 46–61.

Beck, Nathaniel. 1975. "The Paradox of Minimax Regret." *American Political Science Review*, 69 (September): 918.

Berelson, Bernard R., and Gary Steiner. 1964. *Human Behavior: An Inventory of Scientific Findings*. New York: Harcourt, Brace and World.

Bernstein, Richard J. 1983. *Beyond Objectivism and Relativism: Science, Hermeneutics, and Praxis*. Philadelphia: University of Pennsylvania Press.

Boneau, C.A. 1974. "Paradigm Regained: Cognitive Behaviorism Restated." *American Psychologist* (May): 297–310.

Buck, Roger C., and Robert S. Cohen, eds. 1971. *Boston Studies in the Philosophy of Science*, vol. VIII. Dordrecht: D. Reidel.

Burtt, E.A. 1954. *Metaphysical Foundations of Modern Science*, 2d rev. ed. (first publ. 1924). New York: Anchor Books.

Coats, A.W. 1969. "Is There a 'Structure of Scientific Revolutions' in Economics? *Kyklos* (Fasc. 2): 289–96

Collingwood, R.G. 1940. *An Essay on Metaphysics*. Oxford: Clarendon Press.

Dahl, Robert A. 1963. *Modern Political Analysis*. Englewood Cliffs, N.J.: Prentice-Hall.

Davidson, Donald. 1982. "On the Very Idea of a Conceptual Scheme." In Krausz and Meiland, eds.: 66–80.

Doppelt, Gerald. 1982. "Kuhn's Epistemological Relativism: An Interpretation and Defense." In Krausz and Meiland, eds.: 113–146.

Downs, Anthony. 1957. *An Economic Theory of Democracy.* New York: Harper & Row.

Euben, J. Peter. 1969. "Political Science and Political Silence." In *Power and Community*, edited by Philip Green and Sanford Levinson. New York: Pantheon.

Eulau, Heinz. 1964. *The Behavioral Persuasion in Politics.* New York: Random House.

Ferejohn, John A. and Morris P. Fiorina. 1974. "The Paradox of Not Voting: A Decision Theoretic Analysis." *American Political Science Review*, 69 (September): 525–36.

———. 1975 "Closeness Counts Only in Horseshoes and Dancing." *American Political Science Review*, 69 (September): 920–25.

Feyerabend, Paul K. 1963. "How to be a Good Empiricist—A Plea for Tolerance in Matters Epistemological." *In Philosophy of Science: The Delaware Seminar*, edited by Bernard Baumrin, vol II. New York: Wiley.

———. 1970 "Problems of Empiricism II." In *The Nature and Function of Scientific Theories*, edited by Robert G. Colodny. University of Pittsburgh Series in the Philosophy of Science vol. IV. Pittsburgh: University of Pittsburgh Press.

Flanigan, William and Edwin Fogelman. 1967. "Functional Analysis." In *Contemporary Political Analysis*, edited by James C. Charlesworth. New York: Free Press.

Friedman, Milton. 1953. *Essays in Positive Economics.* Chicago: University of Chicago Press.

Friedrichs, Robert. 1971. "Sociological Paradigms: Analogies of Teleology, Apocalypse, and Prophecy." *Sociological Analysis* (Spring): pp. 1–6.

Goodin, R.E. and K.W.S. Roberts. 1975. "The Ethical Voter." *American Political Science Review*, 69 (September): 918.

Gregor, A. James. 1965. *A Survey of Marxism.* New York: Random House.

———. 1968. "Political Science and the Uses of Functional Analysis." *American Political Science Review* (June): 425–39.

Gunnell, John G. 1968. "Social Science and Political Reality: The Problem of Explanation." *Social Research* (Spring): 159–201.

———. 1969. "Deduction, Explanation, and Social Scientific Inquiry." *American Political Science Review* (December): 1233–46.

————. 1968. "Political Science and the Uses of Functional Analysis." *American Political Science Review* (June): 425-39.

Hanson, Norwood Russell. 1958. *Patterns of Discovery.* Cambridge: Cambridge University Press.

Hegel, G.W.F. 1967. *Philosophy of Right.* New York: Oxford University Press.

Holt, Robert T. and Richardson, John M., Jr. 1970. "Competing Paradigms in Comparative Politics." In *The Methodology of Comparative Research*, edited by Robert T. Holt and John E. Turner. New York: Free Press.

Krausz, Michael and Jack W. Meiland, eds. 1982. *Relativism: Cognitive and Moral.* Notre Dame, Ind. University of Notre Dame Press.

Kuhn, Thomas S. 1962. *The Structure of Scientific Revolutions.* Chicago: University of Chicago Press.

————. 1970a. "Postscript" to the 2nd ed. of Kuhn (1962).

————. 1970b. "Reflections on My Critics." In Lakatos and Musgrave 1970.

————. 1974. "Second Thoughts on Paradigms." In *The Structure of Scientific Theories*, edited by Frederick Suppe. Urbana: University of Illinois Press.

————. 1977. *The Essential Tension.* Chicago: University of Chicago Press.

————. 1984. "Scientific Development and Lexical Change." The Thalheimer Lectures, John Hopkins University.

Lakatos, Imre. 1970. "Falsification and the Methodology of Scientific Research Programmes." In Lakatos and Musgrave, 91-196.

———— and Alan Musgrave, eds. 1970. *Criticism and the Growth of Knowledge.* Cambridge: Cambridge University Press.

————. 1971. "History of Science and Its Rational Reconstructions." In Buck and Cohen, 91-136.

Landau, Martin. 1972a. *Political Theory and Political Science.* New York: Macmillan.

————. 1972b. "Comment [on Miller, 1972]," *American Political Science Review* (September): 846-856.

Laudan, Larry. 1977. *Progress and Its Problems: Towards a Theory of Scientific Growth.* Berkeley and Los Angeles: University of California Press.

Lebowitz, Barry. 1971. "Paradigms in Sociology: Some Thoughts on an Undebated Issue." Paper presented at the 1971 American Sociological Association meetings.

Machamer, Peter K. 1971. "Observation." In Buck and Cohen: 187-201.

————. 1973. "Feyerabend and Galileo: The Interaction of Theories, and the

Reinterpretation of Experience." *Studies in History and Philosophy of Science* (May): 1-46.

Masterman, Margaret. 1970. "The Nature of a Paradigm." In Lakatos and Musgrave, 59-90.

Mayer, Lawrence S. and I. J. Good. 1975. "Is Minimax Regret Applicable to Voting Decisions?" *American Political Science Review*, 69 (September): 916-17.

Miller, Eugene F. 1972. "Positivism, Historicism, and Political Inquiry." *American Political Science Review* (September): 796-817.

Moon, J. Donald. 1975. "The Logic of Political Inquiry: A Synthesis of Opposed Perspectives." In *Handbook of Political Science*, vol. I, edited by Fred I. Greenstein and Nelson W. Polsby. Reading, Mass.: Addison-Wesley.

———. 1983. "On Political Philosophy and the Study of Politics." In *Dissent and Affirmation: Essays in Honor of Mulford Q. Sibley*, edited by Arthur L. Kalleberg, J. Donald Moon, and Daniel R. Sabia. Bowling Green, Ohio: Bowling Green University Press.

Ollman, Bertell. 1979. *Social and Sexual Revolution: Essays on Marx and Reich*. Boston: South End Press.

Palermo, David. 1971. "Is a Scientific Revolution Taking Place in Psychology?" *Science Studies*, 135-155.

Plamenatz, John. 1963. *Man and Society*, 2 vols. London: Longmans.

Polsby, Nelson W. 1980. *Community Power and Political Theory*, 2nd enlarged edn. New Haven: Yale University Press.

Popper, Karl R. 1962. *Conjectures and Refutations.* New York: Basic Books.

———. 1963. *The Open Society and Its Enemies*, two vols. New York: Harper Torchbooks.

———. 1970. "Normal Science and Its Dangers." In Lakatos and Musgrave, 51-58.

———. 1972. *Objective Knowledge: An Evolutionary Approach.* Oxford: Clarendon Press.

Riker, William H., and Peter C. Ordeshook. 1968. "A Theory of the Calculus of Voting." *American Political Science Review* (March): 25-42.

———. 1973. *An Introduction to Positive Political Theory.* Englewood Cliffs, N.J.: Prentice Hall.

Rorty, Richard. 1979. *Philosophy and the Mirror of Nature.* Princeton, N.J.: Princeton University Press.

Rudner, Richard. 1972. "Comment [on Miller, 1972]." *American Political Science Review* (September): 827–845.

Ryan, Alan. 1972. " 'Normal' Science or Political Ideology?" In *Philosophy, Politics, and Society*, fourth series, edited by Peter Laslett, W.G. Runciman, and Quentin Skinner. Oxford: Blackwell.

Shapere, Dudley. 1964. "The Structure of Scientific Revolutions." *Philosophical Review* (July): 383–394.

———. 1966. "Meaning and Scientific Change." In *Mind and Cosmos: Essays in Contemporary Science and Philosophy*, edited by Robert G. Colodny, University of Pittsburgh Series in the Philosophy of Science, vol. III. Pittsburgh: University of Pittsburgh Press.

Smolicz, Jerzy. 1970. "Paradigms and Models," *Austrialian and New Zealand Journal of Sociology* (October): 100–119.

Spector, Marshall. 1966. "Theory and Observation." *British Journal for the Philosophy of Science* (May–August): 1–20, 89–104.

Stanfield, R. 1974. "Kuhnian Scientific Revolutions and the Keynesian Revolution." *Journal of Economic Issues*: 97–109.

Stephens, Jerome. 1973. "The Kuhnian Paradigm and Political Inquiry: An Appraisal." *American Journal of Political Science* (August): 467–488.

Stephens, Stephen V. 1975. "The Paradox of Not Voting: A Comment." *American Political Science Review*, 69 (September): 914–15.

Strom, Gerald S. 1975. "On the Apparent Paradox of Participation," *American Political Science Review*, 69 (September): 908–913.

Toulmin, Stephen. 1963. *Foresight and Understanding*. New York: Harper Torchbooks.

———. 1967. "The Evolutionary Development of Natural Science." *American Scientist* (December): 456–471.

———. 1970. "Does the Distinction Between Normal and Revolutionary Science Hold Water?" In Lakatos and Musgrave, 39–48.

———. 1972. *Human Understanding*, vol. I. Oxford: Clarendon Press.

Truman, David B. 1965. "Disillusion and Regeneration: The Quest for a Discipline." *American Political Science Review* (December): 865–873.

Wahlke, John C. 1979. "Pre-Behavioralism in Political Science." *American Political Science Review*, 73: 68–77.

Welmes, W.B. 1973. "Paradigms and Normal Science in Psychology." *Science Studies*: 211–222.

Wittgenstein, Ludwig. 1968. "Wittgenstein's Notes for Lectures on Private Experience and 'Sense Data'." Transcribed and annotated by Rush Rhees. *Philosophical Review* (July): 271–320.

Wolin, Sheldon S. 1968. "Paradigms and Political Theories." In *Politics and Experience: Essays Presented to Michael Oakeshott*, edited by Preston King and B.C. Parekh. Cambridge: Cambridge University Press, 125–152.

James Farr

2

Resituating Explanation

I use the word laws with malice aforethought. There must be laws of politics, for laws are the most universal of all phenomena.

William Bennett Munro

Malicious or not, Munro was no iconoclast. His words, written in 1927 on the eve of his presidency of the American Political Science Association, expressed a rather traditional article of faith (Munro 1928). Indeed, from David Hume to William Riker, the prospect of a science of politics has been said to depend upon the discovery of general laws. Without such laws, the argument runs, political science would be a "science" in name only. But a blue-ribbon name is not the only thing at stake in our disciplinary quest for identity; so is the very aim of science — namely, explanation. The motto of this tradition could well read: No laws, no explanations; no explanations, no science.

This motto — and therefore the identity of political science as science — has not wanted for challengers (for example, Gunnell 1969; Nelson 1975). But within political science, the "deductive nomological" or "covering-law model of explanation" (Dray 1957) has, heretofore, enjoyed a prominence bordering on hegemony. Doubters can readily confirm this by surveying decades of APSA presidential addresses, treatises on the logic of political inquiry, and innumerable scope-and-methods texts (Somit and Tanenhaus 1967; Ricci 1984). Proponents of the covering-law model have taken their cues, however, not so much from the actual explanatory practices of political science — where the absence of laws is repeatedly and ritualistically bemoaned — but from certain contemporary philosophers of science whose reflections on the natural sciences made the covering-law model a *desideratum* in the first place. Karl Popper and Carl Hempel have been two particularly important philosophers in this regard — so important, in fact, that the covering-law model is sometimes called "the Popper-Hempel theory" (Donagan 1964).

In this essay, I want to criticize the Popper–Hempel theory and, by implication, the dominant view of explanation in political science. More constructively, I want to propose an alternative model of explanation. 'Situational analysis,' I hope to show, better suits social and political explanations in principle, and better accounts for political science explanations in practice. I take my cues not only from the practice of political science, but also, ironically, from Popper himself. "For years the unimportant thesis—in a misinterpreted form—has, under the name 'the deductive model' helped to generate a voluminous literature. The much more important aspect of the problem," Popper continues, was "the method of situational analysis" (1976a, 117). What I want to do here, then, is to expose some deficiencies in the covering-law model of explanation; to articulate the outlines of situational analysis roughly along Popperian lines;[1] to discuss in some detail two prominent explanations in political science which have presented themselves in covering-law terms, but which may be better understood in light of situational analysis; and to conclude with some reflections about how we might better understand political science as a whole.

I

Until recently, the covering-law model so dominated philosophical discussion of scientific explanation that many have come to call it the "received" view. So familiar is it that only a brief reminder of its general contours need delay us. Explanations, according to the received view, take the form of deductive arguments. The premises of such arguments have both general laws and statements of initial and scope conditions. Their conclusions are cast as statements describing what we are trying to explain, whether an object, an event, an action, or a causal regularity (itself expressed as a general law). When the conclusion describes something that is yet to happen, we have a *prediction* instead of an explanation. Even so, the logic remains the same, indifferent to its temporal orientation or the pragmatic uses to which it is put. Clearly, everything here depends on the laws which license the deduction.

Laws are true law-like generalizations. The truth of a law-like generalization is ascertained not by collecting confirming instances, as positivists and behavioralists once believed, but by repeated attempts at falsification. Truth, then, is at best a provisional attribute of law-like generalizations. Saying that a generalization is law-like means that it is no ordinary generalization, no mere summary of accidental occurrences in the world. Rather, it must meet exacting standards (Hempel 1965). In particular, it must express a genuine causal regularity, the determination of which depends upon there being at a minimum a "constant conjunction" (to use Hume's famous phrase) between two classes of objects, events, or actions. These conjunctions may be universal or probabilistic, but they must be highly specified. That is, whether universal or probabilistic, a law-like generalization must state its scope conditions by specifying under what range of conditions it claims to hold. Finally, it must support a set of counterfactual conditional statements which allow us to make warranted inferences about unobserved or hypothetical instances. Its failure to support these counterfactuals is tantamount to a confession that our generalization is accidental, a mere summary of previously observed instances.

This is a coherent, consistent, and powerful vision of scientific explanation. But do all scientific explanations necessarily conform to its dictates? In particular, does it shed light on the subject matter, the logic, and the explanatory practices of the social and political sciences? There are at least three reasons for thinking that it does not.

First, the conception of causation as constant conjunction which underlies the model seems most inappropriate to the sorts of causal claims which political science characteristically makes. To appreciate this, consider that in the actual practice of even the natural sciences — as opposed to its positivist reconstruction — causal claims are vindicated not by appealing to constant conjunctions, but to the essential agents or mechanisms which actually bring things about in the material world. Scientific realism promotes this essentialist or activist conception of causation to a first principle, arguing that natural scientists do not in fact rest content with discovering regularities. Rather, they seek out those agents or mechanisms whose discoverable powers cause the phenomena which needs to be explained (Harré 1970). This insight of scientific realism is appropriate to the social and political sciences, as well, even if other insights are inappropriate. Our causal claims are generally — and should always be — vindicated by appealing, not to generalizations as such, but to political agents acting in structured situations. This is so even when there are many observed regularities, as is the case in repeatable and typical situations. But it is also true in other cases, as well — for example, in studies of elites or of entrepreneurial decision-making or of risk-taking. Here we have a single action (or set of actions) to explain where no constant conjunctions are available. But, the relative singularity of the case need not undermine its being understood in causal terms. To vindicate this, however, is to turn to the actor or actors responsible. In short, causes are about actors and actions, independent of laws or constant conjunctions.

A second deficiency follows the first. In encouraging attention to laws and not to actions as such, the covering-law model generally dislocates the conceptual schema appropriate to understanding politics. Indeed, the model is *abstract* in that its account of the logic of explanation does not preserve precisely those concepts which must guide us in explaining and understanding political phenomena. I have in mind rationality, intentionality, and meaning. The covering-law model generally tries to dismiss these notions or to jury-rig them to fit its preconceived account of the nature of science. Intentionality becomes an event temporally locatable "in the head" or even "in the central nervous system," materially different than other events (Simon 1968). Understanding meaning is relegated to a subjective method of *verstehende*-understanding — a helpful source of hypotheses or hunches, perhaps, but no more necessary to science than "a good cup of coffee" (Neurath as quoted in Apel 1972; McCarthy 1973). And explanations by way of rationality are simply subsumed as another sort of covering-law explanation. In particular, the received view contends that the use of an actor's (purported) rationality to explain his or her beliefs or actions just is to be committed to a law. Such a law claims roughly that 'All rational actors in such-and-such a situation (like the one to be explained) will believe or act in such-and-such a way.' All the 'such-and-suches' must be highly specified in non-unique ways and the law, itself, governed by the model's strict criteria of explanation, especially that it be confirmable or falsifiable. But, as we shall see below, rational explanations do not, in fact, meet these criteria nor should we expect them to. More generally, intentionality and meaning pose recurring problems or opportunities (depending on one's view) for political science.

Given this, it is entirely understandable why an earlier generation of positivists and behaviorists thought that categories like intentionality and meaning had to be purged before there could ever be a genuine science of politics or human action. In the name of a would-be science, they were prepared to jettison the very subject matter which made the study of politics so compelling in the first place and so intimately connected with our understanding of ourselves as political actors. Happily, these efforts came to nothing, perhaps because of the unfeasibility of the project, perhaps because of other, more serious reasons. When asked whether positivism had any important defects, one candid positivist replied, "Well, I suppose the most important of the defects was that nearly all of it was false" (A.J. Ayer as quoted in Magee 1978, 131).

Finally and most importantly, actual explanations in political science do not remotely conform to the dictates of the covering-law model. In short, the practice of political science differs radically from the theory of explanation prescribed by the received view. Political science does indeed search for generalizations, and such generalizations as are discovered have increased our knowledge of politics considerably. But these generalizations simply are not law-like. They are frequently correlational regularities which, at best, hint at the sorts of causal actors responsible for their production. They are justifiably hedged around in a number of ways, usually with indeterminate modifiers like 'usually,' 'characteristically,' or 'more-or-less.' They seldom stipulate their boundary or scope conditions with any exactitude. They are unsure about their counterfactual force when straying from the confirming observations which made them possible in the first place. And they are infrequently borne out by the predictions they should underwrite.

None of this is to be regretted as such, at least if one believes that the political world, including its systematic unpredictability, dictates the form which the science of politics must take (MacIntyre 1981). Machiavelli thought this. So too did Aristotle, whom many behavioralists believe to have been "the first political scientist" (Wahlke 1979). Far from longing for a political science with law-governed explanations as exact as those found, say, in physics or mathematics, Aristotle was quite clear that "in studying this subject we must be content if we attain as high a degree of certainty as the matter of it admits. The same accuracy or finish is not to be looked for in all discussions" (1953, 27).

Aristotle's caution is salutary. But it requires, among other things, a model of explanation with such accuracy or finish as is to be expected from political science. Such a model must also, to be an advance on the received view of explanation, avoid the problems besetting the covering-law model. I believe that there is such a model — the model of situational analysis. Its virtues include the preservation of our fundamental explanatory concerns with rationality, intentionality, and meaning. It keeps our attention on actors and actions as the causes of political phenomena. Situational analysis also grounds or undergirds many of the generalizations invoked in political science. Consequently, it better exemplifies the actual practice of political science. After characterizing situational analysis in somewhat general terms, I shall reconsider two classic explanations in political science.

II

Situational analysis has as its primary objective the explanation of the actions undertaken by political actors in given situations. Now in political science we often hear that systems, structures, outputs, or the results of actions form our primary explanatory objectives. This may be true, though it has about it a dogmatic ring in light of the many different things political scientists actually seek to explain. In any case, when we speak of, say, results, we must ask, results of what? The answer, ultimately, is the actions of political actors. In the relevant sense, actions here are behaviors backed by reasons and by beliefs of varying degrees of rationality. This, then, is the proper terrain of situational analysis. The situational analyst, in brief, will go as far as possible to show that an action performed by an actor was the rational or adequate thing to do in that sort of situation. In this way, situational analysis brings together, in a particularly salient way, some of our fundamental explanatory concerns with intentionality, rationality, contextuality, and meaning. This is an idealized characterization, to be sure, for indeed there are repeated and so generalized actions, irrational or nonrational actions, and myriad unintended consequences. But, as we shall see, our ability to explain even these phenomena presupposes situational analysis.

Situational analysis has two parts or aspects: the situational model and the principle of rationality. The *situational model* is a detailed description of (1) the natural environment; (2) the social environment (that is, other strategic actors and the social relations between actors); and (3) the problem-situation in which an actor finds himself or herself, defines his or her problems, and tries out tentative solutions. Describing the situation is a fundamental task of political science, though some political scientists spend more time on this than do others. Of the features of the situational model, the problem-situation demands the most careful attention, for our very identification of the actor's problem and subsequent action hangs in the balance. The problem-situation is usually constituted by a tradition or traditions of various kinds, whether in the form of theories, ideas, rules, norms, procedures, and/or practices.

Situations, then, are partly constituted by problems, ideas, and theories which actors pose or have or hold. These phenomena are all *intentional* phenomena in that they are products of mental states, and that they are about something, whether mental or not (Searle 1983). Thus the task of understanding intentional phenomena is part of the very task of describing the situational model. This is so even when, as so often happens, political scientists wish to explain the *un*intended consequences of action because the very *identification* of unintended consequences logically depends upon the prior identification of what was intended in the situation in the first place. Intentionality, in short, is a benchmark for understanding and explaining political action. Hence, the actors' own construction or interpretation of the situation is of particular importance. To appreciate what is at stake here, consider the oft-heard claim that actors' " 'definitions of the situation' have a very real existence of their own . . . Even a situation that is misperceived may be real in its consequences'' (Eulau 1963, 120; Easton 1971, 27). This serves to remind us both that situations are objective in that features of them may be misperceived, and also that (mis)perceptions are nonetheless real in that they are causally related to outcomes.

However, psychological perceptions (or misperceptions) are not principally at stake here, but the *meanings* which actors attribute to their problems and their situations are. As I.C. Jarvie rightly says, ''The meaning of certain actions to the actors is of course part of the situation as they see it'' (Jarvie 1972, 14). These meanings, then, also help to define or constitute the situation. This, in turn, requires that the situational analyst identify and appraise the problem-situation in large part in the way the actors themselves do. This involves using their concepts, language, and theoretical frameworks. This does not imply, however, that the situational analyst is wholly restricted to the actors' conscious identifications and appraisals. Indeed, insofar as problems are objective, actors may seriously misidentify, misappraise, or underestimate their problem-situation (Weber 1975, 188; Watkins 1970, 171). However, any further objective assessment of the situation on the part of the analyst must still proceed in terms which are meaningful and accessible to the actors, themselves, lest the analyst assess or impose an altogether different problem-situation. In principle, this is the only way actors can discover mistakes or inadequate solutions to their problems and proceed to revise them in a critical manner.

If one thinks that ordinary actors are somehow 'too ordinary' here, then consider political elites who, in making public policy, sometimes turn to political scientists for their expert advice. If the methodological rule intimated above were not followed — that is, the rule that we identify, understand, and appraise the situation in the way the actors do, at least initially — then the 'policy sciences' would be impossible. The relevant policy problems would be misdescribed and thus misunderstood. Subsequent policy analysis would be impossible or, at any rate, irrelevant. We might call this concern with the actors' language and meanings the hermeneutic or interpretative dimensions of situational analysis. These hermeneutic dimensions are unique to the social and political sciences, however true it is that the natural sciences also have some hermeneutic or interpretative dimensions of their own (Popper 1972; Toulmin 1983; Heelan 1983).

Attention to the situation, then, is of paramount importance. Sometimes the situations which political scientists are called upon to describe are typical in that they are frequently repeated or reproduced in political life, and actors act in fairly uniform and substitutable ways in them. These kinds of situations readily lend themselves to modeling —

versions of Weber's ideal-types. Models of intentional and rational action — particularly in economic, organizational, or game-theoretic contexts — represent the more generalized form of situational analysis. On other occasions, however, the situations and problems are more particular and the actors less typical, as when political scientists explain the actions of a world-historic individual, the beliefs of a special group, or when a historian of political thought tries to explain the theory of a political thinker long dead. Thus situations range from the (more) typical to the (more) unique, and this range of situations will dictate the extent to which generalizations, models, or idiographic explanations will dominate a particular field of study.

On the basis of the description of the situation, the political scientist can claim to understand and explain an action to the extent that he or she can show it to have been "adequate to the situation as the agent saw it" (Popper 1972, 179; and 1976b, 97, where Weber is credited for this insight). This is to apply the *rationality principle*, the second feature or aspect of situational analysis. Our understanding of political actors depends upon our ability to capture their reasons or rationales for acting as they do in their given situations.

The rationality principle has been introduced here in a perhaps infelicitous way, for it might appear that the attribution of rationality comes after the description of the situation. But this obscures the main point about the rationality principle because to fully describe the situation in the first place actually *presupposes* its application. It is, to borrow and adapt another notion of Popper's, a *searchlight principle* (1972, appendix). In the practice of situational analysis, the rationality principle functions much as a searchlight does, illuminating those features of the situation which clarify the subsequent action. In this way, the rationality principle is a decidedly *methodological postulate* (Popper 1967, 144; Watkins 1970, 209; Moe 1979). The metaphor of a searchlight is perhaps most appropriate when, in the face of *prima facie* irrationalities, confusions, lapses, or lacunae, we search, often repeatedly, for hidden or uninvestigated beliefs, meanings, theories, or problems which lie in the dark, but which must be brought to light in order to adequately describe the actors' situation. Only to the extent that we can do this can we say we understand political actors, be they voters, bureaucrats, presidents, or revolutionaries.

The concept of rationality presupposed by the rationality principle is admittedly a bounded, limited, and charitable one in light of its use and in comparison with other conceptions of rationality. When we speak of the rationality of an actor in a given situation, we have in mind something like the following. An actor has a more or less coherent or consistent set of beliefs which back his or her actions in a given situation.

Actions are explained and/or justified by (what we might call) im-mediate, action-informing beliefs in that these beliefs, usually about the achievement of immediate goals, supply agents with a reason or reasons for acting that way in that situation. These immediate, action-informing beliefs are explained and/or justified by other, background beliefs in that the background beliefs give a reason or reasons for holding the im-mediate beliefs. Ultimately, some of these beliefs must be open to criticism, to correction, and even to refutation. Our ability to criticize or refute our beliefs is made possible, in large part, by our ability to learn from our mistakes, and so, to solve our problems. Problem-solving in this sense is a tradition-bound enterprise which has a rational trajectory underestimated by speaking solely of informed choices (as is commonly done in a number of theories of rationality). In problem-solving situa-tions, there is often precious little information about available alter-natives and, especially, about their respective consequences. Novel and unpredictable problems often emerge in an attempt to solve old ones. And there is no suggestion that only one action or belief is rational or adequate to an actor's situation, for several may be.

The rationality principle, then, guides our inquiries by focusing at-tention on rational actions generally in problem-solving situations. In this role it clearly functions as a methodological postulate, a practical guide to social inquiry. However, to achieve formal closure of explana-tion, the rationality principle plays its last role in constructing a major premise in a deductive explanation duly conforming to its dictates. (On this reading, the situational model summarizes the initial conditions for such a deductive explanation). The major premise might be fashioned in a *formally* law-like (though rather loose) way, like: ''In such-and-such a situation, a rational actor, faced with such-and-such a problem, with such-and-such beliefs, intentions, and meanings, will act in such-and-such a way.'' Our ability to fill in the 'such-and-suches' for a particular ex-planation presupposes the previous use of the rationality principle as a searchlight principle. Frequently, the actor's problem, beliefs, and mean-ings which figure in this formally law-like premise were discovered *in the first place* by the rationality principle in its charitable search for situa-tional understanding. Thus the premise essentially restates *post hoc* the findings of the rationality principle in that case or cases.

In practice, then — and contrary to the covering-law model — this formal premise is no more falsifiable than is the rationality principle which backs it (Watkins 1970; Moe 1979). The rationality principle is not put forward as a hypothesis or bold conjecture to be falsified or cor-roborated by the facts of the situation, for it brought the facts to light. The rationality principle is just not a candidate for decisive refutation. We retain it as a methodological principle for future cases even when we discover cases of genuine irrationalities, because the very identification of irrationalities depends upon a benchmark established by the rationality principle itself (Weber 1975; Watkins 1970; Elster 1979). If the rationality principle were indeed an empirical law, the discovery of irrational actions would be enough to falsify it, thereby forcing us to give it up once and for all. But we cannot do this because our ability to identify and solve problems, forge intelligibility out of confusing patterns of human interaction, discover beliefs and meanings of others, fit intentions to actions, and so understand and explain human action depends upon it. Without it, there are movements, sounds, behaviors, and mystery. We need the rationality principle, despite its unfalsifiability. To give it up would just be to give up.

Situational analysis, then, circumscribes the domain of falsification by immunizing the rationality principle. However, this does not rule out falsification altogether in situational analysis. Quite the contrary. Falsification plays its part in regulating our acceptance or rejection of the description of the situation. If an analyst makes a false claim about an actor's problem-situation — shown to be false, for example, by documentary or verbal evidence — then that (particular) analysis can be rejected, at least in light of a competing situational analysis.

Popper makes a similar point when referring to those situational analyses of the more generalized, economic-modeling kind. For even though they are instrumentally useful for understanding large-scale economic processes, they are nonetheless "oversimplified and overschematized and consequently in general *false*" (Popper 1976b, 103). This, he emphasizes elsewhere, "seems to indicate a considerable difference between the natural and the social sciences — perhaps *the most important difference in their methods*" (Popper 1961, 141). Situational analysis might be seen, therefore, to demarcate the social from the natural sciences in terms of rationality, intentionality, meaning, and the scope of falsification. This is true and important, even if (as is surely obvious) the natural and social sciences are alike in other, equally important respects.

Finally, situational analysis enjoys explanatory primacy over the important (though less-than-law-like) generalizations discovered in the social and political sciences. These generalizations, we should recall, characteristically lack predictive power, fail to specify their scope, and are unsure about their counterfactual force. Thus it is not surprising that they are themselves frequently in need of explanation. Situational analysis meets this need: It *lies behind* these generalizations, giving them their intelligibility, inasmuch as the generalizations are themselves characteristically artifacts of situational behavior that is recognizably rational. I.C. Jarvie has best made this point, using as his example an empirical generalization which he generously allows to be called a law:

Where the behavior is regular and repeatable we search for laws governing it like "all social changes create vested interests which resist further
social changes." These laws in turn we explain by exposing the logic of
the typical vested interest individual's situation and why it would be rational for him to act against further social change (Jarvie 1972, 18).

Most typical actors are like Jarvie's erstwhile reformer. Their regular and
repeatable behavior may be captured in a generalization. Of course, our
ability to do this with any confidence wholly depends upon our ability to
isolate similar or typical actors in similar or typical situations with
similar or typical problems. The frequency with which this will happen
will be dictated less by any logic of political inquiry than by contingent or
empirical considerations. This is worth emphasizing because no *a priori*
method can determine in advance whether situations will be typical or
particular. This is simply one of the many things discovered as practicing
political scientists go about their work of solving explanatory puzzles.
However, it bears mentioning, that since situations are often sufficiently
and interestingly different across comparative or historical contexts, we
might expect generalizations of a rather more contextually-limited,
historically-bounded kind, rather than truly universal law-like
generalizations (Ball 1972; George and Smoke 1974; Farr 1982; Tilley
1982; Eidlin 1983). Although the former eschew universality, they still
make for considerable generality. Thus situational analysis underwrites
most political scientists' hopes to craft theories which go beyond the infinite detailing of minute particulars.

III

Like all models of explanation, situational analysis should be judged
by its ability to help us to understand our actual explanatory practices.
Its prospects augur well in this regard, largely because a number of explanations have already been understood in the way described above.
Besides a programmatic claim about the whole of microeconomic theory
(Popper 1961; 1976a), such explanations have included particular
episodes in the history of science, warfare, social pathology, art, and
political theory (Popper 1972; Watkins 1970; Wisdom 1970; Gombrich
1974; Farr 1985). With less explicit attention to the philosophical issues
discussed above, many social and political scientists have also spoken of
one or another conception of 'situational analysis.' This is hardly surprising given basic features of social and political life to which our
science must attend. As David Easton once observed, "Since all social
activity takes place within structure, it would indeed be strange if all

social scientists were not compelled in one way or another to fall back on the conception of the situation . . ." (Easton 1971, 192).

Thus, the bare language of situational analysis is by no means alien to political and social science. Many of the diverse practices advertised as situational analyses have been in comparative political science and comparative political sociology, whose patron saint is Max Weber. From the social life world of the immigrant Polish peasant (Thomas and Znaniecki 1927) to foreign policy decision-making (Snyder, Bruck, and Sapin 1962) to deterrence (George and Smoke 1974) to international crises (Hermann 1969) to the international system as a whole (Goodman, Hart, and Rosecrance 1975), situational analysis has figured prominently on the methodological landscape of political and social science. But because names can be deceptive, some caution might be advisable here. For example, at times some of these self-styled situational analyses (or others akin to them) have displayed a tendency to identify situational analysis with behavioralism or to cite positivist precursors like Hempel. There has also been, at times, a tendency to *reduce* actions or decisions to situational variables, as might be seen in the implicit assumptions of some statistical-correlative studies. We might say that this tendency inclines toward a situational or environmental determinism.[2] But this reflects precious little of the concern with agency, intentionality, rationality, and meaning characteristic of the sort of situational analysis championed here. Alexander George and Richard Smoke (1974) have advanced a particularly good example of situational analysis in political science. Their practice of focused comparison and their discoveries of contingent generalizations display the proper balance between the contextuality and generality appropriate to a science of intentional and rational beings who act in situations not of their own design.

Situational analysis promises an even broader scope still. To begin to deliver on this promise, let us take the method of situational analysis into terrain previously claimed by the covering-law model of explanation. By briefly considering two famous 'laws' of partisan political life — 'Duverger's law' and 'the iron law of oligarchy' — I hope to illustrate how situational analysis better captures the explanatory practices to which political science genuinely lays claim.

Speculating about the forces which shape and maintain a two-party system, Maurice Duverger called attention, in mid-century, to "one general factor of a technical kind, the electoral system." Its effect can be expressed in the following formula:

> *the simple-majority single-ballot system favours the two party system.*
> Of all the hypotheses that have been defined in this book [*Political Parties*], this approaches the most nearly perhaps to a true sociological law [Duverger 1954, 217].

Subsequently coined "Duverger's law" in his honor, this hypothesis summarized and explicitly formulated nearly a century of debate and, in turn, inaugurated greater social scientific attention to its exact status and its reformulation in terms of *plurality* counting systems (for a brief history, see Riker 1982). Like W.B. Munro, whose sentiments opened this essay, Duverger chose his words, if not with malice, at least with aforethought, given his considerable command over the methodological issues that beset political science (Duverger 1964 and 1972a). Echoing the striking imagery of an oft-cited preface to *Capital*, Duverger concluded his analysis of bipartisanism by stating that the "dualism of parties is the 'brazen law' (as Marx would have said) of the simple-majority single-ballot electoral system" (Duverger 1954, 228).

Duverger's "brazen law" strikes the social scientific imagination not only because it indeed captures a good deal of partisan political life, but because of two additional features. It does *not* in fact meet the withering standards of the covering-law model; and, as stated, it too stands in need of explanation. Duverger was cognizant of both of these features, though he continued to insist upon law-governed nomenclature (Duverger 1972b, 27). Most of the technical difficulties — especially about prediction and the support of counterfactual conditionals — which have exercised the minds of covering-law theorists have all taken for granted genuinely universal laws, or probabilistic laws with exactingly specified ranges, or laws whose *prima facie* exceptions are readily subsumed in a non-ad-hoc manner in the statements of initial or boundary conditions. But these technical difficulties hardly get off the ground here because Duverger's law exists in the face of important standing exceptions or recalcitrant cases. (This need not be a fault, but for its not being so, the covering-law model needs considerable relaxation to the point of abandonment.) "Not counting Latin America" (Duverger 1954, 220), nor most party systems in their formative years, nor most party systems amidst critical realignment, single-majority (or plurality) single-ballot systems exist alongside and allow for an interesting diversity of party systems beyond the classical two-party system. These include multiparty systems (like Britain between 1910 and 1945); multiparty systems with one party dominant (like the Congress Party in India); two-party systems with stable third parties (like the Social Credit Party or Parti Quebeçois in Canada); and even one-party systems (like the old Confederacy). These are striking former or contemporary exceptions to Duverger's law. Indeed, so striking are they, that if this were not political science but (common sense) physics, we would have to say something like, "water runs downhill, except on weekends."

Many of these exceptions or recalcitrant cases are explainable — but outside the terms of reference of the law. (Duverger suggested a number of plausible social and historical factors, and, less plausibly, the factor of "the *natural* movement of society towards the two-party system" [1954, 216]). Other exceptions have stimulated further refinement of Duverger's law, and many of these have now been (re)subsumed under the various refinements of the law. But interesting exceptions continue to emerge. Consider the Libertarian Party in the United States. It has now been stable across three (or arguably four) presidential elections, without anywhere being one of two principal parties locally (which is one of Riker's amendments [1982, 761]). The Libertarian Party continues to gain support in its search for electoral power, without diluting its ideological appeal. Some might say that it is not 'really' a party because its ideological intransigence entails its consciously failing to try to win elections according to the usual sorts of understood rules. But surely this would beg the question in a most mendicant way.

The substantive issues raised here may be left to students of party systems so as to focus our attention on the second of the above-mentioned features of Duverger's alleged law. To put it in its extreme form, even if the 'law' met covering-law criteria, we would still need an explanation of it. This is a task for situational analysis.

Even *if* there were *no* exceptions, why, we might ask, would major-ity (or plurality) electoral systems bring about two-party systems? Why, to put it another way, do not three or more parties thrive? The generally accepted explanation proceeds, at least partly, by analyzing the situation which governs the casting of votes by individual electors and then judg-ing the collective consequences. To frame the question on an individual basis: In the situation governed by majority (or plurality) electoral rules, why will electors *not* vote for any number of parties, especially including parties ideologically closest to their political views? Though there have been refinements aplenty, Duverger's own account still captures the root of the matter, and it suffices for our purposes:

> In cases where there are three parties operating under the simple-
> majority single-ballot system the electors soon realize that their votes are
> wasted if they continue to give them to the third party: whence their
> natural tendency to transfer their vote to the less evil of its two adver-
> saries in order to prevent the success of the greater evil (1954, 226).

In short, if electors in that situation want a party at least closest to their views to win, then votes for third parties are wasted. And nonwasted votes, collectively considered, maintain a two-party system. "In a system of proportional representation," by contrast, "the *situation* is quite dif-ferent" (Duverger 1972b, 28). The situation is also quite different when voters interpret its meaning for them differently, not as one where im-mediate electoral success is on the line — as if one's vote really counted — but as one calling for, say, ideological purity even in the teeth of elec-toral defeat or one calling for the moral exercise of civic duty, no matter what the electoral consequences (Meehl 1971). Such voters — like their more interest-maximizing fellow citizens — may be deemed rational. But the judgment of rationality, in these various cases, depends on the meaning of the situation as the voters see it. Upon this, hangs much of our explanation of the nature of the party system. Here, then, is the language and general form of situational analysis. Explanatory emphasis falls on actors acting rationally and intentionally to solve problems in situations which are meaningful to them. This is what Duverger *showed* in his practice, despite his description of it in terms of 'psychological forces' and 'brazen laws.' Situational analysis describes matters aright.

Similar conclusions may be reached by considering another, even more brazen law of political life — 'the iron law of oligarchy.' In his 1915 classic, *Political Parties*, Roberto Michels vividly portrayed the oligarchical tendencies of the leaders of modern parties, even of professed democrats. His analysis is still timely, seventy years later, because oligarchs of one stripe or another continue to emerge in modern organizations, whatever their avowed aims and programs. There are, of course, exceptions or recalcitrant cases similar in form to those espied in the case of 'Duverger's law.' But, we may lay these to one side at the outset and allow the initial claim of the covering-law model to go down, namely, that to explain a case of organizational oligarchy would be to bring it under Michels's law. But, it seems that the law-covered explanation would not yet be satisfactory, since something would still be missing. Why do party democrats always or regularly become oligarchs? How, in short, do we explain this purported law? Michels's principal contribution to political science, I suggest, lies not so much in discovering the 'iron law of oligarchy,' but in providing a situational analysis which lies behind the political tendency glossed in generalized form as a 'law.'

Democratic parties, Michels avers, need organization. No mass-based organization can be run as a direct democracy because of the sheer numbers of members, the logarithmic expansion of duties and activities, the need for special aptitudes neither equally nor universally distributed among all members, and the frequent lack of interest displayed by many of the members towards the day-to-day details of party life. The situation dominated by a large and complex organization simply requires increasing expertise and direction which leads to the increasing reliance on delegates, bureaucrats, and leaders in general. "Though it grumbles occasionally, the majority is really delighted to find persons who will take the trouble to look after its affairs" (1915, 58). For their part, the delegates and leaders, by education and inclination, but largely by the force of the situation, accumulate functions. They attend and chair meetings, give orations, produce literary work, provide legal counsel, lead strikes, pore over details, and so acquire supremacy at the cost of extremely hard work.

> All this brings honor to the leader, gives him power over the masses,
> makes him more and more indispensable; but it also involves continuous
> work; for those who are not of exceptionally strong constitution it is apt
> to involve a premature death (1915, 64–65).

The leaders also receive gratitude, even adoration, from the masses, and
"in the object of such adoration, megalomania is apt to ensue" (1915,
74). Add to this situation the lure of pay, prestige, and the trappings of
office offered by the party, as well as the subsequent control of its purse
and press, we find the leaders tending toward long tenures and eventually
wholesale oligarchical control. And so the typical

> leader of working-class origin is enabled, thanks to his new situation, to
> make himself intimately familiar with all the technical details of public
> life, and thus to increase his superiority over the rank and file (1915, 88).

> In this way . . . (the leaders) render it impossible for the masses, whose
> 'theoretical interpreters' they should be, to follow them, and to under-
> stand them, and they thus elude all possibility of technical control. They
> are *masters of the situation* (1915, 91).

The 'iron law of oligarchy' recapitulates and radically summarizes
the actions and the consequences of these "masters of the situation."
Michels succeeds in showing how, in the situation dictated by the problems and needs of large-scale party organizations, leaders emerge and attain positions of great power. Given the effort and skills of the emergent
leaders, along with the deference and inactivity of ordinary members, it
becomes rationally understandable how oligarchy emerges, even in pro-
fessedly democratic organizations. Michels glosses all this not only with
talk about 'iron' laws — a metaphorical usage appropriate to the end of
the era of iron horses and iron chancellors — but also with talk about
"pre-ordination" and "inevitable psychophysiological laws" (1915, 199,
417ff). These flourishes are perhaps understandable, given the
mechanistic and deterministic rhetoric of turn-of-the-century science.
But they are unnecessary, even false. Michels's actual practice affords a
splendid example of situational analysis. Situational elements carry the
burden of explanation, not the psychophysiology of leaders and led.
And for all the purported inevitability and preordination of political
life, Michels concludes with a lesson learned from history which is to
form the kernel of new policy. "It is," he tells us, "the great task of
social education to raise the intellectual level of the masses, so that they
may be enabled, within the limits of what is possible, to counteract the
oligarchical tendencies of the working class movement" (1915, 424). We
can learn from our mistakes, and so craft at least partial solutions to the
problems posed by the unintended and unwanted consequences of

modern political organizations. In this way it is possible to change the so-called "laws" of political life, however iron hard they seem (Gewirth 1954). This was Marx's considered view, contrary to popular opinion (including Duverger's) and despite his Michels-like invocation of "laws . . . working with iron necessity" (Marx 1967, 10). In the *Critique of the Gotha Program*, political change dominated the metallurgy of scientific determinism: "If I abolish wage-labor, then naturally I abolish its laws also, whether they are of 'iron' or sponge" (Marx 1938, 14).

IV

"Methodology," Max Weber once said, should be conceived as "the reflective understanding of the means which have already demonstrated their value in practice by raising them to the level of explicit consciousness" (Weber 1949, 115). Following Weber, I hope to have shown that situational analysis provides such "reflective understanding" for political science. Despite its hegemony, the covering-law model, to adapt Weber's language, reflectively *mis*understands the logic of political explanations. Thus it could hardly be counted on to provide the general form of an explanation of *the development of political science itself*. What sort of laws, we might wonder rhetorically, could conceivably be marshalled to explain even the barest outline, much less the satisfactory details, of, say, the project to reject 'enthusiasm' at the time the figures of the Scottish Enlightenment crafted the first explicitly conceptualized "science of politics"; or the radicalism and avowedly normative pretensions of the utilitarian 'science of government'; or the fascination with history, progress, and induction characteristic of what Macaulay called "that noble science of politics"; or the abandonment of historical sensibility by the "science of politics" movement in the 1920s; or the rapid conversion of a generation of professional political scientists to the tenets of the behavioral revolution; or the emergence of new concepts like "systems" or "structural-functionalism"; or why these concepts have, today, largely lost their meaning, and why the "state" has returned in their stead? Situational analysis, I daresay in conclusion, may help here as well in this current (or perhaps recurrent) identity crisis of political science.

Consider what needs to be done. The life histories of particular theories, research programs, or research traditions within political science[3]—for example, rational choice theories of voting, realism in international relations, cognitive development in political socialization, empirical democratic theory, Marxist political economy, and the like — need to be reconstructed. These projects are not just contributions to the intellectual history of political science, but are absolutely necessary if we are to speak of the progress (or lack of progress) in various areas within political science. Indeed, to understand our theories is to understand their histories in that

> every attempt (except the most trivial) to understand a theory is bound to open up a historical investigation about this theory and its problems, which thus become part of the *object* of investigation (Popper 1972, 177).

The method of situational analysis here finds its final task. To understand a theory is to understand it not so much as a fixed or formal set of rules or regularities, but as an attempted solution to a problem within a given situation. Thus "the history of science" — here, political science — "should be treated *not* as a history of theories, but as a history of problem-situations and their modifications" (Popper 1972, 177). In this way, situational analysis applies itself reflexively to the episodes and overall development of political science. Theorists in political science, past and present, are to be understood as rational actors seeking to solve the methodological and substantive problems of politics as they emerge in changing problem situations. In this way, the method of situational analysis helps us not only to explain political life, but to understand political science.

Notes

I would like to thank Terence Ball for his ever helpful criticisms and suggestions.

1. Despite its importance to his philosophy of the social sciences, Popper has never systematically discussed situational analysis. What brief discussion there is, is to be found in Popper (1961, 1966, 1972, and 1976b). Further development of situational analysis is to be found in Watkins (1970), Wisdom (1970), Jarvie (1972), and Farr (1983, 1985).

2. Determinism is a sensitive issue for Popper. Indeed he has suggested that his original terminology of "the logic of the situation" be changed to "situational analysis" inasmuch as "the latter name may be preferable because the former may be felt to suggest a deterministic theory of human action, it is of course far from my intention to suggest anything like this" (Popper 1972, 178).

3. This would advise political science to follow the best developments in post-positivist philosophy of science. Despite other differences, Popper (1972), Lakatos (1978), Laudan (1977), and others all share in the turn towards an historically-informed philosophy of science. For a programmatic appeal for this turn in political science, see Moon (1975) and Ball (1976). For different examples of what this might yield, see Riker (1982) and Keohane (1983).

References

Apel, Karl-Otto. 1972. "The A Priori of Communication and the Foundation of the Humanities." *Man and World*, 5: 3-37.

Aristotle. 1953. *Ethics*. Translated by J.A.K. Thomson. Harmondsworth: Penguin.

Ball, Terence. 1972. "On 'Historical' Explanation." *Philosophy of the Social Sciences*, 2: 181-192.

———. 1971. "From Paradigms to Research Programs: Toward a Post-Kuhnian Political Science." *American Journal of Political Science*, 20: 151-177.

Borger, Robert and Frank Cioffi, eds. 1970. *Explanation in the Behaviorial Sciences*. Cambridge: Cambridge University Press.

Donagan, Alan. 1964. "Historical Explanation: The Popper-Hempel Theory Reconsidered." *History and Theory*, 6: 3-26.

Dray, William. 1957. *Laws and Explanation in History*. Oxford: Oxford University Press.

Duverger, Maurice. 1954. *Political Parties*. London: Methuen and Co.

———. 1964. *An Introduction to the Social Sciences*. New York: Praeger.

———. 1972a. *The Study of Politics*. New York: Thomas Crowell Co.

———. 1972b. *Party Politics and Pressure Groups*. New York: Thomas Crowell Co.

Easton, David. 1971. *The Political System*, 2nd ed. Chicago: University of Chicago Press.

Eidlin, Fred. 1983. "Area Studies and/or Social Science: Contextually-Limited Generalizations versus General Laws." In *Constitutional Democracy: Essays in Comparative Politics*, edited by Fred Eidlin. Boulder, Co.: Westview.

Elster, Jon. 1979. *Ulysses and the Sirens*. Cambridge: Cambridge University Press.

Eulau, Heinz. 1963. *The Behavioral Persuasion in Politics*. New York: Random House.

Farr, James. 1982. "Historical Concepts in Political Science: The Case of 'Revolution'." *American Journal of Political Science*, 26: 688-708.

———. 1983. "Popper's Hermeneutics." *Philosophy of the Social Sciences*, 13: 157-176.

———. 1985. "Situational Analysis: Explanation in Political Science." *Journal of Politics*, 47: 1085-1107.

George, Alexander L. and Richard Smoke. 1974. *Deterrence in American Foreign Policy*. New York: Columbia University Press.

Gewirth, Alan. 1954. "Can Men Change the Laws of Social Science?" *Philosophy of Science*, 21: 229–241.

Gombrich, Ernst. 1974. "The Logic of Vanity Fair." In *The Philosophy of Karl Popper*, edited by Paul A. Schilpp, La Salle, Ill.: Open Court, 925–957.

Goodman, Ronald and Jeffrey Hart and Richard Rosecrance. 1975. "Testing International Theory: Methods and Data in a Situational Analysis of International Politics." In *Theory and Practice of Events Research*, edited by Edward E. Azar and Joseph D. Ben-Dak. New York: Gordon and Breach, 41–61.

Gunnell, John G. 1969. "Deduction, Explanation, and Social Scientific Inquiry." *American Political Science Review*, 63: 1233–1246.

Harré, Rom. 1970. *The Principles of Scientific Thinking*. Chicago: University of Chicago Press.

Heelan, Patrick. 1983. "Natural Science as a Hermeneutic of Instrumentation." *Philosophy of Science*, 50: 181–204.

Hempel, Carl. 1965. *Aspects of Scientific Explanation*. New York: Free Press.

Hermann, Charles F. 1969. "International Crisis as a Situational Variable." In *International Politics and Foreign Policy*, edited by James N. Rosenau. New York: Free Press.

Jarvie, I.C. 1972. *Concepts and Society*. London: Routledge and Kegan Paul.

Keohane, Robert O. 1983. "Theory of World Politics: Structural Realism and Beyond." In *Political Science: The State of the Discipline*, edited by Ada W. Finifter, Washington, D.C.: American Political Science Association, 503–540.

Lakatos, Imre. 1978. *The Methodology of Scientific Research Programmes*. Cambridge: Cambridge University Press.

Laudan, Larry. 1977. *Progress and its Problems*. Berkeley: University of California Press.

MacIntyre, Alasdair. 1981. *After Virtue*. Notre Dame: University of Notre Dame Press.

Magee, Bryan. 1978. *Men of Ideas*. New York: Viking.

Marx, Karl. 1938. *Critique of the Gotha Program*. New York: International.

———. 1967. *Capital*, vol. I. New York: International.

McCarthy, Thomas. 1973. "Misunderstanding 'Understanding'." *Theory and Decision*, 3: 351–370.

Meehl, Paul E. 1971. "The Selfish Voter Paradox and the Thrown-Away Vote Argument." *American Political Science Review*, 61: 11–30.

Michels, Roberto. 1915. *Political Parties*. New York: Free Press.

Moe, Terry M. 1979. "On the Scientific Status of Rational Models." *American Journal of Political Science*, 23: 215–243.

Moon, J. Donald. 1975. "The Logic of Political Inquiry: A Synthesis of Opposed Perspectives." In *Handbook of Political Science*, vol. I, edited by Fred I. Greenstein and Nelson W. Polsby, Reading, Mass.: Addison-Wesley. 131–228.

Munro, William Bennett. 1928. *The Invisible Government*. New York: MacMillan.

Nelson, John S. 1975. "Accidents, Laws, and Philosophic Flaws: Behavioral Explanation in Dahl and Dahrendorf." *Comparative Politics*, 7: 435–457.

Popper, Karl. 1961. *The Poverty of Historicism*. New York: Harper and Row.

———. 1963. *Conjectures and Refutations*. New York: Harper and Row.

———. 1966. *The Open Society and Its Enemies*, vol. II. Princeton: Princeton University Press.

———. 1972. *Objective Knowledge*. Oxford: Oxford University Press.

———. 1976a. *Unended Quest*. LaSalle, Ill.: Open Court.

———. 1976b. "The Logic of the Social Sciences." In *The Positivist Dispute in German Sociology*, edited by T.W. Adorno. New York: Harper and Row. 87–104.

Ricci, David M. 1984. *The Tragedy of Political Science*. New Haven: Yale University Press.

Riker, William. 1982. "The Two-party System and Duverger's Law: An Essay on the History of Political Science." *American Political Science Review*, 76: 753–766.

Searle, John R. 1983. *Intentionality: An Essay in the Philosophy of Mind*. Cambridge: Cambridge University Press.

Simon, Herbert. 1968. "Causation." *International Encyclopedia of the Social Sciences*, vol. II. New York: MacMillan.

Snyder, Richard C. and H.W. Bruck and Burton Sapin, eds. 1972. *Foreign Policy Decision-Making*. New York: Free Press.

Somit, Albert and Joseph Tanenhaus. 1967. *The Development of American Political Science: From Burgess to Behavioralism*. Boston: Allyn and Unwin.

Thagard, Paul and Richard E. Nisbett. 1983. "Rationality and Charity." *Philosophy of Science*, 50: 250–267.

Thomas, W.I. and Florian Znaniecki. 1927. *The Polish Peasant in Europe and America*. New York: A.A. Knopf.

Tilley, Nicholas. 1982. "Popper, Historicism, and Emergence." *Philosophy of the Social Sciences*, 12: 59–67.

Toulmin, Stephen. 1983. "The Construal of Reality: Criticism in Modern and Postmodern Science." In *The Politics of Interpretation*, edited by W.J.T. Mitchell. Chicago: University of Chicago Press. 89–118.

Wahlke, John C. 1979. "Pre-Behavioralism in Political Science." *American Political Science Review*, 73: 9–31.

Watkins, John. 1970. "Imperfect Rationality." In Borger and Cioffi: 167–217.

Weber, Max. 1949. *The Methodology of the Social Sciences*. New York: Free Press.

———. 1975. *Roscher and Knies*. New York: Free Press.

Wisdom, J.O. 1970. "Situational Individualism and Emergent Group Properties." In Borger and Cioffi: 271–296.

3

Rational Choice Theories

Despite the singular title that is commonly used to refer to it, rational choice theory is not a single coherent enterprise. There are many theories, each depending on its own rationality assumptions. I wish to discuss two of the most influential sets of assumptions and their respective theories. The two are the problem of social choice as formulated by Arrow (1963) and the theory of games as formulated by Neumann and Morgenstern (1953). I choose these two because they are very important, because they have compelling characteristics, and because they are remarkably different. The two theories were designed for different purposes and one might explain their different assumptions as the result of their purposes. However, I think one might sooner suppose that the assumptions were, in part, arbitrarily chosen and that one could as well build social choice theory and game theory on similar assumptions. Indeed, each of these theories has many variants that are based on a fairly wide range of assumptions.

The rationality assumptions of the two theories differ in many ways, as represented in Table 1. They differ with respect to their aggregation rules, what is chosen in them, their value theories, their ranges of choice, and what count as outcomes in them. Two of these differences are centrally important. These two are strikingly different views of what are the objects of choice and radically different aggregation rules. The objects of choice are outcomes in the Arrow theory and strategies in the Neumann-Morgenstern theory. What is aggregated are interpersonally noncomparable preferences in the Arrow theory and transferable utilities in the Neumann–Morgenstern theory.

There are compelling reasons for adopting each of these two pairs of central assumptions. Arrow's focus on outcomes rather than strategies is motivated by his concern with the normative evaluation of results of various choice procedures; the Neumann–Morgenstern focus on

Table 1. Arrow and Neumann–Morgenstern Assumptions

	Arrow	Neumann–Morgenstern
Aggregation Rule	Interpersonally Non-comparable Utility	Transferable Utility
Value	Ordinal Utility	Cardinal Utility
Range of choice	Whole State of Affairs Outcomes	Marginal Pieces Strategies
Outcomes	Complete Rankings of All States	Particular States

strategies is motivated by a normative concern with rational self-interest in social interactions. Arrow's focus on interpersonally noncomparable utility is motivated by epistemological and conceptual doubts about the notion of interpersonal comparability, doubts that have shaped modern microeconomics from the time of Edgeworth and Pareto to the present. Neumann and Morgenstern's focus on transferable utility is perhaps motivated by concern with mathematical tractability but also by the evident belief that interpersonal comparability is not always meaningless. Around poker tables, which Neumann reputedly loved, the notion of transferable utility must often seem compelling, especially when the players are economic and social peers who know one another well.

In what follows, I wish to discuss the various differences in the assumptions of these two theories. Along the way, I will argue that, if we strive for coherence, then the aggregation rules virtually drive us to assume ordinal or cardinal utility and choices that range over whole states of affairs or marginal pieces of whole states. What counts as an outcome and what counts as a choice are not similarly influenced by our choice of aggregation rules. Depending on our theoretical purposes, we may wish to vary all of these assumptions. Two of the most important grounds for choosing our assumptions will be their realism and their coherence. Unfortunately, coherence and realism do not always fit well together: striving for coherence typically drives us to unrealism.

Some Background

Although there were extensive forerunners, the rational choice theory enterprise in the postwar era has grown out of contemporary problems in economic theory and efforts to understand them. Neumann and Morgenstern, in *Theory of Games and Economic Behavior* (first edition, 1944), attempt to restructure microeconomic theory on highly generalized, methodological individualist, finite bases by focusing on individual choices and their interactions with choices of others. Instead of the usual microeconomic concern with equilibria in the economy, Neumann and

Morgenstern are concerned with individual maximization of returns from choices. This is the concern of poker players and, Neumann and Morgenstern reasonably suppose, of actors in economic relations.

Kenneth Arrow, in *Social Choice and Individual Values* (first edition, 1951), wishes to ground social or political choice directly on the usual assumptions of economic choice theory. In particular, he pushes the welfare economic analysis of political choice to cover the broadest range of choices by actors collectively trying to reach the state of affairs each most prefers. In this endeavor, he generalizes earlier results of Condorcet and C.L. Dodgson on committee decision-making.

There have been many other major efforts to understand politics in a rational choice framework. The two most influential have been those of Anthony Downs and Mancur Olson. Downs (1957) uses traditional equilibrium analysis to show that electoral parties are behaving rationally when they tend (under certain circumstances that may often have prevailed in the United States) to adopt similar, rather than distinctively different, platforms so that — as George Wallace liked to say — there is not a dime's worth of difference between the two major American parties' presidential candidates. Downs also shows that it is straightforwardly rational of citizens not to spend much effort on voting or on informing themselves of the merits of various candidates. Olson's theory of collective action is a much more general statement of this latter conclusion of Downs: individual members of a group who will be affected by potential political or other actions in the group's interest may not find it in their interest, individually, to contribute toward the effort to influence their own well being (Olson 1965). This theory readily translates into game theoretic terms (Hardin 1971).

All of these efforts assume that the relevant individual choosers are seeking to do the best they can in achieving results that mirror their own preferences. Indeed, in this literature, this is the meaning of 'rationality': It is the efficient seeking of one's self-interest or one's own preferences. Many of the findings in this literature radically alter prior understandings of politics and individual rationality. For example, the traditional literature on responsible parties and voters has virtually disappeared in the face of Downs's theory. And the traditional treatments of groups and pluralism have been severely undercut by Olson's theory. Taken together, these and many other contributions of rational choice theory suggest, among other things, a strong conservative bias in democratic politics that cannot easily be overcome. In particular, powerful, concentrated interests have substantial advantages over more nearly popular interests.

In what follows, I wish to discuss some of the fundamental assumptions of rational choice theories. The point of this exercise is not to call such theories into question — they have established their relevance and power in many applications — but to point to a centrally important problem in them. At base, this problem may finally mirror a fundamental problem in our understanding of human choice and psychology, not merely of political analysis. This problem is that there are many theories under the rational choice umbrella and that they are based on radically different assumptions. Because one can nevertheless claim that the enterprise is a coherent one, it is important that we understand this problem at its base. The problem is one that the current generation of rational choice theorists must face. Indeed, it is the successes of these theorists that make the problem important. Moreover, one of the chief creative directions in which rational choice analysis is now moving is into the understanding of the cognitive and psychological aspects of individual choice. In this analysis, the problems discussed here may be especially crucial.

Aggregation Rules: Interpersonally Noncomparable vs. Transferable Utility

Twentieth century microeconomics is distinguished by the degree to which utility theory assumptions have been pared down to a bare minimum. Against the classical utilitarian assumption that we can add your utility to mine to get our aggregate utility, Pareto argued forcefully that we cannot meaningfully compare our utilities. How can my utility for a good French dinner be weighed against your utility for schussing down an Alpine slope? How can a millionaire's enjoyment of beluga caviar be compared to a peasant's enjoyment of hot porridge? Pareto recommended that we avoid making such comparisons and therefore restrict our judgments of when there has been an aggregate improvement in the state of affairs to those cases in which everyone has benefited or at least no one has been disadvantaged while others have benefited. Hence, we restrict social judgments to those under what are now called the Pareto criteria. A Pareto improvement is one that benefits at least one person without harming anyone. We are at a Pareto optimal distribution of resources if no one's share can be increased without decreasing someone else's share.

If we accept Pareto's view, several remarkable results follow. First, of course, we can no longer simply add utilities across different people. But then there may be no point in having a cardinal, that is, additive utility function for any individual: ordinal functions will generally suffice for the analysis of markets and of individual choice in the market. Such functions yield a particularly perspicuous analysis of certain problems, such as complementarity, that have historically plagued utility theory.

Kenneth Arrow wished to ground social choice in the same utility assumptions that microeconomists use. With Pareto he wanted to give up maximizing, or summing utilities across individuals, to obtain the best state of affairs in favor of merely optimizing or otherwise transforming a collection of individual preferences into a social preference, for example, by majority vote. He merely wished to ground social choice on standard economic choice principles. A compelling reason for doing so is that economic choice theory is very highly developed and its principles have been subjected to extensive debate over the past century. Moreover, it serves very well in contemporary economic theory. Indeed, it would be odd not to consider social choice from the perspective of economic choice theory.

In his study of two-person zero-sum games, John von Neumann in the 1920's showed that such games have a well-defined best strategy for each player if each player plays for best results. In generalizing the model of such games later, he and Oskar Morgenstern assumed the simple structure of payoffs in complex interactions that Neumann had assumed in his saddle-point theorem for two person zerosum games. Their generalization takes two directions: toward more than two players and toward games in which the sum of payoffs to all players is not a constant (such as zero). The initial model may well have been poker, which is generally played with more than two players but which is still zerosum: what the winners win the losers lose. It was sensible to start from such a simple context to see how much could be derived about choices in more complex contexts.

The model of poker does not generalize to games that are not constant sum for the following obvious reason: there is no endogenous source of extra money to add to the pot of players' contributions to make winnings add up to more than losses. In an economy in which commodities are traded, winnings regularly exceed losses in the sense that all parties to a trade are better off than they would have been had they not traded. But the representation of winnings and losses—or more generally "payoffs" — in the Neumann–Morgenstern game theory can easily accommodate endogenous gains of the kind that one expects in market exchange. It is this simple insight that gives *Theory of Games and Economic Behavior* the second part of its title.

In generalizing their games to cover complex interactions, however, Neumann and Morgenstern keep intact the form that payoffs take in poker: the payoffs are in some unit that they call utility but that for all the world seems like money. This utility is transferable in the sense that it can be passed back and forth between players in many forms of games. For example, to get you to cooperate with me in a coalition to increase our payoffs, I may offer you a side payment that is subtracted from my payoff and added to yours in the most straightforward arithmetic fashion. Such a notion of utility is not uncompelling for many purposes. Economists who accept all of Pareto's strictures on comparisons across people nevertheless speak of "consumer's surplus" from exchange as though it could be aggregated across all consumers. Consumer's surplus is the gain in value to participants in exchange from giving up something less valued for something more valued. To get you to cooperate with me in a joint exchange when you might otherwise prefer to deal with others, I might offer you extra payment that, not unlike a Neumann-Morgenstern side payment, comes out of my consumer's surplus.

Values: Ordinal vs. Cardinal Utility

Arrow's interpersonally noncomparable utility need not be ordinal. But for many purposes nothing is gained by making it cardinal; so, by an application of Ockham's razor, it might as well be merely ordinal. Neumann and Morgenstern's transferable utility, however, must be cardinal if it is to make sense to subtract some of mine to add to yours. As they note, the free transferability of utilities between persons "does force one to assume proportionality between utility and monetary measures" (Neumann and Morgenstern 1953, 629n). One might suppose that this difference between the two value theories is the signal difference, that this is prior to the concern with noncomparability and transferability. For certain purposes, this supposition would be compelling. However, it seems that, historically, the problem of interpersonal comparison drove discussion and that the eventual resort to ordinal utility theory flowed naturally from the abandonment of interpersonal comparability. Similarly, the original impetus for Neumann's game-theoretic utility theory seems to have come from a naive ignorance of economic utility theory and from the presumption that, as in poker, money is a proxy for value.

Ordinal Value Theory

Elsewhere, I have discussed the problems of utility theory (Hardin 1984) and I will not rehearse all the issues here. The problems of chief interest here grow out of the obvious fact that values of various events or objects to us depend on other aspects of the state of affairs in which we find ourselves. That is to say, there are complementarities between goods, experiences, and conditions of life. It is this insight that largely undercuts the view that we can simply add the utilities of various goods to obtain our overall or total utility. A naive cardinal utility theory — with or without interpersonal comparability — would require that we be able to add the separate utilities of everything we consume to determine the total utility we drive from the consumptions. Against the hope that we can do this, we know that there are interactions between our various consumptions. For example, the utility of two dinners this evening is not likely to be twice the utility of one. If our tastes are particularly refined, we might even hold that the utility of a bottle of white wine with this evening's dinner is far greater than than of a bottle of red wine whereas the reverse will be true for tomorrow evening's dinner.[1]

That different consumptions interact is a general problem that has long been recognized. For example, Hume, in his essay "Of Refinement in the Arts," argues that "Human happiness, according to the most received notions, seems to consist in three ingredients; action, pleasure, and indolence: And though these ingredients ought to be mixed in different proportions, according to the particular disposition of the person; yet no one ingredient can be entirely wanting, without destroying, in some measure, the relish of the whole composition" (Rotwein, 1955, 21). Or, as Prince Hal put it, "If all the year were playing holidays, to sport would be as tedious as to work" (Shakespeare, *Henry IV, Part I*, Act I Scene II, lines 205-6).

Despite the widespread recognition of the problem of complementarity, however, the analytical resolution of it was long in coming. It was essentially resolved in the work of Edgeworth and Pareto at the turn of this century and, finally, of Hicks and Allen in the 1930's in what Samuelson (1974) calls the "revolution in demand theory." The result of that revolution is the contemporary ordinal utility theory in indifference curve representations of demand.

Arrow introduced the ordinal utility assumptions into the analysis of collective choice — thereby virtually inventing social choice theory — to see how far one could go in stipulating normative rules for collective choice. His purpose was to oppose ordinal, interpersonally noncomparable welfare theory to the cardinal, interpersonally additive theories of classical utilitarians such as, especially, Bentham, as expressed in such notions as the greatest good for society. There are two fundamental differences between these theories. First, the ordinalists generally suppose that there are epistemological objections even to comparing my utility and yours. Second, the ordinal theory supposes that individuals do no more than rank alternatives for choice, they do not attach additive weights to the alternatives.

Unfortunately, once one recognizes the problem of complementarity, one seems forced to carry its implications to the limit of recognizing that one cannot rank the kinds of things over which we typically make choices without an enormous, all-encompassing *ceteris paribus* clause. One can only rank whole states of affairs, completely determined. Hence, for Arrow,

> the objects are social states. The most precise definition of a social state would be a complete description of the amount of each type of commodity in the hands of each individual, the amount of each productive resource invested in each type of productive activity, and the amounts of various types of collective activity, such as municipal services, diplomacy and its continuation by other means, and the erection of staues to famous men. It is assumed that *each individual in the community has a definite ordering of all conceivable social states*, in terms of their desirability to him. (Arrow 1963, 17, emphasis added.)

Obviously, ordinal choice theory, as Arrow describes it, makes outrageous demands on our cognitive abilities. But it not easy to see how we might adopt ordinal utility theory without going all the way. One might often seemingly rightly suppose that the enormous *ceteris paribus* clause governs all else and rank only small variations in the whole state of affairs as though there were no complementarity effects between these small variations and the remainder of the state of affairs. But in principle one must grant that we cannot stipulate *a priori* that there are no relevant complementarities. Hence, a coherent ordinal theory is an unrealistic cognitive theory.

Neumann–Morgenstern Cardinal Utility

As discussed above, the assumptions that were not necessary to economic theory were successively pared away from utility theory by Edgeworth, Pareto, and the modern indifference curve theorists. Along the way, epistemological reasons were discovered for abandoning cardinal utility and, especially, interpersonal comparisons. In their theory of games, however, Neumann and Morgenstern resurrected cardinal utility and they generally assumed a variant of interpersonal comparability or, rather, what they called "transferability" of utility. Like the earlier economists who abandoned it, Neumann and Morgenstern adopted cardinal utility, not because they first considered how the mind works but because cardinal utility was elegantly suited to their theory. Samuelson calls Neumann's invention of his cardinal utility "adventitious." Neumann "needed metric-utility payoffs for his elegant, but not very useful, two-person zero-sum game theorem" (Samuelson 1974, 1266n).

Against the criticism of their failure to use ordinal utility theory, Neumann and Morgenstern added an appendix to the second edition of their book to demonstrate that an individual who has a complete ordering over outcomes effectively has a cardinal evaluation of them. The Neumann-Morgenstern device for turning an ordinal ranking into a cardinal measure is to establish a lottery over two outcomes and any outcome ranked between them. Suppose I prefer outcome x to y to z. We can establish a cardinal measure of the distances x-y and y-z in the following way. Determine the value of p ($0 < p < 1$) at which I would be indifferent between a lottery over $px + (1-p)z$ and the certainty of y. Now stipulate that the value of x is 1 and the value of z is 0. It follows that the value of y is p. We can continue this process to put cardinal values on all outcomes in my ordering.

It happens that such probabilistic weightings over pairs of outcomes are necessary for Neumann's solution of the two-person zerosum game and for more general Neumann–Morgenstern solution theory for games. Hence, to object to this procedure is *eo ipso* to object to some of the most powerful results of game theory. One may, however, find the procedure compelling in the context of typical games and still object to the generalization of the procedure to cover an individual's entire utility schedule over all possibilities (as I will discuss further below under "Range of Choice").

When pushed to its limits, the ordinal theory becomes intellectually bizarre: it is inconceivable that people actually think that way. Alas, the same is true of Neumann and Morgenstern's version of cardinal utility, an apparently quite simple conception of unidimensional utility that is ridiculously too complicated for actual choice. Neumann and Morgenstern (1953, 8) "assume that the aim of all participants in the economic system . . . is money, or equivalently a single monetary commodity. This is supposed to be unrestrictedly divisible and substitutable, freely transferable and identical, even in the quantitative sense, with whatever 'satisfaction' or 'utility' is desired by each participant." The result of this assumption is the magnificently ethereal development of the 600 pages that follow it. To gaze at this edifice, branching out in seemingly chance directions with refinements on top of refinements, is to lose sight of problems of choice.

Transferability is simply a dodge from the epistemological and conceptual problems of interpersonal comparability. It lets us suppose payoffs are in some currency or resource that any player could use to obtain particular values.[2] Genuine games that interest us in social and political life are sometimes, but far from always or even usually, about allocations of resources. Often, they are straightforwardly about achieving one outcome rather than others. If payoffs are genuinely in resources, such as money, we can make abstract combinations of them to yield compromise outcomes. If they are not in such resources, compromise outcomes may make little sense. For example, there might be no combination of part victory and part defeat for each side in a war that could sensibly be seen as having a value halfway between those of full victory and full defeat for both sides. There is no loaf to cut in half and share between the sides. Many solution theories, such as the Nash–Zeuthen bargaining theory, require that such compromises make sense or that we choose a relevantly weighted probabilistic lottery over some set of outcomes so that at least the expected value of the outcome to each party is, say, halfway between the values of full victory and full defeat.

It is a standard objection of the Neumann and Morgenstern utility assumptions that they limit game theory to choice problems in which everything at issue is valued in money (Luce and Raiffa, 1957, 168). But there is another odd characteristic of this utility that renders game theory abstruse beyond understanding: it is unrestrictedly divisible. There is a peculiarity of money that makes it possible for us to think we notice a difference when we do not. We know how to order any two real numbers. Hence, we can presume that a gift of $1,000,000,001 is better than one of $1,000,000,000. It is an absurd presumption. In the spending of a billion dollars there must be so much rounding off and approximating, as well as simple errors of choice, that many dollars more or less could not be expected to make a difference to our satisfactions. If when we saw colors we could see with them the numbers representing the wavelengths of the light associated with them, we might then claim to be able to perceive fine distinctions of tone when in fact all we could do is perceive differences in numbers. The same is true of fine distinctions in quantities of money. Yet the bulk of mathematical game theory depends on the presumption of our perceiving *and even caring about* infinitesimal distinctions among payoffs.

In this respect, game theory is a branch of mathematics but not of choice theory. The notion of a continuum of utility values has no human meaning. As in empirical measures, Bridgman's (1927, 33) "penumbra of uncertainty" must preclude such precision of perception of utility as is recquired for the vastness of mathematical game theory. Indeed, the situations we will face are finite in number and the rules we draw on to face them are finite in scope. The larger project of game theory can have meaning for actual choice only to the extent that finite choice theory results are included within the larger enterprise as special cases. However, little or no effort has been made to reduce the Neumann–Morgenstern theory to its finite set theory implications. In particular, the Neumann–Morgenstern solution theory commonly has no transparent implications for choice. It is not sensibly argued that we command choice rules of infinite scope and that such rules can handle the smaller set of situations, in which we will depend on them for resolution, as though the limited world we inhabit fell out of the grander world of infinite possiblities.

The mathematician Kronecker is supposed to have said, "The integers were created by God; all else is man-made" (Weyl 1949, 33). Were he with us now, he would derogate virtually all of mathematical game theory. Although in some respects it might not be complex enough to fit choices over multiple values, surely the theory is vastly too complex to describe whatever social choice situations arise even in vaguely unidimensional value realms such as economic exchange. One may think, or at least hope, that actual choice problems are limiting cases in the ethereal realm of game theory, but it is not easy to say what distinguishes relevant from ethereal results. Many of the mathematically engaging results are not relevant.

Already in the hands of Neumann and Morgenstern, its first-generation creators, game theory went through a development that, as characterized by Neumann himself, might not be uncommon in mathematics:

> As a mathematical discipline travels far from its empirical source, or still more, if it is a second and third generation only indirectly inspired by ideas coming from "reality," it is beset with very grave dangers. It becomes more and more purely mathematicizing, more and more purely *l'art pour l'art*. This need not be bad, if the field is surrounded by correlated subjects, which still have closer empirical connections, or if the discipline is under the influence of men with an exceptionally well-developed taste. But there is a grave danger that the subject will develop along the line of least resistance, that the stream, so far from its source, will separate into a multiple of insignificant branches, and then the discipline will become a disorganized mass of details and complexities. In other words, at a great distance from its empiracal source, or after much "abstract" inbreeding, a mathematical subject is in danger of degeneration. At the inception the style is usually classical; when it shows signs of becoming baroque, then the danger signal is up . . . . [W]henever this stage is reached, the only remedy seems to me to be the rejuvenating return to the source: the reinjection of more or less directly empirical ideas. I am convinced that this was a necessary condition to conserve the freshness and the vitality of the subject and that this will remain equally true in the future. (Neumann 1956, 2063).

Granting that game theory is a morass if we base our solution concepts on unrestrictedly divisible utility, we might hope to reconstruct it on finite foundations. Would it still be a morass? In certain respects it might, but the problems are of a kind to which we are accustomed. For example, we readily think in finite terms when we think of the number of players in a game — the very idea of a continuum of players, as assumed in non-atomic games (Aumann and Shapley 1974), is beyond our usual conceptions. With finite numbers of players, our solutions are likely to be messy but at least understandable. For example, when I once analyzed the problem of Condorcet choice over a finite choice set in a finite group of individuals (Hardin 1971), an associate who was a mathematician found the results of the analysis unsatisfactory — not because the derivation was wrong but because the result was not elegant. The inelegant result is that the rule for the existence of a Condorcet choice — an outcome that is preferred to all other outcomes by a majority of all players — depends, as any choice theorist might guess, on whether the group making the choice has an odd or even number of members. In a real society, this problem seems as artificial as a bonus dollar in a legacy of a billion. However, even in theory, the practical import of whether the number of choosers is odd or even becomes negligible as the number of choosers becomes large.

A finite choice theory is likely to be inelegantly cluttered, or perhaps fuzzy, just as much of Neumann and Morgenstern's theory is cluttered with bits of results for peculiar kinds of games played by certain numbers of players. Moreover, to say that the set of choices available to me is finite is not to say that in some sense it is complete or that I know the list. It is finite but open, because there may be outcomes which are unknowable at the moment but which I may soon come to know just as children and scientists come to know new things. Hence, my choice of strategy may result in an outcome I did not anticipate.

Range of Choice: Whole States vs. Marginal Pieces

The most striking difference between the Arrow and Neumann–Morgenstern choice theories is that the former is generally about choices over whole states of affairs whereas the latter is typically about choices over marginal wrinkles in the status quo. On this difference, game theory seems descriptively more realistic than set theoretic choice theory. If there are ever intellectual limits to what we can do, there are limits that prevent our seriously considering the ranking of various whole states of affairs.

In this respect, the value theory of games is psychologically more realistic than that of set theoretic choice theory. We do make choices over certain sets of alternatives as though they were decoupled from the larger state of affairs. It may matter, finally, whether I buy a Ford or a Datsun in the radical sense that it may change the universe in the manner of the children's story about the kingdom being lost for want of a horse-shoe nail. The way in which it matters in that tale is causally. But I cannot plausibly make a choice over which of my two cars to buy as though I thought the causal relations were so devastingly different as those in the states with and without the horseshoe nail. If there were a *ceteris paribus* clause to govern such causal relations — as there is likely to be for people as ignorant of relevant causal relations as I am in this case — I could blithely consider the values of the alternative states of affairs as though most of both were independent of whether I buy the one or the other car.

But, the set theoretic value theory is not predicated on causal relations between parts of alternative states of affairs and other parts of them. Rather it is predicated on value relations between these parts. If all else is either partial state X or partial state Y, I might prefer X plus the Ford to X plus the Datsun, but prefer Y plus the Datsun to Y plus the Ford. I can say I prefer the Ford to the Datsun only if I think I know enough about the remainder of the whole state of affairs to judge that it is X rather than Y. Typically, I will know so little about the whole state of affairs that I will choose between the Ford and the Datsun on the grounds only of differences between them as though there were a strong *ceteris paribus* clause such as implicitly underlies game theory.

Of course, it is not only individuals who make choices over minute aspects of the whole state of affairs as though these aspects were decoupled from the larger state of affairs. In part, just because they are collections of individuals, collectivities also typically make choices in this way. For example, elections are commonly treated as though they are marginal blips in the larger state of affairs, as though their "purpose" or intendment is to make piecemeal modifications in the larger state of affairs rather than to choose between different whole states of affairs.

Let us push the implications of the distinction between holistic and piecemeal choosing. When we choose over parts of whole states of affairs, in effect, we are choosing whole states only as a result of a sequence of piecemeal choices. There is not one choice to be made, but many, and these many choices build into the larger state of affairs. Some of our piecemeal choices may be fraught with great import while some may be of trivial significance. The very important choices may seem virtually to be choices over whole states of affairs. Still, they will never be quite what Arrow has in mind with his complete states fully determined. Piecemeal choosing is always *in media res*, as are our actual choices, whether individual or social. The implications of Arrow's General Possibility Theorem — that there is no choice rule that meets his conditions and that produces a social ordering — might seem to apply as well to piecemeal choices. But it will not be a simple matter to say just how they apply if we cannot be sure that there are no complementarity effects, as we can if we are ranking whole states of affairs. Of course, game theory is afflicted with the same difficulty: we cannot select a best strategy in the present game unless we are sure that there are no complementarity effects between the outcomes in the game and features in the greater state of affairs in which the game is being played.

Outcomes: Complete Rankings vs. Particular States

The simplest difference between Arrow's and the game theoretic representations of interactive choice is the following. Arrow's concern is to achieve a collective ranking of all possible states of affairs while the game theoretic concern is to select one outcome out of all possible outcomes. The "outcome" of an Arrovian social choice is a complete ranking. For example, one can say that majority rule works if it yields a complete ranking over all the states of affairs under consideration. It is not sufficient that it might produce a single-best-candidate state of affairs that is preferred by a majority to each alternative state of affairs. It must also produce a majority choice for second best, third best, and so forth. This is an idiosyncratic aspect of Arrow's theory in the sense that one can construct a social choice theory that is based on all of his other assumptions but that does not require that social choices be analogous to individual preference orderings.

In a game, of course, an outcome is simply the intersection of all players' strategy choices. That outcome can be represented as a state of affairs (victory for one player and defeat for another, say) or as a set of payoffs to all of the players in the game. There are as many outcomes as there are possible combinations of strategy choices by all the players, although every outcome may not be unique or have unique values or payoffs associated with it.

On this difference, game theory is the more realistic at representing what we generally do and what we generally expect to have follow from our actions. In actual practice, we are seldom concerned with obtaining a complete collective ranking — we generally only wish to discover a particular result of our interactive choice. Nevertheless, there may often be value in being able to assess the complete collective ranking of all candidate states of affairs. In particular, we might be concerned with such a ranking in certain normative evaluations of our choice procedures. This is, of course, Arrow's (1963) concern in *Social Choice and Individual Values*. A successful game theory gives normative prescriptions for individual choice; Arrow's concern is to give normative evaluations of procedures that produce aggregate outcomes.

Choices: Outcomes vs. Strategies

One of the strengths of the game theoretic representation is that it makes clear a distinction that pervades our actual lives: that between strategies (or actions) and outcomes (or events). What one wants is to achieve certin outcomes; what one chooses is a strategy that, one hopes, interacts with the strategies of others to produce the best feasible outcome for oneself. The significance of this distinction is not generally so clear in set theoretic choice theory. To see its import, consider a game that represents the Voters' Paradox. My preferred outcome is the election of candidate X. My available strategies are votes for X, Y, or Z. My set of available strategies might also include the strategy of not voting, but let us restrict the set to the three possible votes.

Suppose there are three voters voting under majority rule. There are now at least three possible outcomes: the election of X, Y, or Z by majority vote. But, there is also the possibility that none of these candidates gets a majority vote. That will also produce an outcome. That outcome might be the stipulated election of one of the candidates, the continuation in office of someone else, or the random selection of one of the candidates. Suppose I rank the candidates X, Y, and Z in the order 1, 2, 3. If failing to get a majority entails the election of a specified one of the three candidates, I rank that outcome the same as the election of that candidate. If it entails the random selection of one of the three, I would rank

GAME 1: Voters' Paradox (Outcome ill-defined if there is no majority)

B's choice	Z	1,2,3	-?-	3,1,2
	Y	1,2,3	2,3,1	-?-
	X	1,2,3	1,2,3	1,2,3
		-?-	2,3,1	3,1,2
		2,3,1	2,3,1	2,3,1
A's choice	Y	1,2,3	2,3,1	-?-
		3,1,2	3,1,2	3,1,2
		-?-	2,3,1	3,1,2
	Z	1,2,3	-?-	3,1,2
		X	Y	Z
			C's choice	

NOTE: The Choosers are A, B, and C; the candidates for choice are X, Y, and Z. The preferences are as follows:

	A	B	C
X	1	2	3
Y	2	3	1
Z	3	1	2

Hence, in the matrix, a payoff of 1, 2, 3 indicates the selection of candidate X, a payoff of 2, 3, 1 indicates the selection of candidate Y, and a payoff of 3, 1, 2 indicates the selection of candidate Z.

that outcome as 2 or, at least, as somewhere between the election of X and that of Z. If it entails the continuation in office of someone else, I could rank that outcome anywhere from above the election of X to below that of Z.

To see how different is the focus of the set theoretic problem from the game theoretic problem of cyclic majorities, consider the three-dimensional game matrix in Game 1. Suppose there are three voters or players, A, B, C, who rank the candidates in the orders XYZ, YZX, and ZXY, respectively. If X wins, A's rank order payoff is 1 (for first choice), B's is 2, and C's is 3, and similarly for the other candidates.

In Game 1, the only outcomes that are determinate are those in which there is a majority choice. Hence, only the payoffs for these outcomes can be specified. There remain six outcomes which are ill-defined (as indicated by the question marks). But suppose that each player ranks the outcome of no majority as equivalent to that player's third choice candidate's winning. Now we have a fully specified payoff matrix for the game if we substitute the payoff 3, 3, 3 for each ill-defined payoff.

Note that in the game representation of the voters' problem, what they choose is how to vote, not necessarily what outcome should happen. But the product of their combined votes is an outcome. Once the matrix of all outcomes that can result from various voting strategies is specified, the players can more sensibly decide what voting strategies best serve their interests. In set theoretic choice theory, we are not generally concerned with the question of how to serve the interests of the parties. We are merely concerned with how to aggregate their preferences. The concern in Arrow's theory is, crudely, with whether one of the candidates is elected or, more accurately, with whether the collective choice has the characteristics of an individual choice or, most accurately, with whether the collective preference has the characteristics of an individual preference ranking over *all* the candidates. The concern in game theory is with what outcome results from our strategy choices, and it is certain that there will be some outcome even if it is not the majority election of one of the candidates.

To put this another way, in Arrow's choice theory, we stipulate what would count as an ''outcome'': it is a complete rank ordering of all the candidates for choice. Arrow's theorem says that no procedure for choice can guarantee that there will be an outcome in all cases in this sense. This is not what most of us would mean by an outcome in ordinary life. Game theory typically represents as outcomes just the kind of thing we normally mean by that term: for example, the election of a specific candidate or a follow-up procedure for putting someone in the relevant office. In game theory, we can be sure that there will be a state of affairs that follows from our present actions. Hence, in this respect, the two representations of our collective choice problem are incompatible.

Clearly, the game theoretic representation is, on this point, the more realistic: in ordinary life, we know there will be a next state of affairs, we do not reach impasse with time. But the set theoretic representation is generally intended for normative evaluation of choice procedures, not for prediction of actual behavior. Whether it is useful for the normative evaluation of choice procedures depends on whether we can devise or stipulate reasonable normative criteria for evaluating procedures. Arrow supposes that his several conditions comprise a reasonable set of such criteria.

One might complain against Arrow's enterprise that normative evaluation in social theory has, of course, generally been about the evaluation of outcomes or states of affairs rather than of procedures for getting to states of affairs. Concern with procedure has often been derivative from concern with outcomes, with procedures considered as means to ends.[3] Against this complaint, Arrow might argue that he is actually interested in the evaluation of procedures in a strictly derivative sense. Arrow's enterprise can be characterized as an effort to evaluate procedures according to the kinds of outcomes they produce. His conditions apply not to procedures for aggregation of individual into collective preferences but to the nature of the social preferences that procedures for aggregation ought to produce. Still however, the Arrow literature is generally not concerned with the kinds of choices we actually make, which are choices of strategies, not of outcomes. Indeed, the proof of Gibbard (1973) that every serious social choice problem is subject to manipulative voting or misrepresentation of individual preferences for the purpose of bringing about a preferred outcome for the individual is particularly perspicuous just because it is accomplished in a game theoretic representation. One must necessarily focus on strategies in this representation. If our choice procedure depends on the presentation by each chooser of that chooser's ranking of all *outcomes*, then each chooser may see that it is better to give a false ranking in order to bring about a better aggregate choice. This is because what each chooser chooses is a strategy while what the collective body of choosers chooses is an outcome.

An Example: Choosing a Constitution

To see just how massive are the differences in focus between Arrow's theory, game theory, and actual choice problems, let us consider the choice of a full constitution, as in the American choice in 1787. This problem gives Arrow's theory some benefit of doubt in that choosing a constitution might plausibly seem to be a choice over complete states of affairs. Hence, it is the kind of thing that Arrow's theorem is about, the

kind of thing that we cannot have a general choice rule to determine if we
are to meet all of Arrow's conditions.

Consider what actually happened in 1787. The Constitutional Convention and thereafter the separate states selected a constitution. They
did not select a complete ranking of all possible constitutions, nor would
it even have made sense to consider many contrivable constitutions: these
would have been utterly implausible because they would have fit no one's
idea of what to have. Of course, this means that Arrow's condition of
Unrestricted Domain was effectively violated in this particular instance,
as it is likely to be in most instances. This condition requires that our
choice rule be able to handle the choice no matter what set of preference
rankings each individual chooser has over all the states of affairs, or constitutions in our case. That is to say, it would have to handle the choice
even when many of the choosers prefer the practically implausible constitutions over that which was chosen, for example, when some choosers
prefer a constitution stipulating that whatever a majority of forty-four
year olds want on February 29th should be legislated and should govern
for the subsequent quadrennium. Because there are likely to be many
such real agreements in actual choice situations, we can generally narrow
the range of choice drastically.

For example, in adopting a constitution in 1787, the conventioneers
and the states might readily have found a particular constitution that was
preferred by a majority of choosers to every other possible constitution
or that was considered by a majority to be at least as good as any other.
If they did, it could not have mattered to anyone that there was no majority choice for second best. Such a constitution would have been a
Condorcet winner. Indeed, we might expect in many contexts to find a
Condorcet winner, that is, a winner over every other alternative, even if
our choice rule is not simple but extraordinary majority rule. In general,
one might suppose that anyone concerned exclusively with democratic
choice would consider a Condorcet choice of constitution ideal.[4] But
having a Condorcet winner is not equivalent to having a ranking of all
possible states of affairs. Hence, the result one might ideally desire from
a constitutional convention is a result that Arrow's theorem does not
govern.[5]

The constitutional choice of 1787 depended on more than merely
relaxing Arrow's condition that the social choice be a complete ordering
of all possible states. It also required that there be substantial agreement,
which is to say that Arrow's condition of Unrestricted Domain be *de fac-
to* violated. One reason we might expect that this condition will typically
be violated in piecemeal problems of social choice is that often our
choices are not about issues over which we conflict or disagree but over
ways of coordinating on matters on which there is widespread agree-

ment. There are many cases of such coordination choices, such as coordinating how we decide guilt or innocence of crime, which side of the road each of us drives on, or what each community takes to be noon, problems we resolve by establishing conventions (Hardin 1982, 191–193). Much of the point of a constitution is to coordinate everyone on doing certain things one way rather than many other ways that would have been possible and acceptable. Such coordination is desirable when we are all better off if we coordinate than if we do not. In addition, there are many outcomes on whose ranking we would, in principle, all agree, such as whether to have our army attack us or our enemy. Because it is virtually certain that we do have such uniform preferences over certain aspects of the general state of affairs, we may generally expect to violate the condition of Unrestricted Domain for individual rankings over all outcomes defined as states of affairs fully determined. For decisions that are as nearly holistic as those Arrow considers, we may often suppose, as in 1787, that uncertainties about the implications of various constitutional rules make an enormous variety of constitutions more or less equivalent. We will merely satisfice rather than struggle to maximize, just because the uncertainties make decision costs for doing "better" too great. Coordination may be far more important than supposed maximizing in such cases. Our ignorance about the finer implications of various alternative constitutions may so reduce our confidence in our preference for one over another constitution as to eliminate the problem of cyclic majorities.

When we consider parts of whole states of affairs, the condition of Unrestricted Domain is obviously often violated in the sense that some options might be preferred by no one to certain others. Nevertheless, there are obviously important decisons over piecemeal parts of the state of affairs to which the Domain condition might be reinterpreted to apply. But then, it is not clear that we want to have the same rule apply to all our decisions over piecemeal changes in the status quo or even that we should be concerned if the rule for a particular class of decision is not always successful. What may concern us most is not choices over particular outcomes but the constitutional choice or rule, or what we might call "metadecision." We may easily agree on the choice of a rule in the sense of finding one that is Condorcet preferred by a simple or extraordinary majority to any alternative. Then we simply live with its failure to produce consistent choices in certain piecemeal cases.

Arrow's concern is with outcomes defined as complete rankings over all states of affairs fully determined. Our concern at the constitutional level is rather with the selection of rules to deal with choices over piecemeal changes in the status quo. It should not be surprising that in such a selection, the condition of Unrestricted Domain is violated almost in principle. And if it is violated, the odds that there will be a Condorcet winner among all states of affairs are radically greater than that there would be such a winner among all complete orderings of all states of affairs.

If the conditions of the choice problem of 1787 do not fit Arrow's assumptions, neither do they fit the assumptions of Neumann–Morgenstern game theory. It is implausible that we could characterize the utility functions of the conventioneers as cardinal. While the choice of a constitution was not literally a choice of a whole state of affairs, it was probably too far-reaching a choice for each conventioneer meaningfully to weight lotteries over various alternatives. More importantly, it would be odd to claim that utilities to the conventioneers were transferable, hence interpersonally comparable. Surely they were not.

In various other respects, the choice problem does fit the assumptions of game theory. It was not quite a one-shot decision over states of affairs fully determined but was one of an ongoing sequence of decisions about aspects — perhaps somewhat larger than "marginal" pieces — of the larger state of affairs. Moreover, the conventioneers made choices of strategies, not merely of outcomes. Indeed, Madison's diaries are a wonderful account of strategic maneuverings. And, as already discussed above, they chose a particular constitution, they did not choose a ranking of all constitutions.

Conclusion: Some Implications

If the picture of the set of things over which one is choosing is far more complex in the set theoretic choice theory, the mathematics of the range over which choices are made is far more complex in game theory in the following sense. The range in the set theoretic theory must be finite for most of the interesting results that have impressed us. The range in game theory can be not only infinite but even nondenumerable: It can be the continuum. Indeed, as noted above, some of the most interesting and profound results in game theory assume a continuum of strategies from which to choose, with expected values attached to the strategy choices that, themselves, may comprise a continuum of values.

Can we simply reject the Neumann–Morgenstern cardinalization of values in games? Neumann and Morgenstern suppose that a player can cardinalize the values of various outcomes by determining the weighted lottery over any pair of outcomes that would make the player indifferent between the lottery and some outcome that ranks between the two in the lottery in the player's preference order. It is psychologically implausible that real players can do any such thing with sufficient precision to make mathematical game theory be realistic. To reject the cardinalization is to suppose that one has only an ordinal preference over various outcomes or, perhaps, that one has only a crudely or approximately cardinal preference over them. Since choice theory is more nearly a branch of psychology than of mathematics, surely we should reject the Neumann–Morgenstern cardinalization. If we reject it, then virtually the entire apparatus of zerosum game theory collapses.

Recall what it means to cardinalize my ordering over all outcomes as Neumann and Morgenstern do. It means that each utility value depends only on which outcome obtains. That is to say, each outcome must be completely evaluable, independently of any other aspect of the state of affairs associated with it. This implies that there is no complementarity between the outcome and anything else in the larger state of affairs. This can be true if the cardinally ranked outcomes are all complete states of affairs or if the outcomes are exclusively in some resource or benefit that is linearly valued. It seems unlikely that money is such a resource for anyone. Indeed, only utility might be conceived as linearly valued. But there is nothing that is utility *tout court*. Utility is a subjective evaluation of something else. Hence, it is implausible, in general, that we can cardinalize outcomes that are specified in terms of something actually achieved unless they are states of affairs fully determined.[6] But, if the outcomes are complete states of affairs, lotteries over them can have little meaning. Cardinal utility, like money, has its meaning in context, relative to other things.

Of course, at the margin, we might approximately cardinalize amounts of money or other generalized resources. Much of the time, this is all we need to do since the particular game we are playing may genuinely be over marginal changes in the current state of affairs. But, if we suppose that we can go much further than this, we are probably mistaken. Irrespective of whether we have cardinal or only ordinal rankings over the objects of choice, we can intellectually only suppose that we have marginal choices to make with a massive *ceteris paribus* clause to cover the bulk of the state of the universe.

Unfortunately, that *ceteris paribus* clause can be violated by unanticipated causal relations, unexpected strategy choices of others, and possibly even complementarities that we have not fully grasped before experiencing certain outcomes. Our real ranges of choice are far more muddy and approximate than those assumed in the Arrow or Neumann–Morgenstern choice theories. It is not generally clear what is the message of the refined results of the set and game theoretic literatures for our real choice problems. Many of the verbal, discursive accounts of the problems we face are as compelling as any of the abstruse results of these technical literatures. For example, the real burden of the Arrow theorem for our own institutional arrangements may be little more than the problem of cyclical majorities — a problem well understood by C.L. Dodgson and Condorcet one and two centuries ago. And the chief insight of game theory for us may be the matrix representation of interacting strategy choices with a handful of particular game structures, such as the Prisoner's Dilemma. Game theory has remade our thinking about many problems by giving us the relevant analytical vocabulary and sense of structure, but its solution theories may be of remarkably limited import.

Perhaps, at this point in the development of these theories, we must admit how limited is the value of many of the most technical developments in directly resolving problems and how great is the conceptual clarification that we have gained from the theories. Hence, it is a time when we should follow Neumann's advice and return to the source to look at the nature of the problems we wish to resolve. For example, we might more carefully consider such choice problems as that of 1787. A realistic choice theory for such collective choices as that of 1787 would combine certain of the assumptions of Arrow and of Neumann and Morgenstern. Generally, it would use ordinal and noncomparable utility, it would focus on piecemeal rather than holistic choices, it would result in choices of particular states and not complete rankings of all states, and it would be about choices of strategies rather than of outcomes. In certain respects, such a theory would seem to be incoherent: despite its focus on ordinal, noncomparable utility, it would focus only on piecemeal choices. Depending on the choice problem, it might, as Sen (1982, pp 203–281, 327–352) recommends, use a mixture of cardinal, transferable utility, and ordinal, noncomparable utility, but it could not exclusively depend on transferable utility and still be realistic. The unrealistic shortcomings of both the Arrow and Neumann–Morgenstern utility theories are that both make extreme demands on our cognitive and informational capacities. Relaxing these demands makes for less coherent choice theories and probably much less elegant proofs and results. For the moment, we may have to do with less elegance.

Notes

The arguments here have benefited from presentations to the Department of Government, Wesleyan University, in December 1984, and the conference "Constructing Right Categories" at Northwestern University in March 1985. I wish to thank Donald Moon and Mary Douglas, respectively, for organizing those occasions and to thank the participants for many comments. I also wish to thank Chris Achen, James Douglas, Arthur Fine, Jonathan Riley, Duncan Snidal, and Steven Walt for extensive commentaries on an earlier draft of the paper.

1. Technically, there are two problems here: substitutability in the case of the two dinners and complementarity in the case of the two wines with dinner.

2. It is a common dodge not restricted to game theory. For example Dworkin (1981) makes a similar move in his effort to base our concern with equality in equality of resources rather than of outcomes or welfare. The dodge may be justified when resources are linearly valued and when all seem to be similarly situated.

3. In modern liberalism, there are strands of rights theory that are concerned more nearly with means or procedures than with outcomes or ends. But even these are often defended with arguments from ends. For example, Kantian liberalism might be characterized as the attempt to trick up a concern with actions as a concern with ends by defining actions in terms of rational agents who are ends in themselves.

4. That one should not be exclusively concerned with majoritarian democratic choices is argued forcefully by Barry (1979).

5. As Sen (1970, pp. 47–49, 52–54) notes, Arrow's theorem does not hold if we do not require, as Arrow does, that the social choice be a complete, transitive ordering of all states of affairs. Still, one might suppose that choice rules that would work for selecting a best state of affairs (rather than for ranking all states of affairs) would be unattractive. For example, the Pareto extension rule, which says that if an outcome is not Pareto inferior to another it is at least as "good" as the other, would work. Unfortunately, in principle, it could rank all outcomes as equally good so that it would not be a helpful rule.

6. The underlying utility theory, even for the Neumann–Morgenstern cardinalization, requires a complete ordinal ranking of whole states of affairs like that of Arrow (Neumann and Morgenstern 1953, 19; Hardin 1984, 463).

References

Arrow, Kenneth J. 1963. *Social Choice and Individual Values*. New Haven, Conn.: Yale University Press, second edition; first edition 1951.

Aumann, R.J. and L.S. Shapley. *Values of Non-atomic Games*. Princeton, N.J.: Princeton University Press.

Barry, Brian. 1979. "Is Democracy Special?" *Philosophy, Politics and Society*, fifth series, edited by Peter Laslett and James Fishkin. New Haven, Conn.: Yale University Press.

Bridgman, P.W. 1927. *The Logic of Modern Physics*. New York: Macmillan.

Downs, Anthony. 1957. *An Economic Theory of Democracy*. New York: Harper and Row.

Dworkin, Ronald. 1981. "What is Equality?, Part I: Equality of Welfare; Part II: Equality of Resources." *Philosophy and Public Affairs*, 10: 185–246, 283–345.

Gibbard, Allan. 1973. "Manipulation of Voting Schemes: A General Result." *Econometrics*, 41: 587–601.

Hardin, Russell. 1971. "Collective Action As an Agreeable n-Prisoners' Dilemma." *Behavioral Science*, 16: 472–81.

———.1982. *Collective Action*. Baltimore, Md.: Johns Hopkins University Press for Resources for the Future.

———. 1984. "Difficulties in the Notion of Economic Rationality." *Social Science Information*, 23: 453–67.

Luce, R. Duncan, and Howard Raiffa. 1957. *Games and Decisions*. New York: Wiley.

Neumann, John von. 1956, "The Mathematician." In *The World of Mathematics*. Edited by James R. Newman. New York: Simon and Schuster, vol. 4: 2053–63.

——— and Oskar Morgenstern. 1953. *Theory of Games and Economic Behavior*. Princeton, N.J.: Princeton University Press, third edition; first edition 1944.

Olson, Mancur, Jr. 1965, *The Logic of Collective Action*. Cambridge, Mass.: Harvard University Press.

Rotwein, Eugene, ed. 1955. *David Hume: Writings on Economics*. Madison, Wis.: University of Wisconsin Press.

Samuelson, Paul. 1974. "Complementarity: An Essay on the 40th Anniversary of the Hicks–Allen Revolution in Demand Theory." *Journal of Economic Literature*, 12: 1255–89.

Sen, Amartya K. 1970. *Collective Choice and Social Welfare*. San Francisco: Holden Day.

———. 1982. *Choice, Welfare and Measurement*. Cambridge, Mass.: MIT Press.

Weyl, Hermann. 1949. *Philosophy of Mathematics and Natural Science*. Princeton, N.J.: Princeton University Press.

Part II

Interpretation and Critique

4

Deadly Hermeneutics;
Or, *SINN* and the
Social Scientist

Wᴇ political scientists pride ourselves on our tough-mindedness. Collecting, counting, and classifying data, processing it by computer, discovering statistically significant correlations, and devising causal explanations, we see ourselves as unsentimental scientists toiling in the labyrinthine laboratory of modern society. Not surprisingly, many of us admire and wish to emulate what we take to be the "hard" natural sciences. And some of us sometimes seem to view such "soft" humanistic disciplines as literary interpretation and criticism with a mixture of pity and contempt. For, after all, we political scientists study the real world, while literary critics study texts dealing in fancy and fiction rather than hard fact.[1]

Against this standard, if somewhat simplified, self-image, I will try to show that the task of the political scientist is in fact more closely akin to that of the interpreter of texts than to that of the chemist or physicist (or rather, as I shall suggest, of their imaginary engagement in the idealized activity depicted by a now-passé philosophy of science). My route to this controversial conclusion proceeds by way of a defense of four interrelated claims. The first of these is the claim that political reality is itself interpretively constituted. This I attempt to show by adducing a number of examples, beginning with an apparently arcane and seemingly irrelevant interpretive controversy and proceeding, case by case, to a consideration of less recondite and more obviously relevant examples. My aim is simply to suggest that hermeneutics — the art of textual interpretation — is often a deadly enterprise having serious political import.

The second claim I wish to defend is a corollary of the first. Because political science studies and seeks to understand an object-domain which is itself interpretively constituted, the methods of the political scientist must of necessity be interpretive or hermeneutical ones which, in certain cricial respects, resemble those employed by interpreters of religious, literary, legal, and philosophical texts. My third claim is that political scientists have so far failed to recognize and appreciate the inescapably interpretive character of their discipline because they are bewitched by a largely passé philosophy of science and, especially, by its conception of scientific explanation. By means of an extended example, I attempt to elucidate and illustrate the import of the first three claims. My fourth and final claim takes the form of a conjecture. Once the philosophical spell is broken and political scientists see more clearly the hermeneutical character of their enterprise, they can then cease to fret about their inability to emulate the natural sciences as idealized by earlier neopositivists.

Before beginning, though, a word of warning: The following remarks are addressed more to my "scientifically" oriented colleagues than to my peers in political philosophy. To the latter, many of my conclusions will seem rather obvious and old-hat (although the arguments used in reaching them are, I hope, original). The former are apt, not always without reason, to be suspicious of armchair critics who (as it seems to them) sound more like German philosophers or French *littérateurs* than English-speaking social scientists. Today, this chasm yawns as wide as ever. My hope here is to build a bridge, however shaky and small, across the divide and to suggest that the two camps share some unexpected common ground. My quarrel with my social-scientific colleagues is less that they are doing the wrong thing than that they are given to misdescribing what they are, in fact, already doing. The source of this misdescription resides in their continuing adherence to a certain conception of science and method. Roughly characterizable as positivist or perhaps neopositivist, this conception, long since abandoned by philosophers of science, never did — and still does not — begin to correspond either to what natural scientists or political scientists actually do or how and why they do it. Even so, most "scope and methods" texts we assign to our students still continue to preach positivism even as we practice hermeneutics. The following essay amounts to a plea that we begin to preach what we practice.

Hermeneutical and Political Conflict

It might be best to begin by recalling that hermeneutics is the art or technique of interpreting texts, whether they be religious, literary, legal, or philosophical. The word itself comes from Hermes, the messenger of the gods. Because Hermes, like the Sphinx, spoke allusively and in riddles, his messages had to be interpreted in order to be understood. Hence "hermeneutics," the art of interpretation. This art was refined, if it did not originate, in the sixteenth century with the need to interpret recently rediscovered classical texts and canonical texts in theology and jurisprudence. Since the late nineteenth century, however, hermeneutics has been understood more broadly as the art of interpreting all sorts of texts, including literary ones.[2]

But what, one might ask, could be less relevant to the real world than the esoteric and arcane art of textual interpretation? The only thing deadly about such a subject must surely be its dullness — so, at least, one might be tempted to conclude. This temptation should, however, be resisted for a single simple reason: It is mistaken. The scope, import, and impact of hermeneutical controversies — that is, disputes over the meanings of texts — is by no means confined to the classroom. On the contrary, these controversies are not only literary but legal, political, and even scientific ones.[3] Political conflicts and controversies often take the form of hermeneutical disputes raging between rival theories of interpretation. And it is these hermeneutical conflicts which constitute the very subject matter of the social sciences and of political science in particular. Several examples should serve to illustrate the point.

Consider first an apparently arcane case. The Reformation was essentially, though not of course exclusively, a hermeneutical controversy. At the center of this protracted conflict were questions not only about what the scriptures mean but about who has the ability and the authority to interpret them. Martin Luther's vision of "a priesthood of all believers" amounts to the hermeneutical claim that all reasonably intelligent and literate laymen are perfectly capable of reading and interpreting the meaning of the Bible (which, by 1534, Luther had obligingly translated into German). The Roman Church disagreed. Only the extended education and ecclesiastical apprenticeship of the priest provides the needed exegetical expertise. And, even then, the priest must take the word of the Pope as final and authoritative in matters of scriptural interpretation. Thus, the stage was set for a controversy which raged for more than a century and which continues to smoulder even today.

Luther's task, as he saw it, was to undo the damage already wrought by mistaken methods of interpretation. As he wrote in the Preface to his translation of the New Testament, an interpretive preface is required only because "many unscholarly expositions and introductions have perverted the understanding of Christian people till they have not an inkling of the meaning of the gospel. . . . This distressing state of affairs calls for some sort of guidance by way of preface, to free the ordinary man from his false though familiar notions [and] to lead him into the straight road . . . ." (Luther 1961, 14). The straight road of the Scriptures had been made crooked, Luther thought, by the complicated multi-layered interpretive theories of the Church Fathers, the greatest of whom was surely St. Thomas Aquinas. St. Thomas, like later Thomists, discerned and distinguished between four layers of textual meaning — historical, moral, allegorical, and analogical — and various combinations thereof. Like every interpreter, Luther insisted that he offered, not interpretation, but pure unvarnished truth. Against the Thomists, Luther argued that "the literal sense of Scripture is the whole essence of faith and of Christian theology." Each passage has a true, definite, and discoverable sense of its own; hence, allegories and other speculative constructs are "the scum of Holy Scripture" (Miller 1966, 35).

If Luther's objections to other theories of interpretation had theological premises, they nevertheless yielded legal and political conclusions. "The Romanists," he wrote, "profess to be the only interpreters of Scripture . . . They claim authority for themselves alone, juggle with words shamelessly before our eyes, saying that the Pope cannot err . . .; although they cannot quote a single letter of Scripture to support their claim. Thus it comes about that so many heretical, unchristian and even unnatural laws are contained in the canon law . . ." Luther thought it "a wicked, base invention . . . to aver that it is the function of the Pope alone to interpret Scripture, or to confirm any particular interpretation" (1961, pp. 412–13). Bad laws, abuses of papal authority, political corruption — all are traceable to misinterpretations of Scripture and can, accordingly, be overcome only by a correct interpretation. Hermeneutics was, for Luther and his opponents, a deadly serious business.

More parochial but scarcely less deadly was the Antinomian controversy that racked New England in the seventeenth century. This, too, was essentially a hermeneutical dispute between Puritan orthodoxy and other, rival theories of scriptural interpretation, the most notable of which was Roger William's "typological" theory. This theory provides a specific way of interpreting the Bible, particularly the relation of the Old to the New Testament, so as to find heretofore hidden meanings and messages for the faithful. The Old Testament provides "types" which prefigure New Testament "antitypes" in the life and teachings of Christ and his disciples. Thus, for example, Daniel's descent into the lion's den and Jonah's descent into the belly of the whale are "types" whose "antitype" is Jesus' descent into hell. From these correspondences, various messages and morals are inferred by the interpreter, and these are, in turn, meant to be bases of belief and, ultimately, to serve as guides to action. Roger Williams was not the first to use the typological method; indeed there are versions of it in the writings of earlier religious thinkers, including St. Augustine. But in Puritan New England typology was believed, by the more orthodox Calvinists at least, to be the devil's own method of interpretation. After all, Luther himself had earlier denounced the theory of types as a "harlot" seducing "idle" men, and Calvin had dismissed it as a "frivolous guessing-game" (Miller 1966, 35).

What so disturbed and distressed conservative Calvinists like Governor John Winthrop, Thomas Hooker, and John Cotton, was that Williams' typological method posed a political threat of the first magnitude. It was, in their view, an attempt to undermine the authority of the governors and the fidelity of the governed. Their interpretation of Williams' theory of interpretation was, in this respect, entirely correct. For Williams' theory, if widely accepted, would almost certainly have undermined the authority of the Calvinist clergy and the magistrates, who subscribed to a very different theory of scriptural interpretation. Little wonder, then, that Roger Williams was deemed a dangerous subversive and banished from the Massachusetts Bay Colony.

The skeptic might at this point be tempted to say that this is all very well, but that I have surely stacked the deck in favor of my initial thesis. For these are, after all, examples drawn from the history of religion rather than politics. By way of self-defense, I can only say that religion and politics were not then — and are not even now — so easily separable as my critic suggests. If historical references to the Reformation or the Antinomian controversy or the Great Awakening carry little weight, one need only think of the religious revivals of our own day. These are to be found not only in the Islamic revivals of the near and the middle East — in the hermeneutical-*cum*-political conflicts between Sunni and Shi'ite Moslems, for example — but in the fundamentalist Christian revival represented by the Moral Majority in our own country. Anyone who fails to understand the hermeneutical aspects of these conflicts will find the antagonists' actions unintelligible, inexplicable, and perhaps irrational (and therefore dismiss them as psychopathic behaviors requiring psychoanalytic explanation). But, in fact, there are alternative theories of interpretation animating and legitimating these movements. And each purports to divine the "true" meaning of some canonical text, be it the Bible or the Koran.

But let me concede, if only for the sake of argument, that my critic is right in saying that my examples are narrowly theological and are therefore of interest only to theologians and historians of religion rather than to political scientists. No matter. Other, more recognizably "political" illustrations are readily available.

Consider, for example, Stalin's situation in the mid–1930s. In the midst of consolidating his power and pushing through his program of rapid forced industrialization, Stalin not only purged his most outspoken opponents; he also advanced a new interpretation of Marxism (by then already termed "Marxism–Leninism," thereby acknowledging Lenin as an authoritative interpreter of the Marxian canon). And, indeed, Stalin's attempt to concentrate and consolidate his power required that he establish his interpretations of the canonical texts of Marx, Engels, and Lenin as the only truly authoritative ones. Rival theories of textual interpretation — most notably those advanced by Bukharin and Trotsky — had to be discredited and driven from the field (Cohen 1973, chs. 9–10; Knei-Paz 1978, Part III). Accordingly, Stalin published in 1938 — at the height of the purge trials — his first foray into Marxian theory, *Dialectical and Historical Materialism*.[4] The publication of this apparently abstract philosophical work by a distinctly third-rate theorist was not, as some (for example, Deutscher 1960, pp. 381–82) would have it, mere image polishing or ideological window dressing. On the contrary, Stalin, who had originally been educated for the priesthood, was shrewd enough to recognize that unrivaled political power requires unrivaled exegetical and interpretive authority. It was in hopes of establishing such hermeneutical preeminence that Stalin, under the guise of theoretical refinement, redefined, or dropped altogether, virtually all the concepts and categories of classical Marxism (MacIntyre 1964). Henceforth, Marx's materialism was held to embody the ontological claim that "matter" alone is "real"; that all phenomena — including human actions — are explainable via the laws governing "matter in motion"; that mechanical-causal explanations of social and political phenomena are the only ones acceptable to truly "scientific" Marxists; and so on. As I have argued elsewhere (Ball 1984), these views are more akin to those of the later Engels and the early Lenin than to those of Marx himself (or of the later Lenin, for that matter). At any rate, Stalin very nearly succeeded in turning Marx's corpus into a corpse, much as he had, for good measure, turned his hermeneutical rivals Bukharian and Trotsky into corpses. Until his death in 1953, Stalin was, for most Marxists, the unrivaled authority in matters textual and interpretive. And it was his virtually unchallenged claim to hermeneutical authority that underlay, and legitimated, his increasingly personal hold on political power. No one before or since — not even Lenin, and certainly not the recently departed Mikhail Suslov — has enjoyed such unrivaled interpretive authority as Stalin. His hermeneutical monopoly, I have argued, goes some way toward explaining his political preeminence.

Even the addition and elaboration of this last-mentioned example will not, I suspect, satisfy a critic, who might object that my chosen cases have little bearing upon present-day American politics. We Americans are, after all, fortunately free of the religious and ideological differences dividing other societies. We have no canonical texts over which interpretive controversies rage. Or do we?

II. The Constitution as Canonical Text

What, after all, is the U.S. Constitution, if not a (or, for us, *the*) canonical text? And how are we to characterize the ongoing dispute between literal-minded "strict constructionists" and their liberal critics, if not as protracted hermeneutical controversy between rival theories of interpretation? The controversy is a venerable one, and virtually as old as the Republic itself.[5] Thomas Jefferson feared that "construction" (that is, interpretation) would turn America away from the straight and narrow constitutional path. And Chief Justice John Marshall, in *McCulloch v. Maryland* (1819), held that government ought not be judicially restrained "unless the words [of the Constitution] imperiously require it." Following in Marshall's footsteps, modern strict constructionists (Jefferson would have thought the label a contradiction in terms) likewise hold that the Constitution "means" what the Founders intended it to mean. Variations on this view can be found, for example, in the decisions and dissents of Justices Joseph Story, Felix Frankfurter, Hugo Black, William Rehnquist, and Warren Burger, and in the works of such constitutional scholars as Thomas Grey and Raoul Berger.[6] Their more liberal hermeneutical rivals, by contrast, view the Constitution as having a certain "spirit." The task of constitutional interpretation is, accordingly, to discover and define this spirit. Without such periodic redefinition the Constitution would quickly become a dead letter rather than the living document it is. Justice William O. Douglas, arguably the most extreme exponent of this view, was fond of such metaphors as "penumbras" surrounding the rights specifically enumerated in the Bill of Rights, and of constitutional "emanations." Variations on this view are provided by Justices Benjamin Cardozo, John Marshall Harlan, William Brennan, by the late Chief Justice Earl Warren, and by such academic analysts as John Hart Ely, Laurence Tribe, and Ronald Dworkin, among others.

Hermeneutical controversies rarely, if ever, admit of definitive resolution. In this respect, constitutional controversies resemble persistent religious disputes. Indeed, it might not be too far-fetched to view the Constitution as a kind of secular scripture around which hermeneutical controversies rage (Levinson 1979). The Supreme Court might, at a stretch, be viewed as a modern legal and political papacy claiming interpretive infallibility, while Luthers of the left and right challenge any and all decisions with which their theories of interpretation lead them to disagree. Given the logic of constitutional thinking, these challenges will perforce appear in the guise of amendments "amplifying" if not altering, the meaning of key concepts or specific articles. Thus, the now-defunct Equal Rights Amendment and the quickening Human Life Amendment represent attempts to reconstitute the Constitution, to give its articles definite but different meanings than those already decided upon in the light of earlier interpretive theories. No one who fails to understand these aspects of constitutional controversy can even begin to understand much of present-day American politics.

From these considerations an important, if contentious, conclusion follows. It is this: *Hermeneutical controversies constitute, to a very considerable degree, the very subject-matter of the social sciences, and of political science in particular.* A political scientist wishing to explain the controversy over (say) prayer in the public schools will characteristically begin — as Frank J. Sorauf does in his study, *The Wall of Separation* (1976) — by locating this issue within the context of the long-lived dispute over the meaning of the constitutional doctrine of separation of church and state. Similarly, anyone writing about the history of civil liberties in the United States can hardly ignore the Supreme Court's changing interpretations of what the First Amendment "means." As Paul Murphy (1978) observes, the history of "civil liberties" is the history of the changing meaning of the concept, as determined by decisions of the Court. In both of these cases, as in countless others, the subject-matter is itself hermeneutically constituted.

Nor is this all. Political science is, as it were, doubly hermeneutical, for not only does its subject matter consist of the interpretively constituted "behavior" of those who it studies; but its various methods are themselves necessarily hermeneutical. Political scientists who study judicial behavior, for example, supply us with second-order interpretations, that is, interpretations of interpretations. Why did Judge X dissent in a particular decision? If we take at face value X's own word — as expressed in his or her written dissent — then the political scientist or historian can tell us nothing that we do not know already from reading X's own words; the political scientist or historian would, in that case, be a lower-level clerk or court reporter and therefore superfluous or redundant. But, in fact, she/he is neither. The task of the social scientist is to interpret the meaning of the "behavior" in question in the light of this or that hermeneutical theory or framework. Such a theory tells us what sorts of things are significant, noteworthy, and/or problematic; what to look for; which concepts and categories (for example, judicial restraint and discretion) are central; and how, in short, these hermeneutically constituated human actions and activities are themselves to be understood.

III. Political Actions as Text-Analogues

But surely, my critic will at once object, my double-barreled claim applies only to a small segment of the social sciences. It applies well enough, perhaps, to political scientists and historians who study constitutional controversies, but not at all to those whose subject is (say) electoral politics or international relations or, indeed, any sort of "behavior" which is not itself concerned with disputes over the meaning of texts.

This apparently weighty objection can be overcome by widening what we mean (*sic*) by "texts." Following the lead of Paul Ricoeur (1977) and Charles Taylor (1985), we might think of human actions as "text-analogues." They are analogues because, though not literally (written) texts, actions are like texts in several respects. Human actions, like texts, have meanings both for the persons who perform them and for those witnessing the performance. Yet, some of these meanings may not cohere with or correspond to others, may not be transparent of self-evident, and so on. And so human actions — again, like texts — characteristically require interpretation in order to understand their meaning. Usually it is the "audience" who seeks an interpretation; but sometimes — as in psychoanalysis — it is the "author" who seeks an interpretation of the heretofore hidden meaning of his or her own text-acts. In either case, the interpreter brings an interpretive theory to bear upon an action or activity whose meaning is unclear or problematic. Marxist, Freudian, Jungian, Adlerian, Laingian, or otherwise, this theory tells the inquirer what to look for and how to understand the meaning or significance of particular actions, attitudes, and utterances.

Several examples should serve to clarify the character of my claim. Consider, for instance, a question still animating many political scientists: What might Ronald Reagan's 1980 and 1984 landslide victories mean? Did they mean that most American voters rejected the legacy of the New Deal and believed the welfare state *passé*? Did these victories signal a massive popular turn to the right? Or, did they merely mean that many Americans were, by 1980, fed up with Jimmy Carter's vacillating and ineffectual leadership and, in 1984, still linked Walter Mondale with Carter? These are essentially hermeneutical questions admitting of different answers, none of which is likely to be definite or definitive.

In the study of international relations and foreign affairs, hermeneutical questions loom even larger. For example, rival schools of Sovietology differ, at bottom, in their respective theories of interpretation. The differences between (say) Stephen Cohen and Henry Kissinger are in no small measure hermeneutical ones. Each gives quite different answers to questions like the following. What do the Soviets mean to convey by clamping down (or loosening up) on Jewish emigration? What is the meaning of a particular official communiqué, taking into account not only its written text but its timing, who read or released it, to whom it was released, and so on? What was the meaning of former KGB chief Yuri Andropov's rapid elevation to membership in the Party Secretariat? Did it mean that Andropov would most likely succeed Brezhnev?[7] Did it mean that the KGB's influence and importance was being upgraded? Similarly, specialists in Eastern European affairs ask what the Polish government meant to do in suppressing and subsequently outlawing Solidarity. Did they mean to show Moscow that the Polish house was in order? Or did they mean that independent trade unionism poses a threat to a centrally planned socialist economy? Or did they mean something else entirely? The answer one gives will depend on how one "reads" the "meaning" of Soviet and Polish perceptions, intentions, policies, and actions. And one's "reading" will, in turn, depend on the particular interpretive theory or schema to which one subscribes.

Like Molière's M. Jourdain, who was amazed and delighted to discover that he had been speaking prose all his life, political scientists may be no less suprised to learn that they have been engaged in hermeneutical inquiries all along. To the degree that they are unaware of this fact, however, they are apt to execute their task less ably than they otherwise might.[8] But why should this be? My contention is that political scientists are still beholden to and enamored of a particular model of scientific explanation — the nomological-deductive or "covering-law" model — which darkens more than it illuminates and confuses more than it clarifies. More particularly, the covering-law model misrepresents what political scientists do, and how and why they do it.

IV. An Extended Example: Allison on The Cuban Missile Crisis

Let me add some flesh to these logical bones by adducing yet another, though more extended, example. Any number of examples are readily available and would surely suffice but I shall, for the sake of brevity, mention only one. Published more than a decade ago, Graham Allison's *Essence of Decision: Explaining the Cuban Missile Crisis* has, by now, the twin virtues of familiarity and respectability. By looking briefly at Allison's analysis, we can, I believe, illustrate and bring into bold relief the sorts of methodological misperceptions and self-misunderstandings to which we political scientists seem peculiarly prone. Let me reiterate, however, that these slips and shortcomings are not Allison's alone but are, on the contrary, amply evident in the literature of contemporary political science.

Allison accepts, without demur or dissent, Carl Hempel's characterization of the logic of scientific explanation. According to Hempel (1965), any adequate scientific explanation consists of deducing a description of the event to be explained (the *explanandum*) from premises containing one or more general laws (the *explanans*). All "satisfactory scientific explanations," Allison adds, "exhibit this basic logic" (1971, pp. 278-79, n. 5). This is all very well except that he has, by these lights, succeeded in explaining nothing. For nowhere does Allison allude to or provide even a single general law or law-like generalization. Does this then mean that he has explained nothing? On the contrary, I should say that he has succeeded in explaining a great deal while, at the same time, systematically misunderstanding the logical and epistemological character and import of his own explanations. What Allison actually provides are not law-covered causal explanations of the Hempelian variety but interpretations of a distinctly hermeneutical sort. He supplies his reader with second-order interpretations — that is, with interpretations of the actors' interpretations of their situation, which are in turn constituted by their understanding of Soviet and American intentions, interests, strategic objectives, hopes, and fears.

Consider first, for example, Allison's Model I, the "rational actor" model. This model is, at bottom, a simplified but suggestive interpretive framework. It tells us what to look for — agents having certain aims and the means (or lack thereof) to achieve them, the obstacles they are apt to encounter in attempting to achieve them, and so on — and what a satisfactory explanation would look like. An adequate explanation must be couched not in terms of causes but in terms of the actors' own reasons — reasons having to do with A's beliefs about his own interests and about B's interests and intentions, framed in the light of B's beliefs concerning A's beliefs, interests, and intentions, and vice versa.[9] These are, of course, the first-order interpretations of the actors themselves. More than once President Kennedy was heard to ask what the Russians *meant* in installing missile bases in Cuba. Did they mean to threaten and compromise the security of the United States so as to pursue with impunity their designs in Berlin and elsewhere? Or did they mean to offer tit for tat: If the Americans could place missiles in Turkey and elsewhere around the Soviet border, then why can't two play at that game? Or, did the Russians merely mean to protect their beleaguered Cuban ally? Which American response was appropriate, therefore, depended in important ways upon which interpretation of Soviet intentions was judged to be correct. If, for example, the second were correct, then the appropriate response might be to offer to withdraw American missiles from Turkey if the Russians would, in turn, agree to dismantle their missile installations in Cuba. If the third of these interpretations were correct, the appropriate response might be to promise that the United States would never again attempt to invade Cuba. At any rate, Allison's Model I is, in fact, irreducibly interpretive: It enables the analyst to arrive at second-order interpretations by placing the agents' own interpretations, calculations, and self-understandings within this particular interpretive framework.

Much the same can also be said of Allison's Models II and III. According to Model II, the "organizational process" model, the actors are not free-floating individuals but are instead occupants of this or that role within this or that organization; they are, accordingly, constrained and restrained by the roles they occupy and by the aims, aspirations, and functions of their respective organizations, whether these by the State Department, the Department of Defense, or the CIA. Each has its particular priorities and perceptions, its own rules, routines, and operating procedures. Actors within this institutional matrix act neither in their own individual interest nor in the national interest *simpliciter*, but in the institutionally defined interest of the organization to which they belong and of which they are a greater or lesser part. And finally, Allison's Model III, the "governmental (bureaucratic) politics paradigm," interprets decisions, policies, and other governmental outcomes as the "resultant" of different games played simultaneously and often according to different rules by various strategically placed players. Who, for example, is in a position to give, or to withhold, information from the President? To whom does this ambassador report, and to whom does that journalist have access? These are the sorts of questions likely to be asked by a Model III analyst. At any rate, Models II and III, like Model I, are, at bottom, hermeneutical strategies for arriving at second-order interpretations.

Models II and III differ from Model I, however, in three important respects. First, they depart from the individual means/end conception of rationality and rational action embodied in Model I. To the "thin" or minimal means/end conception of rational action, Models II and III offer a contrasting "thick" or institutionally embedded conception. That is, Models II and III replace the thin description of agents' intentions and actions with what Clifford Geertz (1973, ch. 1) calls "thick description." The description is thickened, so to speak, by exhibiting actions and utterances as performances characteristic (and, on occasion, uncharacteristic) of normatively constrained role occupants or games players. To understand the actions and activities of pitchers and batters, you must first understand something about the rules of baseball and the roles of the different players; to understand the actions of presidents and policy makers, you must likewise understand something about the rules of the game as it is played in Washington (or Moscow) and the ways in which the players are organized and situated vis-à-vis one another.

The second way in which Allison's second and third models depart and differ from the first is that they make us wary of accepting as valid or definitive the actors' own explanations or interpretations. Model I takes actors pretty much at their word: *A*'s intention is what *A* says it is.

Models II and III make no such assumption and are, indeed, skeptical of the agents' own first-order interpretations: what *A* says and what *A* means are apt to be two different things. This is so, not merely because of the very real possibility that *A* may be lying, but because *A* might well be deceiving himself. In politics — and in political science — sincerity does not suffice; it is not the acid test of truth. Proponents of Models II and III are accordingly practicing (perhaps without knowing it) what Paul Ricoeur (1970) calls "the hermeneutics of suspicion." That is, their interpretations of the agents' interpretations rather closely resemble the psychoanalyst's somewhat skeptical view of his patients' own interpretations and self-understandings. If *A* professes to love his mother — or to act always in the national interest — he need not be taken at his word, however sincere. A better way of understanding *A*'s actions is to see where *A* stands vis-à-vis other actors, how he and they are normatively constrained, and, not least, how *A*'s own institutionally embedded interpretations serve to inform his intentions and direct his conduct.[10]

There is, finally, a third respect in which Models II and III differ from Model I. Model I views political outcomes as the wholly intended result of intentional human actions, thereby leaving little room for, and indeed scarcely recognizing the possibility of, utterly unintended outcomes. Model I makes the "psychologistic" assumption, rightly decried and criticized by Popper (1969, pp 90–95), that actions always proceed according to plan and that outcomes must perforce conform to someone's design. This assumption undergirds the "conspiracy theory of society" which holds that should some complex event occur — a war, depression, or nuclear holocaust, for example — it must be because some identifiable agent or agency wanted or intended to bring about that particular event and not some other outcome (Popper 1969, pp. 94–95). Models II and II embody no such assumption. Like Model I, Models II and III view actions as intentional, but they — unlike Model I — lead us to view outcomes not as results but as "resultants" of the combined and often conflicting intentions of differently situated players. The upshot is that Models II and III take into account, as Model I cannot, the very real and ever-present possibility that actions can go awry and that the best-laid plans of even the most expert planner or "crisis manager" can come a cropper.[11] But this realization, far from undermining the interpretivist emphasis on the importance of intentions, actually presupposes it. For, as I have argued elsewhere, the identification and description of an outcome as unintended logically requires reference to the agents' initial intentions, along with some specification of the ways in which the *actual* outcome differs from the *intended* outcome.[12] Models II and III meet this logical requirement.

If I am right, then, Allison and many other analysts are engaged in hermeneutical or interpretive inquiries without really knowing it. It might be more accurate to aver that they could and would know it, if their allegiance to an inappropriate model — the covering-law model — did not blind them to that otherwise obvious fact. And, indeed, Allison implies as much when he says that his three models, as applied to the Cuban Missile Crisis, "present a number of differences in emphasis and *interpretation*" (1971, 246; italics added). Allison succeeds in making explicit, applying, and then comparing, contrasting, and evaluating three different hermeneutical strategies. None of these is of course above reproach or beyond criticism (for example, Krasner 1972) and, indeed, Allison often proves to be his own best critic. That none of these models conforms to the criteria and requirements of the covering-law model of explanation is scarcely surprising and certainly no cause for alarm. Without intending to do so, Allison shows that political science is a hermeneutical discipline and none the worse for that.

V. Conclusion

I began by arguing that some of the most violent, prolonged and intractable political disputes are hermeneutical disputes about meaning — the meaning, as often as not, of some piece of holy writ, whether it be the Bible, the Koran, *Capital*, or the Constitution. Thus the subject matter of the social sciences, and of political science in particular, is itself interpretively constituted. I then went on to argue that the social sciences are hermeneutical not only in their subject matter but in their methods as well. The social sciences are, indeed, doubly hermeneutical, insofar as they offer interpretations of interpretations. All human actions, whether they be the text-specific action of interpreting the Constitution or the text-analogue of declaring martial law in Poland, are alike in requiring interpretive decoding. Interpreting the meaning of these varied actions, I argued, is the necessary and proper task of the political scientist.

These considerations give rise to a final, and possibly unwelcome, conclusion. The social sciences, and political science in particular, are more closely akin to literary interpretation and criticism than to physics or chemistry, or indeed any of the "hard" sciences whose hardness is both idealized and exaggerated by neopositivists. The social sciences are bound to be so, argued Max Weber (1968, vol. 1, ch. 1), so long as they continue to be concerned not merely with questions of empirical regularity or of cause and effect, but with the meaning (*Sinn*) of human action. And, considering that our interpretively constituted subject matter is by its very nature meaningful, the hermeneutical nature of our vocation is inescapable.

To many of my peers, particularly those political scientists who envy and wish to emulate a philosophically idealized version of the natural sciences, this will not come as a welcome reminder. I should not be sur-prised if the more adamant among them might, in an earlier day, have wished to stone me. Very well, then. Let him who is without *Sinn* cast the first stone.

Notes

I thank James Farr, Frank Sorauf, and W. Phillips Shively for criticizing an earlier version of this essay.

1. Any reader who thinks this an overblown portrait or otherwise exag-gerated caricature of a straw man is referred to the opening remarks of Riker (1982).

2. For a useful introductory summary and overview of the history of hermeneutics, see Palmer (1969); for more advanced discussion, see Gadamer (1975, 1976).

3. On the hermeneutical aspects of inquiry in the natural sciences, see Toulmin (1983), Popper (1972), Farr (1983); for the social sciences, see Geertz (1973) and the essays collected in Dallmayr and McCarthy (1977), Rabinow and Sullivan (1979), and Taylor (1985).

4. Two points are particularly worth noting in this connection. The first is that Stalin's debut as theorist coincided with his suppression of David Ryazanov's still-unsurpassed edition of Marx and Engel's collected works, the *Marx-Engels Gesamtausgabe* (*MEGA*), after the eleventh volume appeared in 1935. The gentle and scholarly Ryazanov was then purged and (rumor has it) subsequently shot. The second point is that Stalin's *Dialectical and Historical Materialism* first ap-peared as a chapter in the *History of the C.P.S.U. (B)*, the first major Stalinist at-tempt to rewrite the history of the Russian Revolution and the Soviet communist party.

5. The account which follows relies heavily upon Walter F. Murphy (1978) and Harris (1982).

6. A memorable and heated flare-up of this continuing interpretive con-troversy occurred in the autumn of 1985, when Attorney General Edwin Meese III told the American Bar Association that the various provisions of the Constitu-tion mean what(ever) the Founders *intended* them to mean and that he and other conservatives alone had correctly understood these intentions. Predictably, a hermeneutical-*cum*-political furor ensued.

7. The first draft of the present essay was completed shortly before the death of Leonid Brezhnev on November 10, 1982, and the remarkably rapid ac-cession of Yuri Andropov (d. 1983) to the Party Chairmanship. I have chosen to leave the wording of this example unaltered, not only because it is now of some

added historical interest but also because it illustrates and underscores the appositeness of this particular instance.

8. This is perhaps particularly evident in the case of policy analysis (Dryzek 1982).

9. For a defense of the two-fold claim that explanations couched in terms of the actors' interests are reason-explanations and that explanations of this sort are not law-covered causal explanations, see my (1979).

10. For a particularly good example of this sort of interpretive inquiry, see Connolly (1981, ch. 1).

11. The idea that human plans, projects, and actions are apt to produce consequences that are both unintended and inherently unpredictable — stressed in our day by writers as different as Alasdair MacIntyre (1981, ch. 8), Hannah Arendt (1958, ch. 5), and Karl Popper (1969, pp. 90–97) — is not entirely novel. In *The Prince* (ch. 25) Machiavelli maintains that "fortune (*fortuna*) is the ruler of half our actions, but that she allows the other half or thereabouts to be governed by us."

12. For a development of this argument, see my (1981) and the reply by Sir Karl Popper (1982).

References

Allison, Graham T. 1971. *Essence of Decision: Explaining the Cuban Missile Crisis*. Boston: Little, Brown.

Arendt, Hannah. 1958. *The Human Condition*. Chicago: University of Chicago Press.

Ball, Terence. 1979. "Interest-Explanations." *Polity*, 12: 187–201.

———. 1981. "Popper's Psychologism." *Philosophy of the Social Sciences*, 11: 65–68.

———. 1984. "Marxian Science and Positivist Politics." In *After Marx*, edited by Terence Ball and James Farr. Cambridge: Cambridge University Press.

Cohen, Stephen F. 1973. *Bukharin and the Bolshevik Revolution*. New York: Knopf.

Connolly, William E. 1981. *Appearance and Reality in Politics*. Cambridge: Cambridge: Cambridge University Press.

Dallmayr, Fred R., and Thomas A. McCarthy, eds. 1977. *Understanding and Social Inquiry*. Notre Dame, Ind.: University of Notre Dame Press.

Deutscher, Issac. (1960). *Stalin: A Political Biography*. New York: Vintage Books.

Dryzek, John. 1982. "Policy Analysis as a Hermeneutic Activity." *Policy Sciences*, 14: 309–329.

Dworkin, Ronald. 1983. "Law as Interpretation." In Mitchell 1983: pp. 249–270.

Farr, James. 1983. "Popper's Hermeneutics." *Philosophy of the Social Sciences*, 12.

Gadamer, Hans-Georg. 1975. *Truth and Method*. New York: Seabury Press.

———. 1976. *Philosophical Hermeneutics*, transl. and ed. D.E. Linge. Berkeley and Los Angeles: University of California Press.

Geertz, Clifford. 1973. *The Interpretation of Cultures*. New York: Basic Books.

Harris, William F. II. 1982. "Bonding Word and Polity: The Logic of American Constitutionalism." *American Political Science Review*, 76: 34–45.

Hempel, Carl G. 1965. *Aspects of Scientific Explanation*. New York: Free Press.

Knei-Paz, Baruch. 1978. *The Social and Political Thought of Leon Trotsky*. Oxford: Claredon Press.

Krasner, Stephen D. 1972. "Are Bureaucracies Important? (Or Allison in Wonderland)." *Foreign Policy*, 7: 159–179.

Levinson, Sanford. 1979. " 'The Constitution' in American Civil Religion." *The Supreme Court Review*, pp. 123–151.

Luther, Martin. 1961. *Martin Luther: Selections From His Writings*. Edited by John Dillenberger. Garden City, N.Y.: Anchor Books.

MacIntyre, Alasdair. 1964. "A Mistake About Causality in Social Science." In *Philosophy, Politics and Society*, second series, edited by Peter Laslett and W.G. Runciman. Oxford: Blackwell.

———. 1981 *After Virtue*. Notre Dame, Ind.: University of Notre Dame Press.

Miller, Perry. 1966. *Roger Williams*. New York: Atheneum.

Mitchell, W.J.T. ed. 1983. *The Politics of Interpretation*. Chicago: University of Chicago Press.

Murphy, Paul. 1978. "Dilemmas in Writing Civil Liberties History." *Civil Liberties Review*, 5: 16–22.

Murphy, Walter F. 1978. "Constitutional Interpretation: The Art of the Historian, Magician, or Statesman?" *Yale Law Journal*, 87: 1752–71.

Palmer, Richard E. 1969. *Hermeneutics*. Evanston, Ill.: Northwestern University Press.

Popper, Karl. 1969. *The Open Society and Its Enemies*. Vol. II. 5th rev. edn. London: Routledge & Kegan Paul.

———. 1972. *Objective Knowledge*. Oxford: Clarendon Press.

———. 1982. "Popper's Psychologism: A Reply to Ball." *Philosophy of the Social Sciences*, 12: 69.

Rabinow, Paul, and William M. Sullivan, eds. 1979. *Interpretive Social Science: A Reader*. Berkeley and Los Angeles: University of California Press.

Ricoeur, Paul. 1970. *Freud and Philosophy: An Essay on Interpretation*. New Haven, Conn.: Yale University Press.

———. 1977. "The Model of the Text: Meaningful Action Considered as a Text." In Dallmayr and McCarthy 1977: pp. 316–34.

Riker, William. 1982. "The Two-Party System and Duverger's Law: An Essay on the History of Political Science." *American Political Science Review*, 76: 753–66.

Sorauf, Frank J. 1976. *The Wall of Separation: The Constitutional Politics of Church and State*. Princeton, N.J.: Princeton University Press.

Taylor, Charles. 1985. "Interpretation and the Sciences of Man." In Taylor, *Philosophical Papers*. 2 vols. Cambridge: Cambridge University Press. II: pp. 15–75.

Toulmin, Stephen. 1983. "The Construal of Reality: Criticism in Modern and Postmodern Science." In Mitchell 1983: pp. 99–117.

Weber, Max. 1968. *Economy and Society*. Edited by Guenther Roth and Claus Wittich. 3 vols. Bedminister Press.

Stephen K. White

5

Toward a Critical
Political Science

In recent years, it has been suggested that the theoretical landscape of the social sciences, as well as the natural sciences, can best be conceptualized as a terrain of competing research programs or general strategies for interpretation and explanation. Unlike the natural sciences, however, the core of any research program in the social sciences must include some model of the subject, that is, some conceptualization of what it is to be human. Such a model is not only conceptually necessary, it is also necessarily normative (Moon 1975, 1977; Ball 1976).

It may be the case that, in the future, some research program will be devastatingly successful in its range of convincing explanations and interpretations. Were this to be so, and were the normative implications entailed by the corresponding model of the subject to diverge radically from our most reflective moral judgments, we would probably do well to question the cogency of those judgments.[1] However, I suspect that no research program will have such unqualified success. If this is true, then the choice of one or a combination of programs as the "best" will be strongly underdetermined. But that means that the relationship of our considered moral judgments to the normative implications of a given model is not going to be one in which thorough questioning is advisable in the former, but rather one in which the latter are assessed in terms of the former. That is, it seems reasonable to think that one plausible criterion for assessing the overall adequacy of a research program is to ask how well the normative implications of its model of the subject stand up under the scrutiny of our most reflective moral judgments. Other criteria of assessment will, of course, be related to the cogency of the interpretations and explanations which can be developed on the basis of the core conceptual components of a given program. How one weights

113

the normative criterion against the interpretive and explanatory ones will
no doubt be a complex matter. It does seem plausible, however, to suggest that if the model of the subject one begins with is too heavy with
normative implications, then the associated interpretations and explanations will suffer in terms of their scope. The trick, it would seem, is to
elaborate a minimal model of the subject which neither diverges radically
from our considered moral judgments nor is incapable of generating
cogent, general interpretations and explanations.

In this paper, I will differentiate between a research program derived from critical theory and one which dominates much of political
science today, either explicitly or implicitly. In its most explicit form, the
latter strategy of inquiry is known as rational choice theory.[2] It is the
most explicit form because of its clear delineation of a minimal subject
and its attempt to be theoretically rigorous in tying its assumptions about
the subject's characteristics to its hypotheses about political phenomena.
Its characterization of the subject is clear in relation to what are two
essential aspects of any minimal model: a conception of action and of rationality. Action is conceptualized as the self-interested, purposive
behavior of individuals in an objectivated world; that is, one in which
objects and other individuals are related to in terms of their possible
manipulation.[3] The rationality of action is correspondingly conceptualized as the efficient linking of actions-seen-as-means to the attainment of
individual goals. The strategic model of the subject as possessive individualist is familiar enough, and although rational choice theory makes
its character explicit, much of mainstream political science seems to rely
upon it implicitly.

What I want to argue is that critical theory, at least as it is developed
in Jürgen Habermas's recent work, provides a minimal model of the subject which is both normatively more adequate than that of rational
choice theory and which can provide a more useful theoretical orientation for interpreting and explaining at least some important phenomena
in political life. Here I will only examine two such phenomena: power
(Section II) and modernization (Section III). My arguments, if successful, are not intended to show the uselessness of the dominant
research program, but rather to show that it has definite limits which its
proponents would do well not to ignore.[4]

The Core of An Alternative Research Program

Habermas has been developing the ideas of "communicative
action" and "communicative rationality" since about 1970; however,
until recently, these concepts did not receive the sort of systematic ex-

planation they required.⁵ I want to flesh these concepts out a bit since they form the core of Habermas's research program. Given space limitations, this exposition will have to be extremely brief and ignore a number of important criticisms.

What is at issue when a theorist chooses a particular conception of action? With this choice, Habermas argues, the theorist makes certain fundamental assumptions about the possible "relations between actor and world" which have a quasi-ontological status for that theorist's vision of social life. And the "world relations" the theorist imputes to the actor, in turn, establish a particular framework for the "possible rationality of . . . actions" (1984a, pp. 75, 84). Habermas explicates his communicative conceptions of action and rationality by contrasting them with other conceptions. None of the others, he argues, adequately grasps the central role of ordinary language in coordinating human behavior; and all of the others posit a world populated by actors whose capacities are not as extensive as those of the theorist herself (1984a, 94 ff.). Habermas delineates three other models of action and shows how each achieves only a partial view of the complex phenomenon of social behavior.

A. The instrumental/strategic model

This is the model which has dominated mainstream political science. From Habermas's viewpoint, this view presupposes a relation between the actor and a world of "states of affairs," either presently existing or producible through action. The actor relates to this world both cognitively, through opinions about it, and volitionally, through intentions to intervene in it. These two possible relations to an *objective world* can be rationalized, respectively, according to criteria of "truth" and "effectiveness" or success. The former criteria demarcate epistemic rationality while the later demarcate practical rationality in the purposive sense. This purposive sense refers both to nonsocial action and its corresponding "instrumental rationality," as well as to social action and its corresponding "strategic rationality." In the latter case, the objective world includes not only physical objects and naturally occurring events, but also the intentions, strategies, decisions, etc. of other individuals, to which the actor relates in an "objectivating" manner: that is, solely in terms of their bearing on the success or failure of that actor to manipulate states of affairs (1984a, pp. 87–88, 285; 1982b, 263).

B. The norm-guided model

This sort of model has been used in role theory and also has been influential in philosophical discussions focusing on the conventional character of social action. Here, the actor can relate not only to an objective, but also to a *social world*. "A social world consists of a normative context that lays down which interactions belong to the totality of legitimate interpersonal relations" (1984a, 88). Insofar as actors share such a context, they share a social world. Now this normative context exists as a categorically distinct world only when it is *recognized as valid* by actors; that is, it maintains an 'ought' quality for them. (Otherwise this context simply becomes another feature of the objective world.)

The relation of action to social world allows rationalization in two senses, both of which Habermas subsumes under the concept of *"normative correctness"* [*Richtigkeit*] or *"normative legitimacy"* (1984 a, pp. 85, 88–90). On the one hand, an action can be assessed in regard to how well it conforms to or deviates from an intersubjectively valid role or other norm. On the other hand, these normative expectations may themselves be called into question in terms of other, more basic ones.

C. The dramaturgical model

Habermas attributes the initial development of this model to Erving Goffman. Here, the focus is not specifically on how an individual pursues a strategy or follows a set of normative expectations, but rather on how the performance of any action reveals something about the actor's subjectivity. More particularly, in the performance of actions, an individual *represents* his *subjective world* in a specific way to an *audience* of other actors. This subjective world is "defined as the totality of subjective experiences" to which the individual actor has "privileged access." This world of subjective experiences includes wishes, feelings, hopes, needs, etc. to which the subject can reflectively relate and selectively represent to others. This actor-subjective world relation is open to objective judgments of rationality by assessing the degree of consistency which exists between what a subject expresses about himself in an utterance and his ensuing action; that is, "whether he means what he says, or whether he merely feigns the experiences he has." Rationalization is thus measured in relation to a subject's "truthfulness" [*Wahrhaftigkeit*] or deceptiveness in relation to the others (1984a, pp. 90–93).

D. The communicative model

Each of the foregoing models, according to Habermas, highlights only one aspect of the multi-faceted phenomenon of social action. In order to achieve a more adequate understanding, we must grasp more systematically the role of ordinary language in interaction; more specifically, how ordinary language functions as a "mechanism for coordinating action." Habermas defines communicative action as linguistically mediated interaction which is "oriented toward reaching an understanding." Actors are conceived of as "seeking an understanding in regard to some practical situation confronting them, in order to coordinate their actions consensually" (1984a, pp. 69-70, 86, 94; 1979a, 1).

In this communicative model, actor-world relations are substantially more complex than in any of the preceding models. Actors are now conceived of as being able to relate to all three of the aforementioned worlds (objective, social, and subjective). Moreover, they can relate to them *reflectively*, in the sense that they have the competence to differentiate the three types of relations and select one or the other as the most appropriate for interpreting a given situation and working out an agreement on a common definition of it. Thus, the three modes of world relations together constitute a "commonly imputed system of coordinates" which actors have at their mutual disposal to aid them in understanding one another. (1984a, pp. 69-70, 95, 98, 101).

Actors within the communicative model are not only accorded the competence to dispose reflectively over the three world-relations, but also the competence to assess the rationality or irrationality of one another's actions according to the three respective sets of criteria (truth/success, normative legitimacy, and truthfulness) which are implied by each of the different possible world-relations. This competence (in both senses) is what Habermas refers to as "communicative competence," and it is employed by actors whenever they attempt to reach an understanding (1979a, 29).

Habermas thinks that his idea of communicative competence can be substantiated by the development of a "formal pragmatics" of language. In other words, he wants to argue that this competence can be represented as the mastery of a set of formal and universal rules for the use of sentences in utterances aimed at reaching an understanding. As the analysis of speech acts since J.L. Austin has shown, speakers in *saying* something also *do* something (Austin, 1975; Searle 1969). Habermas wants to argue that the universal core of the many and varied things speakers do in uttering sentences is the embedding of those strings of symbols into the system of three world-relations, thereby opening up their utterances to the possibility of objective assessment according to the three corresponding criteria of rationality. When a speaker orients himself toward understanding — that is, engages in communicative action — his speech acts must raise, and he must be accountable for, three "validity claims" [*Geltungsanspruche*]: truth, normative legitimacy, and truthfulness. Because a listener can contest these claims, a speaker must be able to convince her that his claims are worthy of recognition. Only if such intersubjective recognition is achieved can there develop a "rationally motivated . . . agreement" [*Einverstandnis*] or a rational "consensus" on how to coordinate their future actions (1984a, pp. 69–70, 99, 137, 282; 1979a, 3; 1982b, pp. 236–37).

Thus, in the model of communicative action, speech acts are the medium in which actors who are oriented toward a cooperative coordination of their different plans of action "mobilize the potential for rationality" inherent in ordinary language. This potential is only partially identified in the other models of action. It is only the communicative model which can fully illuminate the "rational internal structure" of the process of coming to an intersubjectively valid agreement. Such an agreement can, in turn, constitute the basis of a form of cooperation, the rational motivating force of which, according to Habermas, is reducible neither to its accordance with strategic calculations (as in the first model) nor to its fit with a normative structure whose validity is socially predefined (as in the second model) (1984a, pp. 94–99).

From what has been said so far, it should be clear that the model of communicative action is closely intertwined with the concept of understanding. Since Habermas uses this concept in a rather unusual way, it is important to delineate his position clearly. He uses "understanding" to encompass a range of achievements between speaker and hearer: the comprehensibility achieved when the speaker utters gramatically well-formed sentences (conditions of syntactical well-formedness); the listener's understanding of what sort of orientation or action the speech act typically requires of him ("conditions of fulfillment"); the listener's understanding of the conditions under which the claim raised in the speech act ought to be agreed to ("conditions for agreement"); and, finally, the understanding — in the sense of "reaching an understanding" — that takes place if the listener is convinced that the claim is justifiable. It is this full range of understanding, including the last or "maximal" sense, which Habermas has in mind when he speaks of understanding-oriented action having as its goal the bringing about of an "agreement" [*Einverstandnis*] or consensus on, respectively, the truth of an opinion, the legitimacy of an action or norm, or the veracity of an expression (1984a, pp. 299–300; 1979a, 3).

It is important to be clear about what Habermas means by understanding-oriented action because some critics have interpreted him as arguing that simply trying to understand a speech act somehow implies a commitment to finally *agreeing* on the validity of the claim raised in that speech act. Although some of Habermas's remarks might seem open to this interpretation, he has, nevertheless, made it quite clear that such an interpretation is incorrect.[6] What Habermas is interested in investigating is how the competence to use language and its rational potential can be employed to reach an agreement (understanding in the maximal sense) which will provide the basis of a cooperative coordination of individual plans of action (1984a, 101). This does not imply, however,

that anyone who seeks to understand the utterances of another under-
takes an obligation to come to an agreement with him.

What Habermas wants to emphasize is how, when actions are
oriented toward understanding, the ongoing exchange of speech acts is
based upon a mutual reliance on an intersubjectively shared cognitive
framework. It is in relation to this framework that the speaker's persuasion of the listener must take hold. The former must convince the latter
of the truth of what he says, its normative correctness or legitimacy, and
his sincerity or veracity. This does not mean that in ongoing communicative action there is always a continual testing of each specific
claim. Rather, it means that there is a *reciprocal supposition of accountability* between actors. This supposition involves two expectations: that
the other's actions are intentional and that he could, if called upon,
justify the claims he raises. Insofar as this supposition is unquestioned in
given situations, the basis of cooperation remains undisturbed (Habermas
and Luhmann 1971, pp. 114–20; 1983b, 110).

When a listener demands that the speaker justify a given claim,
however, what exactly is the source of justification to which a speaker
can appeal in order to motivate the listener to accept his claim and
restore the basis of cooperation? If we think in terms of the norm-guided
model, the motivation to accept the claims can be explained by reference
to such things as how those claims cohere with the social context of
received opinions about what is true and of traditional norms prescribing
what is right and legitimate. Specifically, if the speaker's claims are
judged to be contextually rational by the listener, the latter will be sufficiently motivated to accept them. Clearly, however, Habermas wants to
argue that the sense in which the listener can be rationally motivated is
not exhausted by the foregoing conceptions.

In situtations where there is no shared background of received opinions and norms, there is, nevertheless, a common intuition about what
kind of justification is needed to establish opinions as true and norms as
legitimate. This intuition or "know-how" can be relied upon by the
speaker as a non-conventional, intersubjective court of appeal within
which his claims can be shown to be rational, if the listener should wish
to test them. This court of appeal is referred to by Habermas as
"theoretical discourse" for truth claims and "practical discourse" for
normative claims. 'Truth ' is defined in relation to what could be ageed
upon in theoretical discourse; and 'normative legitimacy' or 'justice' in
relation to what could be agreed upon in practical discourse (1981b, 23
f.). Given the focus of my analysis, I will be concerned primarily with
this "consensus theory" as it relates to normative questions.

The intuitive knowledge available to all communicatively "competent members of modern society" constitutes, for Habermas, the
ultimate source from which any norm derives its 'oughtness' or

legitimacy for a particular group of actors. While conformity to a given norm may, in fact, result from many factors (for example, habit or strategic considerations), the capacity of that norm to provide the kind of action coordination Habermas is talking about must derive from a conviction on the part of the actor subject to that norm that it is legitimate. One of the underlying goals of Habermas's model of the subject is to reconstruct the basic sense of what makes a norm legitimate in modernity, and thus, what general criteria an actor must work through if he is to make a particular normative claim rationally convincing to those to whom that claim is directed.

From the arguments presented so far, one can see that Habermas wants to make two broad claims about action and rationality: first, that the conception of communicative action warrants a central theoretical position in social theory; and second, that a focus on communicative action implies (just as with other conceptions of action) the adoption of a corresponding conception of rationality. The basic outlines of "communicative rationality" have already been touched upon. It refers to the different types of validity claims raised in communicative action and the criteria for assessing them which are included in the intuitive knowledge of all competent speakers.

> This concept of *communicative rationality* carries with it connotations based ultimately on the central experience of the unconstrained, unifying, consensus-bringing force of argumentative speech, in which different participants overcome their merely subjective views and, owing to the mutuality of rationally motivated conviction, assure themselves of both the unity of the objective world and the intersubjectivity of their lifeworld (1984a, pp. xl, 10, 22, 37–38).

Different models of action and rationality have, as I indicated earlier, different normative implications. The strategic rational model is often attacked as presenting a thoroughly demeaning, egoistic image of human beings. However, this is a somewhat one-sided portrayal, as proponents of rational choice theory have been quick to point out. They argue that one can also see this basically Benthamite image as part of the legitimate core of the modern democratic thinking, in which 'each is to count as one' and in which policy is to be in accord with the interests of the majority (Barry 1973, pp. 173–174).

The more unsettling normative implications of the strategic model emerge if the critical focus is narrowed. The problem is not so much that self-interest is bad per se, but rather that the strategic model encounters difficulty when it comes to relating self-interest to some sort of normative obligation to support legitimate collective arrangements (Benn

1979). Despite prodigious efforts to resolve this dilemma, it seems to be the case that a subject's decision to act out of a concern for fairness, for example, is a phenomenon which remains difficult for rational choice theorists to accommodate within their category of "rational."[7]

The communicative model, on the other hand, opens conceptual access to precisely this sort of problem. Its normative implications arise from the idea of a mutual supposition of accountability for normative claims made in communicative action, and from a reconstruction of our intuitive sense of what constitutes a convincing normative justification, when one is called to account for one's claims. The idea of a necessary reciprocal supposition is what allows Habermas to commence an argument about the "normative force" inherent in communicative action (1975, 120).

The kind of argument Habermas has in mind is somewhat similar to Alan Gewirth's attempt to derive a basic principle of morality by analyzing the "structure of action" and the normative constraints it necessarily requires an actor, himself, to acknowledge (Gewirth 1978, ch. 2). Habermas asserts that an actor who refuses to acknowledge such constraints is guilty of a "performative contradiction." This means that the speech act in which he announces his refusal "rests on non-contingent [thus in given contexts unavoidable] presuppositions whose propositional content contradicts" the propositional content of the speech act itself.[8] Although Gewirth and Habermas share this mode of argument, their positions are sharply divergent because the former thinks only in terms of a strategic model of action and its associated conception of reason. As I have argued elsewhere, Gewirth's efforts fail, and probably do so unavoidably, given this conception of action and rationality (White 1982). Habermas's conception of communicative action, on the other hand, implies an unavoidable structure of *intersubjectivity* from which he derives a mutual "speech-act-immanent *obligation to provide justification*" for the different sorts of claims which are continually raised in understanding-oriented action. This obligation is one which every actor has "implicitly recognized," simply by virtue of having engaged in communicative action (1979a, 64; 1976, 339).

A number of important questions arise about such a line of argument. Is this normative obligation really a necessary one, in the sense of being unavoidably implied by the communicative structure of action? And what exactly are the normative implications of the obligation "to provide justification"? I cannot adequately take up either of these questions within the limits of this paper. I will, therefore, only sketch the normative implications of Habermas's model as far as is necessary to link them to an analysis of power.

Habermas's reconstruction of how an agent is obliged to defend a claim he raises in a speech act takes the form of a reconstruction of what are the minimal formal conditions of any convincing argumentation. The conditions or rules of such an "ideal speech situation" are as follows:

1. "Each who can speak is allowed to participate [in the argument]."
2. a."Each is allowed to call into question any proposal."
   b."Each is allowed to introduce any proposal into the [argument]."
   c."Each is allowed to express his attitudes, wishes, and needs."
3. "No speaker ought to be hindered by compulsion, whether arising from inside [the structure of argumentation] or outside [of it] from making use of the rights secured under [1 and 2]" (1983b, 99; 1984b, pp. 177-179).

The last of these three rules obviously presupposes further rules for excluding the distorting effects of various forms of coercion and ideology. The most important of these requires that the *action* context from which the argumentation is taken up be one in which there is an equal distribution of opportunities "to order and resist order, to permit and forbid, to make and extract promises, and to be responsible for one's conduct and demand that others are as well." In other words, the fulfillment of the conditions of ideal argumentation implies that the action context must have congruent normative qualities; that is, qualities which do not undermine the autonomy of each as a source of claims which have equal initial plausibility and of demands for justification to which others are obliged to respond (1984b, 178).

From this reconstruction of rational argumentation or discourse in general, Habermas proceeds to the assertion that when a *normative* claim is involved — that is, one which concerns proposed alternative orderings for the satisfaction of interests — the only norms which will be found to be acceptable to all participants in the argumentation are ones which incorporate "generalizable interests." This notion of generalizable interests represents the communicative model's interpretation of the principle of universalizability, a principle which has constituted the heart of every form of post-conventional ethics since Kant. But is is important to emphasize that the communicative interpretation does not categorically separate questions of rightness from needs and interests (1975, 89, 108; 1983a, 102-103; 1982b, 257). In this respect, it is closer to a Rawlsian post-conventionalism than a Kantian one. Having said this, however, it is necessary to emphasize that this Rawlsian comparison is strongly misleading, since Habermas's "communicative" or "discourse ethics" does not attempt to provide any derivation of substantive norms of justice, as does Rawls. All the communicative model can provide us with is a clarification of *what justice is*, in the sense of universally valid procedural criteria appropriate to judging the justness of proposed norms; it cannot go further and tell us with the same certainty *what justice demands*, in the sense of picking out determinate norms for guiding action. What justice demands in given social and historical settings cannot be legitimately decided in advance of an actual argumentation or discourse among all concerned.[9]

In this sense, a discourse ethics has a strong element of indeterminacy. It merely states certain minimal, procedural criteria for assessing norms. Submitting norms to these criteria does not entail that all participants, upon sincere discursive reflection, will find common needs and generalizable interests. They may or they may not. If they do not, resort must be had to compromise. But, it is important to keep in mind, that compromises — at least from within the discursive perspective — are not simply clever bargains. The "basic guidelines for compromise must themselves be justified" in terms of the discursive emphasis on procedural equality, participation, non-deception and non-manipulation. Hence, the process of legitimately disagreeing is, like that of agreeing, tied to certain normative criteria. (1983b, 83; 1975, pp. 111–12).

II. Power

So far, I have explicated the communicative model of action and rationality and shown how its construal of intersubjectivity yields a definite, though minimal normative orientation. However, to repeat again, this sort of orientation does not mean unambiguous, substantive norms for action. Rather, it means a focusing of moral-political attention and a prioritizing of questions to be asked in situations of conflict.

By this point, one may have begun wondering how the communicative model can get us from these abstract moral reflections back to questions of political interpretation and explanation. I want to suggest briefly, now, how this can be done in relation to the analysis of power.

As it arose in American political science in the 1960's, the debate over power was originally phrased in terms of pluralist and elitist models, and decision-making and nondecision-making processes.[10] This controversy has been sharpened in the ensuing years by extended philosophical and methodological discussions.

A conceptual connection which appears basic to this debate is the one between power and interests. Simply stated, an exercise of power by one actor is in some way adverse to the interests of some other actor. Pluralists have argued that the only sensible way to attribute interests to an actor is if he or she expresses a preference for some available policy alternative. This way of operationalizing the concept of interest, and thus also power, is defended both on scientific and moral grounds. Scientifically, this way of thinking about interests is more easily connected with empirically verifiable analyses of power; and morally, it steers clear of the latent authoritarianism which inevitably seems to lurk behind any attempt to attribute 'real' interests to people which diverge from their expressed interests — with this gap being explained in terms of ideology or false consciousness (Polsby 1980, chs. 11-13).

Critics of the pluralists have countered that the concepts of real interests and manipulated consciousness are not so easily swept under the social theorist's rug. Analyses of power using these concepts can be conducted in such a way that they are empirically verifiable, at least to some degree.[11] In relation to moral implications, the critics have argued that the pluralists have simply closed their conceptual eyes to a host of ways in which interests are subtly but effectively shaped by social processes so as to maintain the status quo in an existing society. And, it is not necessary to pay this cost, critics contend, if a way of conceptualizing real interests can be found which does not lend itself to authoritarian manipulation.

It is at this point that Habermas's communicative model is particularly useful. This model provides two key components of any defensible conceptualization of real interests: some model of the agent and some criteria for thinking about conditions which foster or hinder the exercise of her rationality. Among the critics of pluralism, William Connolly has probably developed the best representative of this type of analysis. However, I want to argue that his framework can be given greater coherence if it is rethought in communicative terms.

Connolly argues that when we are considering alternative policies we can say of an individual, A, that:

> Policy X is more in A's real interest than policy Y if A, were he to experience the results of both X and Y, would choose X as the result he would rather have for himself (1983, 64).

Yet, Connolly stresses that this definition is only a "first approximation," and he is aware that it could be interpreted simply as a helpful calculation rule for a narrowly self-interested political actor concerned with being as efficient as possible in reflectively clarifying and pursuing his self-interests. The way Connolly avoids this sort of interpretation is to argue that the exclusively strategic-rational model of man, which it presupposes, does not adequately characterize "our shared ideas about persons and responsibility." These ideas have a certain conceptual shape which can be understood by reconstructing "the depth assumptions and commitments embedded in the language and relationships of social life." In other words, Connolly wants to claim that the way his definition of an agent's real interests is to be understood can be constrained by a "loosely bounded transcendental argument" about agents and responsibility. (Connolly includes the notions that it is in an agent's real interest "to develop the *capacity* to act as a morally responsible" person and to take into consideration not just his "private wants" but his "higher order interest[s] . . . as a social being"; that is, his interest in how alternative policies either foster or undermine forms of life which incorporate mutually gratifying human relationships) (Connolly 1983, pp. 54–69, 192–95, 228, 240–41).

Clearly then, Connolly's short definition is only the beginning of a rich account of the proper conditions and criteria for deliberation about real interests. To his credit, he offers no closed normative framework from which is derived a substantive claim about real interests; rather, he carefully attempts to build into his account a dimension of normativity and intersubjectivity. Although there is much insight in this analysis, it nevertheless results in a picture of the agent and responsibility which lacks a certain coherence. One is simply not too sure how all the conceptual pieces fit together and why.

It is precisely such coherence which the communicative model offers. Its core is the agent's claim to rationality in disputes about proposed collective arrangements, and how that claim makes him intersubjectively responsible to others. The conditions for deliberating about interests are ones which require the agent to cultivate his reflective potential in relation to what he initially might take to be his interests and the needs on which they are based. Moreover, the normative dimension is more sharply demarcated in the communicative model, with its concept of generalizable interest. In disputes over collective arrangements, the agent *who maintains his claim to reason* must admit that he has a real interest in committing himself to alternatives which incorporate generalizable interests. This is one important dimension of what it means to be morally responsible. At the same time, however, this model does not dictate that one cannot have clarified reflectively, real interests which are particular.

Habermas's model is also useful because it interprets the conditions for deliberation about interests as a structure of *communication*. This orientation is particularly appropriate for a theoretical perspective which aims at supplementing the pluralist's exclusive focus on overt clashes between interests. If the study of power is to include the study of ideology, then one needs a general orientation from which one can begin to talk about the kinds of things which directly and indirectly shape consciousness. The notion of an ideal speech situation constitutes just such an orientation; on its basis, one can begin to focus on the ways in which some structures of communication are "systematically distorted" (Habermas 1970).

This would mean that when a theorist interprets a group's situation, one of his foci of attention will be the possible gap between the self-understanding of individuals in that group — expressed in terms of dominant symbol systems — and the theorist's own hypothetical understanding of how those individuals might interpret their social situation and interests under conditions which more closely approximate those of practical discourse (Habermas 1975, 113). Clearly, this sort of inquiry will be somewhat speculative. However, that does not mean that the critical theorist's imagination can run wild. As I mentioned previously, there can be empirical tests for the proffered interpretations, as John Gaventa's study of power in Appalachia has amply illustrated (Gaventa 1980). And, given the moral orientation provided by the communicative model, the researcher's attribution of interests can claim no stamp of infallibility and is, therefore, not susceptible to authoritarian perversion. As Habermas has repeatedly emphasized, the validity of critical interpretations cannot be divorced entirely from the assent of those to whom the interpretations are directed.[12]

The foregoing discussion of power does not directly confront the problem of how to comprehend the *structural* aspect of social phenomena and the associated question of the degree to which such structures should be considered manifestations of power. This is an immensely complex issue which cannot be adequately discussed here. With regard to the structure-as-power question, it seems to me that the most defensible way to proceed is to examine a given structure in the light of a model of the subject and its associated criteria of intersubjective responsibility; these conceptualizations will have to carry the burden of a claim that some structure actually constitutes power.[13] If one forgets this point, as do some deconstructionists and genealogists, the concept of power begins to lose its coherence.[14]

If we turn to the broader question of how, in general, social theory is to conceptualize structural phenonomena, we find that the research program of the rational choice theorist is tied to the assumption of methodological individualism. In other words, all structural phenomena must be explained only in terms of individual actors and their properties (Elster 1982, 453). There are, however, good reasons to doubt whether this way of proceeding will provide an adequate grasp of structures. As Anthony Giddens suggests, there is no more reason to expect that the properties of social structures can be expressed as qualities or descriptions of agents than there is to expect that the syntactical structure of language can be so expressed. "Syntactical rules . . . are not attributes of individual speakers . . . they are instantiated *in*, and reproduced *through*, speech and writing"; but, that is a different relationship than the one envisioned by methodological individualists (Giddens 1982, 534-35).

This problem of accounting for structural phenomena forms a bridge to the next topic I will be examining. For to grasp the complex phenomena of modernity and rationalization, one must have a theoretical framework which can illuminate, systematically, the peculiar ways in which modern life is structured. In this investigation, it is important to remember that cognitive and social structures can both *enable* and *constrain* action (Giddens 1982, 535).

III. Modernity and Rationalization

In the 1950s and early 1960s, the study of modernization was very much in vogue. Theoretical frameworks were developed which specified the attitudes and institutions necessary for a society to become fully modern, fully rationalized. The end-state of this process of modernization was seen as in need of no justification; its thoroughly desirable character was taken as self-evident. With the political and cultural turmoil of the 1960s, however, that end-state became deeply problematic for growing numbers of people within 'fully modern' societies. And the notion of modernization as a norm appropriate for all societies increasingly fell under the suspicion of cultural imperialism.

Although this early concern with the phenomena of modernity and rationalization focused on the development of institutions — especially the modern state and market economy — which incorporated purposive-rational action orientations, the theoretical frameworks (for example, Parson's) which were employed were not ones which contemporary rational choice theorists would consider valid. This being the case, the next question to ask is what sort of orientation toward the phenomenon of modernity and rationalization does the rational choice research program offer? Clearly, it can focus on processes of social change which we associate with modernization and try to explain them based on hypotheses about shifting constellations of power and interests.[15] If we shift the focus, however, from particular changes to broader questions about the overall structure, direction, and meaning of changes we associate with modernity, then it is no longer so clear what orientation the strategic-rational perspective gives us. For example, what significance does it attach to the systematic expansion of strategic rationality into more and more areas of social life?

Rational choice theorists tend not to raise this question directly and they could, if pressed, probably argue that they are not necessarily constrained by their assumptions to take any one position. Nevertheless, the position most rational choice theorists seem, at least tacitly, to adhere to is one which takes the systematic expansion of strategic rationality to be a beneficial process which clears the necessary cognitive and institutional ground for an ever greater degree of individual freedom and welfare, coming to fruition in the modern democratic state (Popkin 1979). This interpretation of societal rationalization has a systematic one-sidedness, however, insofar as it seems to be conceptually blind to the possibility of perceiving a negative side to modernization.

In short, the strategic perspective, by itself, seems inadequate for taking seriously the sort of questions that Max Weber raised about the loss of freedom and the loss of meaning which has accompanied Western rationalization. This is already a crucial shortcoming, at least if one feels that any serious moral and political reflection today must confront these questions at some point. Just as clearly, it was precisely this sort of practical concern which attracted renewed attention to critical theory in the late 1960s. In the work of Marcuse, Horkeimer, and Adorno, the processes and end-states of modernization were subjected to devastating critiques. These critiques, however, were so total in their indictments that they had the ironic result of making it somewhat unclear how any critical theory and practice would be possible in the future.[16]

One of the underlying goals of Habermas's work has been to construct a middle position between an uncritical, endorsement of modernity and a "totalized critique" of it (1982a). In other words, the challenge is to offer a more complex account of modernity, which can accommodate the insights of earlier critical theorists about the destructive effects of strategic reason and yet locate a sense in which modernity can be identified with an increase in the potential for a nondestructive, communicative rationalization of life. For Habermas, this task is important not only in the general sense of giving his work a distinct place in relation to his predecessors in the Frankfurt tradition, but also because his analysis of normative legitimacy is ultimately tied, as we have seen, to the deep structure of *modern* consciousness. Therefore, an argument for the universal validity of this conception of normative legitimacy requires a prior, systematic defense of modernity's legitimacy.

Here I can only suggest the most general contours of Habermas's analysis of modernity. Given the concerns of this paper, my main intention will simply be to illustrate how this analysis is linked to Habermas's model of the subject and at what point the action-theoretical framework in which it is embedded must be supplemented by a system-theoretical framework in order to grasp adequately the structuring of contemporary social life which results from modernization.

Habermas's reading of modernity revolves around his distinction between the rational *potential* manifested in "modern structures of consciousness" and the selective or "one-sided" *utilization* of this potential in the societal processes of rationalization in the West (1984a, pp. 140,

180, 221). Clearly, the distinction requires a multi-dimensional understanding of rationalization.

Habermas's portrayal of the first dimension is constructed from the same core conceptual components as his model of the subject; only this time, they are employed as a framework for understanding the sense in which certain structures of consciousness attained in modernity constitute an advance in learning for the human species. Max Weber, in his sociology of religion, began to investigate this dimension, but he did not clarify adequately the sense of rationalization that was involved in the "disenchantment" of the world, a process which was initiated with the breakdown of magical-mythical thinking (Habermas 1984a, pp. 66–68, 143 f.). Habermas thinks this process of structural change from a magical-mythical consciousness to a "decentered" consciousness (in which demarcations are recognized between the natural, social, and subjective worlds) can be understood within the framework of the sort of genetic structuralism which Jean Piaget and Lawrence Kohlberg have used for the study of the cognitive and moral development of individuals.[17] The developmental-logical importance of such decentering is that it gives actors something lacking in the magical-mythical orientation. Here it should be noted that Habermas wants to emphasize the *enabling* character of modern structures of consciousness: their capacity to enhance human learning potential. In particular, such structures provide actors with the conceptual means of *constructing a self-critical perspective*; that is, the "categorical scaffolding" constituted by the system of three world-relations and validity claims makes possible an articulated consideration and evaluation of alternative interpretations of what is the case, what is legitimate, and what is authentic self-expression. This possibility, which is opened up with the "rationalization of world-views" [*Weltbilden*], is made stronger as cultural value spheres, with specialized forms of argumentation, crystallize around the threefold differentiation. Science and technology, morality and law, art and literature, become thereby secure spheres in which knowledge can be accumulated.[18]

From the viewpoint of an agent's "lifeworld" [*Lebenswelt*], the rationalization of world-views lays the basis for a process of societal rationalization which Weber neglected. The hitherto impenetrable horizon which the lifeworld constituted for primitive man is now opened up to a degree of reflexive penetration. In other words, the system of the three world-relations and their corresponding validity claims becomes available as a medium in which each agent can take a more active role in accommodating new experiences to the unproblematic background convictions which constitute his lifeworld. "More active" here means that each agent's own critical, reflective capabilities are increasingly in-

tegrated into the ongoing reproduction of the lifeworld. This reproduction thus comes to depend *more* on the exercise of interpretive and
evaluative skills displayed in arriving at a "communicatively attained
understanding" in problematic situations, and *less* on normative
prescriptions grounded in opaque sources of authority (1984a, pp.
70–71; 1981b II, 518).

It is in the foregoing processes of rationalization that Habermas
locates modernity's crucial advance. From this broader understanding of
rationalization, he can then argue that what Weber *equated* with societal
rationalization — that is, the expansion of purposive rationality in the
economic and political spheres — is actually a one-sided or selective
mode of societal rationalization. In short, Habermas's multi-
dimensional analysis of rationalization gains him the leverage he needs to
focus on the problem of societal rationalization without having to agree
with Weber's own interpretation of what can or cannot be done to
alleviate the problem.

But the question of modernity is not adequately grasped just by shifting from the strategic or purposive model to the communicative model
of action, supplemented by a framework of genetic structuralism. In
order to comprehend the inordinate "rise to dominance of cognitive-
instrumental aspects [of rationality]," it is not sufficient to think simply
in terms of more and more economic and political actions being organized under purposive-rational criteria. It is here that the shift from action
theory to systems theory is required (Habermas 1979b, 43; 1981b II,
451).

Societies, according to Habermas, must be thought of as undergoing
both symbolic and material reproduction processes. The former refers to
the reproduction of the symbolic structures of the lifeworld: culture,
society, and personality. This process assures, respectively, the transmis-
sion of knowledge and carrying on of traditions; the integration of individuals into a normative order; and the formation of identities. Symbolic reproduction, to be secure, must occur through the *medium* of
communicative action, for only in this way do symbolic structures obtain
the resiliency that comes from internalized convictions on the part of actors. The material reproduction of complex societies, on the other hand,
can be conceptualized as being carried out within two social subsystems
of strategic action, the economy and the state, which function according
to the *media* of money and power. In contemporary Western societies,
these subsystems respond to the imperatives of class-based capital accumulation.[19]

A systems framework such as this one is, by itself, fairly similar to
that employed by a number of recent Marxian theorists. However, when
placed within the action framework and conception of modernity already
developed, Habermas thinks new light can be thrown on the problems of

contemporary societies. In particular, he wants to focus on the way in which systemic phenomena of a modernization tied to class conflict have *"class-unspecific side-effects."*[20]

These side effects are understood as arising from the fact that the pressures of capital accumulation are resulting in the lifeworld reproduction processes being increasingly organized by the media of money and power, rather than communicative action. This restructuring of the lifeworld by the *over*expansion of strategic-rational modes of socially integrating actors is called by Habermas "the colonization of the lifeworld." It is in relation to this colonization phenomenon that we must understand not only the intensification of those "social pathologies" of modernization which Weber wanted to clarify, but also the appearance of those new social movements "for which a critique of growth based on *environmental and peace concerns* provides a common focus."[21]

The dual framework of lifeworld and system is designed to be able to draw the distinction between the simple expansion of strategic-rational action in social life — an expansion which is made possible by the differentiated structures of modern consciousness — and its overexpansion or unbalanced expansion, especially in advanced capitalism. This expansion clearly has a structuring effect on contemporary social life, but it is only after we presuppose the potential offered by modern structures of consciousness and lifeworld that such structuring appears as a significant constraint.

Of course, to identify a process as somehow *un*balanced implies that one is in possession of some corresponding norm of balance. That norm, for Habermas, comes from the three cultural spheres of modernity and the idea of a proper relationship between them. Although this idea is not very clearly spelled out, the guiding theme is one of a more balanced relationship between cognitive-instrumental orientations to life, on the one hand, and moral-practical and aesthetic-expressive orientations, on the other. The practical potential for such rebalancing exists, Habermas suggests, within those new social movements whose common focus is the critique of growth (1982b, 250; Luke and White 1985).

Here, we can see the practical moment of Habermas's critical project. His model of the subject and his analysis of structures of modern consciousness constitute what I have called elsewhere the "quasi–Kantian face" of critical theory. They are worked up, however, into a particular critical interpretation of contemporary capitalism addressed to the self-understanding of contemporary actors. This constitutes the Hegelian-Marxian face (White 1983, 159f.). Habermas intends his analysis to be addressed especially to those new social movements which focus on the critique of growth, because they are struggling with problems of universal significance to industrial civilization. It is aimed at helping to orient the self-understanding of these groups in the following ways: (1) help clarify, by means of the colonization analysis, what is at stake in these groups' struggles; (2) open up a way of understanding modernity which allows such groups to be critical of it without having to reject it totally; and (3) proffer the discursive model as the most legitimate, minimal ethical guide for political action aimed at turning back the tide of colonization.

IV. Conclusion

In this paper, I have attempted to render plausible a research program emerging from Habermas's recent work. This program was contrasted with one tied more or less closely to the basic assumptions of rational choice theory. The contrasts were developed by focusing initially on the model of the subject which forms the core of each program. Some of the strengths of the communicative model were then demonstrated in relation to its normative implications and the theoretical framework it provides for analyzing power.

Furthermore, the communicative model, unlike the strategic one, provides an interpretation of modernity which illuminates a range of key contemporary concerns — moral, aesthetic, and political — about the future of industrial society and the quality of life within it. If the ultimate point of a social science is to address significant social problems, then it would seem that a research program which is relatively blind to such problems would be crucially deficient. Habermas, on the other hand, locates the practical origin of his project in precisely these problems.

Notes

1. I am not, of course, arguing that if our moral judgments diverge from what appear to be enduring features of social life, we are obliged to change them.

2. The literature here is vast and growing. For a useful introductory sampler, see Barry and Hardin (1982).

3. The assumption that action is self-interested is not *conceptually* necessary to the rational choice model. Some proponents do, however, consider it a key part of that program (see, for example, Mueller, 1979, 1). Moreover, the clearest successes of the program have come when this assumption is included (Hardin 1982, 11).

4. A number of important political phenomena ("new social movements," for instance) can be better explained with Habermas's model than with the rational choice model (Cohen 1985).

5. The most important recent works are Habermas (1979a), (1981b), (1982b), (1983b), and (1984a).

6. See Keat (1980, 196) for a critic who interprets Habermas in this way, ignoring the latter's remarks (1979a, 3).

7. Although Barry and Hardin (1982, 383) seem to acknowledge that the strategic model of rationality needs to be supplemented, they look to Weber's "value rationality," a concept that has not proven particularly fruitful in social theory.

8. Habermas (1983b, 90) borrows the concept of "performative contradiction" from Apel (1980, 262 f.).

9. Habermas (1983b, 78), (1982b, 257). I borrow the distinction between "what justice is" and "what justice demands" from Pettit (1982, 217f.).

10. See Lukes (1974) for a summary of this debate.

11. See Lukes (1974), Connolly (1983, chs. 2-3), and Gaventa (1980).

12. See White (1980, 1981).

13. See Connolly's discussion of structural constraints (1983, 116 f.).

14. For a critique of Foucault on this and related issues, see Taylor (1984) and White (1986).

15. See, for example, Popkin (1979).

16. Marcuse (1964); Adorno (1972).

17. See, *inter alia*, Habermas (1979a, pp. 69-94; 1983a; 1983b, pp. 127-205).

18. Habermas (1984a, pp. 48-50, 159-163, 166-180, 194-217; 1981b, II, 191).

19. Habermas (1981b, II, pp. 208-209, 391, 427, 489 f., 565-66, 575 f.; 1982b, pp. 227, 280-81).

20. Habermas (1981b, II, pp. 276-78, 400-419, 489).

21. Habermas (1982b, pp. 280-281; 1981b, II, pp. 292-293, 422, 452, 470-88, 565 f.; 1981a 33-35).

References

Adorno, Theodor. 1972. *Dialectic of Enlightenment*. New York: Seabury Press.

Apel, Karl-Otto. 1980. *Towards a Transformation of Philosophy*. Translated by Glyn Adey and David Frisby. London: Routledge and Kegan Paul.

Austin, John L. 1975. *How to Do Things With Words*. Cambridge, Mass.: Harvard University Press.

Ball, Terence. 1976. "From Paradigms to Research Programs: Toward a Post-Kuhnian Political Science." *American Journal of Political Science*, 20: 176–205.

Barry, Brian. 1973. *Sociologists, Economists, and Democracy*. Chicago: University of Chicago Press.

———. and Russell Hardin, eds. 1982. *Rational Man and Irrational Society*. Beverly Hills, Calif.: Sage.

Benn, Stanley. 1979. "The Problematic Rationality of Political Participation." In *Philosophy, Politics, and Society*, fifth series, edited by Peter Laslett and James Fishkin. New Haven: Yale University Press.

Cohen, Jean. 1985. "Strategy or Identity: New Theoretical Paradigms and Contemporary Social Movements." *Social Research*, 52.

Connolly, William E. 1983. *The Terms of Political Discourse*, 2d ed. Princeton, N.J.: Princeton University Press.

Elster, Jon. 1982. "Marxism, Fuctionalism, and Game Theory." *Theory and Society*, July.

Gaventa, John. 1980. *Power and Powerlessness*. Champaign, Ill.: University of Illinois Press.

Gewirth, Alan. 1978. *Reason and Morality*. Chicago: University of Chicago Press.

Giddens, Anthony. 1982. "Commentary on the Debate." *Theory and Society*, July.

Habermas, Jürgen. 1970. "On Systematically Distorted Communication." *Inquiry*, 13: 205–18.

———. 1971. *Knowledge and Human Interests*. Translated by Jeremy J. Shapiro. Boston: Beacon Press.

———. 1975. *Legitimation Crisis*. Translated by Thomas McCarthy. Boston: Beacon Press.

———. 1976. *Rekonstruktion des historischen Materialismus*. Frankfurt: Suhrkamp.

———. 1979a. *Communication and the Evolution of Society*. Translated by Thomas McCarthy. Boston: Beacon Press.

———. 1979b. "Interview with Jürgen Habermas," conducted by Detlev Horster and Willem van Reijen. Translated by Ron Smith. *New German Critique*, 18.

———. 1981a. "New Social Movements." *Telos*, 49.

———. 1981b. *Theorie des kommunikativen Handelns.* 2 vols. Frankfurt: Suhrkamp.

———. 1982a. "The Entwinement of Myth and Enlightenment." *New German Critique*, 26.

———. 1982b. "Reply." In *Habermas: Critical Debates*, edited by David Held and James Thompson. Cambridge: M.I.T. Press.

———. 1983a. "Interpretive Social Science vs. Hermeneuticism." In *Social Science as Moral Inquiry*, edited by Norma Haan. New York: Columbia University Press.

———. 1983b. *Moralbewusstein und kommunikatives Handeln.* Frankfurt: Suhrkamp.

———. 1884a. *The Theory of Communicative Action*, vol. 1. *Reason and the Rationalization of Society.* Translated by Thomas McCarthy. Boston: Beacon Press.

———. 1984b. *Ergänzungen zur Theorie des kommunikativen Handelns.* Frankfurt: Suhrkamp.

——— and Niklas Luhmann. 1971. *Theorie der Gesellschaft oder Sozialtechnologie.* Frankfurt: Suhrkamp.

Hardin, Russell. 1982. *Collective Action.* Baltimore: Johns Hopkins University Press.

Keat, Russell. 1980. *The Politics of Social Theory.* Chicago: University of Chicago Press.

Luke, Timothy W. and Stephen K. White. 1985. "Critical Theory, the Informational Revolution, and an Ecological Path to Modernity." In *Critical Theory and Public Life*, edited by John Forester. Cambridge, Mass.: M.I.T. Press.

Lukes, Steven. 1974. *Power: A Radical View.* London: Macmillan.

Marcuse, Herbert. 1964. *One-Dimensional Man.* Boston: Beacon Press.

Moon, J. Donald. 1975. "The Logic of Political Inquiry: A Synthesis of Opposed Perspectives." In *Handbook of Political Inquiry*, vol. 1, edited by Fred Greenstein and Nelson W. Polsby. Reading, Mass.: Addison Wesley.

———. 1977. "Values and Political Theory: A Modest Defense of a Qualified Cognitivism." *Journal of Politics*, November.

Mueller, Dennis, 1979. *Public Choice.* New York: Cambridge University Press.

Pettit, Philip. 1982. "Habermas on Truth and Justice." In *Marx and Marxisms*, edited by G.H.R. Parkinson. Cambridge: Cambridge University Press.

Polsby, Nelson W. 1980. *Community Power and Political Theory*, 2d ed. New Haven, Conn.: Yale University Press.

Popkin, Samuel, 1979. *The Rational Peasant*. Berkeley and Los Angeles: University of California Press.

Searle, John. 1969. *Speech Acts*. Cambridge: Cambridge University Press.

Taylor, Charles. 1984. "Foucault on Freedom and Truth," *Political Theory*, May.

White, Stephen K. 1980. "Reason and Authority in Habermas." *American Political Science Review*, December.

————. 1981. "Reply to Comments." *American Political Science Review*, June.

————. 1982. "On the Normative Structure of Action: Gewirth and Habermas." *The Review of Politics*, April.

————. 1983. "The Normative Basis of Critical Theory." *Polity*, Fall.

————. 1986. "Foucault's Challenge to Critical Theory." *American Political Science Review*, 80: 419–32, June.

Michael T. Gibbons

6

Interpretation, Genealogy and Human Agency

In the past decade, an increasing number of political and social theorists have argued that social science and political inquiry are in some fundamental sense interpretive or hermeneutic sciences. Even critics of pure interpretation have admitted that there is an inherent interpretive-hermeneutic dimension to the study of social and political life. Interpretive, that is, hermeneutic, approaches to the study of social life would not only contribute to a better understanding of political life, it is argued, but also would be an essential part of rearranging the connection between theory and practice that many critics of contemporary society claim has gone astray in modern politics (Fay 1977; Habermas 1977).

Yet, just as this recognition of the importance of the interpretive perspective was being recognized by the opponents of empiricism and positivism, more fundamental criticisms of interpretive theory emerged from a Nietzschean perspective than had been previously leveled by even interpretive theory's most adamant opponents. Specifically, the work of Michel Foucault makes possible an argument that contemporary interpretive approaches to the human sciences have failed to avoid the same traps, pitfalls, and dead ends that typify and constitute the modern epistemic maze. Moreover, flowing from Foucault's work is the implication that contemporary interpretive political theory would not significantly alter the countours of what Foucault calls "the modern disciplinary society."

The following essay is a response to the challenge that issues from the writings of Michel Foucault. It proceeds in five parts. I begin by summarizing the contours of that version of interpretive theory which I believe holds the most promise for political inquiry. Second, I will draw out the implications of this version of interpretive theory for the notion

137

of the self and the practice of human agency. Third, I will summarize Foucault's account of his own project, which he characterizes as genealogy. Fourth, I will draw out the critique of interpretive theory that flows from genealogy, focusing on their fundamental disagreements concerning the possibilities for human agency. Finally, I will argue that Foucault's own proposals for resisting the traps of the disciplinary society have their own pitfalls and dangers and, to the extent that these traps are avoidable, they rely on a form of reflection that interpretive theory cultivates.

I. The Critical-Expressivist Approach to Interpretive Theory

In spite of the growing recognition among many political theorists of at least a hermeneutic dimension to the study of political and social life, there remains a good deal of confusion concerning the aims, purposes, claims, arguments, scope, and implications of interpretive theory. Some commentators recast it in the idiom of phenomenology, others in that of ordinary language philosophy, and still others as textual exegesis. Virtually all critics fail to explore the several versions of interpretive theory and few recognize that the several versions are not reducible to a single account of interpretive theory.[1] For the purposes of this essay, I will focus on what I characterize as critical-expressivist interpretive theory. The following five charateristics help summarize what I mean by critical-expressivist interpretive theory and help delineate it from competing versions of interpretation.

1. Language and Meaning

Most important for this version of interpretive theory is the expressivist view of language. Language is the expression of a mode of being in the world; language, in some fundamental sense, helps constitute our social life, practices, and our world. Hence, it is only through language that we come to know, reflect upon, and act upon the world.[2] Moreover, in part because our language is shared by a community, it is always more than we can oversee; we cannot hope to command our language, to have it at our disposal, as the early empiricists would have it. Consequently, we cannot expect that our language, and therefore the institutions that it helps constitute, will ever be completely transparent to us. Significant dimensions of our social and political life will remain obscured, hidden in the shadows that reason can never fully illuminate.[3]

2. The Interpretation of Meaning

Because language is in some fundamental sense constitutive of political and social life, political inquiry, claims critical-expressivism, is primarily interpretive or hermeneutic. For the expressivist approach this interpretation is not exclusively concerned with the intentions of actors. Recognizing that there are several levels of meaning, expressivists argue that political inquiry must focus first on intersubjective and common meanings that help constitute a way of life, that is, that form the social background or matrix that in large part makes any particular set of intentions, practices, or actions available to the participants of that way of life (Taylor 1971). These meanings are not simply the psychological icing on the cake of social behavior that exists independently of the meanings that are said to constitute it or are embedded in it. To say that common and intersubjective meanings are constitutive of, or embedded in, a political practice is to say that without those specific meanings the practices under scrutiny would be radically different or would cease to exist.

A simple example might be helpful here. One of the common meanings embedded in academic life concerns the prohibition against plagiarism. It is not a rule that academic life could claim to leave or take and still remain the social and intellectual practice that it is. A host of values, goals, and practices within academic life (for example, integrity, honesty, truth, the possibilities of research, intellectual exchange, just to name a few) are tied to the prohibition against plagiarism. Consequently, if the prohibition were dropped, perhaps through the commercialization of academic life, or if it were to have only legal standing as an external constraint, academic life would be altered beyond recognition. The result would not simply be academic life as we know it with the change that plagiarism was no longer to be shunned. Rather, the result would be to make the new practice something other than academic life.

This view of what constitutes a complete explanation has an important implication for the evaluative dimension to political inquiry. The common and intersubjective meanings that help constitute a way of life and are required for a complete explanation become part of the foundation of normative appraisal of social and political action, appraisal that is not characterized by emotivism. To say, for instance, that academics ought not to commit plagiarism is a statement that reflects more than the mere subjective preferences of the speaker. It is also something other than an instrumental evaluation suggesting an efficient means (avoiding plagiarism) to a predetermined end (academic life). Rather, the prohibition against plagiarism is compelling because of the very nature of academic life. To refuse to recognize and be guided by it, or to challenge its legitimacy, is to reject academic life as we know it, or to seek to transform it into something entirely different.

Let us turn to a second, more political, example. One of the focal points of interpretive political inquiry is the issue of the legitimacy of the welfare state. Conventional approaches to the issue of legitimacy treat it as a question that can be divorced from the description and explanation of the workings of a polity. To the extent that the question is raised, it is generally conceived in terms of the psychological attitudes of individual actors. But, even here, the attitudes are seen primarily as icing on the cake. That is, whether or not political actors view the political system as legitimate is seen as a separate question from explaining that political system.

The interpretive account of the question of legitimacy is somewhat different. From the interpretive perspective, the legitimacy of the welfare state in the American political economy rests upon three intersubjective meanings that are constitutive of that way of life. Briefly, these are:

   a. a democratic relationship between citizens and the state;
   b. the promise of economic security for oneself and greater economic opportunity for one's progeny, secured through the achievement of individual affluence made possible by increased economic growth; and
   c. a family life that provides support for and meets the psychological and intimate needs of family members.

These meanings are not simply a set of subjective attitudes about politics. They are, according to proponents of this interpretation of American politics, constitutive of that way of life; they help make that political economy what it is and, at the same time, help explain the behavior of citizens within that political economy. Without these intersubjective meanings and the variety of political, economic, and social practices that they inform, the actions, behavior, and everyday life of citizens within the American political economy would be radically different. For example, many current proposals for economic renewal also have considerable implications for the practice of democracy and family life. To the extent that these programs would support the second of the constitutive meanings at the expense of the others, they are proposing fundamental changes in the American political economy.

Two points are in need of emphasis here. First, with this account, interpretive theory is able to disclose the connection between the personal identity of citizens and the polity within which citizens act. This is a dimension to poltical life that many conventional approaches to the study of politics ignore.

Second, the intersubjective meanings that help describe and explain a way of life also provide the foundations for normative evaluation. Because they are constitutive of a way of life, because they form part of the tacit self-understanding of citizens, and because they are embedded in the social practices of that way of life, they are not merely the subjective preferences of the social theorist nor are they merely instrumental means to a predetermined end. Like the prohibition against plagiarism in academic life, they shape standards of evaluation inherent in the American political economy, if the interpretation is correct.

3. Standards of Rationality

The centrality of language and the focus on intersubjective meanings implies, claim critical-expressivists, that standards of rationality are in large part internal to a way of life. Consequently, there is no single standard of rationality (for example, science) that can be taken as exhaustive of standards of rationality for all cultures or ways of life.

4. Interpretation and Political Theory.

Because of the expressivist view of language and the implications that that view of language has for human agency and rationality, expressivist interpretive theory sees the need to reexamine many of the central concepts of political life and political theory. Most prominently, expressivists have offered reinterpretations of the concepts of authority, human agency, legitimacy, and the common good and, in doing so, have simultaneously offered reinterpretations of the political life of modern society as well (Winch 1967; Taylor 1971; Connolly 1981, 1983b).

5. Expressivism and Human Agency

Because of the expressivist and constitutive role that language plays in our experience of the political-social world, expressivist interpretive theory insists that human reflection is both constrained by and made possible by the language within which it is located. Moreover, human identity is in large part constituted by the way of life within which reflection is located. Given this priority of language, critical-expressivism interprets human reflection as something more than the ranking of mere preferences. Human reflection is enhanced by the availability of a rich and often subtle language that makes a deep form of reflection possible. Hence, from the standpoint of critical-expressivism, there are connections amongst the philosophical foundations of one's political interpretation, the substantive interpretation that one offers of a political life, and the possibilities for human agency. First, it is the intersubjectivity of language, and the political life that it constitutes, that provides the deep evaluation necessary for the capacity for strong human agency that is essential for being a person. Second, the interpretation of political life in terms of the intersubjective notions of legitimacy, the common good, power and responsibility, and authority helps delineate the possibilities for a political life that can be reflectively understood and sustained by informed political agents. Any specific interpretation of political life will support some alternatives to politics and undermine others; the political interpretation of critical-expressivism is not morally neutral. In other words, there is a moral dimension to the type of political reflection that interpretive theory endorses. It is these connections among human agency, deep evaluation, and moral responsibility on which I now want to elaborate.

II. Human Agency, Morality and Politics

The claim that language is constitutive of human experience and social life has far-reaching claims for the possibilities of human agency and reflection. First, and foremost, it denies the possibility of human experience taking place outside of language at some prelinguistic time, uninfluenced by the prejudgments embodied in one's language. Our desires, wants, needs, etc. are not first experiences for us to which we subsequently attach labels. Rather, we have the types of experiences we have because of the language available to us; the experience of our desires is inseparable from our language.

It is not just the case that experience takes place within language, In addition, language provides the foundation for human reflection and a critical perspective on one's desires, etc. In effect, language provides the possibility for the transformation of our desires, wants, needs, and purposes. "The expressivist theory opens a new dimension. If language serves to express/realize a new kind of awareness, then it may not only make possible a new awareness of things, an ability to describe them; but also new ways of feeling, of responding to things. If in expressing our thoughts about things we can come to have new thoughts; then in expressing our feelings, we can come to have transformed feelings" (Taylor 1985, pp. 232–33). In short, language provides the possibility for the transformation and revision of those feelings, desires, wants, etc. that it enables us to experience; just as human experience is not prelinguistic, neither is human reflection extralinguistic.

The type of reflection that I am trying to elucidate here is perhaps best exemplified by Taylor's contrast between two examples of self-reflection: weak and strong.[4] Paradigmatically, weak evaluation does not depend upon additional, qualitative appraisal of the thing desired. Examples of weak evaluation might be my preference for this or that basketball team, this or that flavor of ice cream, or where I choose to vacation, say Cape Cod rather than the Berkshires. Strong evaluation, on the other hand, goes beyond evaluation in terms of mere preferences. It deploys a language of qualitative worth (for example, of justice or injustice, courage or cowardice, nobility or ignobility) of the desires entertained or alternatives under consideration. In other words, to qualify as the result of strong evaluation, it is insufficient that something merely be desired to justify or warrant the fulfillment of that desire.

There is a second distinction, related to that outlined above, between strong and weak evaluation. In the case of weak evaluation, the evaluation of alternatives is in non-contrastable terms such that there is no inherent incompatibility between any two alternatives. For example, my desire to vacation on Cape Cod does not inherently conflict with also desiring to vacation in the Berkshires. Though perhaps a shortage of time, and certainly insufficient money, may prevent my satisfying both desires, there is nothing intrinsic to the desires themselves that undermine my desire for the other. In other words, the conflict between desires is a contingent one.

In the case of strong evaluation, on the other hand, evaluation deploys a vocabulary of deeply constrastable ways of life or ways of thinking about alternatives. The language of justice and injustice, courage and cowardice, noblity and ignoblity, describe inherent incompatibilities between the alternatives to which they are applied. Consequently, the incompatability of alternatives is not contingent but rather lies in the fact that the alternatives embody inherently incompatible ways of life.

This distinction between weak and strong evaluation has several implications for the possibilities of the self. First, the self implicated in strong evaluation is more articulate than the self presupposed by weak evaluation. The former has a qualitative vocabulary unavailable to the self who evaluates only in terms of mere preferences. Whereas the weak evaluator begins and ends with mere preferences and is unable to offer any richer description of alternatives, "the strong evaluator is not similarly inarticulate. There is the beginning of a language in which to express the superiority of one alternative, the language of higher and lower, noble and base, courageous and cowardly . . . . The strong evaluator can articulate superiority just because he has a language of contrastive characterization . . . ." (Taylor 1985, 24).

Second, the self who typifies weak evaluation is a relatively shallow self. Something can be judged good or bad simply by the fact that the actor prefers it and there is no means by which to adjudicate between the value of alternatives other than to say that each is desired. For example, the weak evaluator deciding between a policy of infanticide and a policy aimed at eliminating malnutrition among children need only consider his own preferences to justify the choice of one policy over another. By contrast, the self implicated in strong evaluation more deeply reflects upon the variety of implications and the quality of life to which one policy commits him or her:

> To characterize one desire or inclination as worthier, or nobler, or more integrated, etc. than others is to speak of it in terms of the quality of life it expresses and sustains. I eschew the cowardly act . . . because I want to be a courageous and honorable human being. Whereas for the simple weigher what is at stake is the desirability of different consummations, those defined by *de facto* desires, for the strong evaluator reflection also examines the different modes of being an agent. Motiva-

tions or desires don't only count in virtue of the attraction of the consummations but also in virtue of the kind of life and kind of subject that these desires properly belong to (Taylor 1985, 25).

Third, deep evaluation plumbs the depths of personal identity. By personal identity, I mean the most fundamental evaluations that help constitute me as a person, that help make me who I am. Of course, the range of evaluations reasonably available to me, including the very possibility of experiencing this or that emotion, want, need, etc., will always be circumscribed by the language and social institutions that I inherit. Nonetheless, within the language and tradition handed down to me there is a range of alternative evaluations available to me, and these fundamental evaluations are constitutive of the very person I am. "Shorn of these," writes Taylor, "we would cease to be ourselves, by which we do not mean trivially that we would be different in the sense of having some different properties other than those we now have . . . but that shorn of these we would lose the very possibility of being an agent who evaluates; that our existence as persons, hence our ability to adhere as persons to certain evaluations, would be impossible outside the horizon of these essential evaluations, that we would break down as persons, be incapable of being a person in the full sense" (Taylor 1985, pp. 34–35). Consequently, a change in these fundamental evaluations significantly changes the person I am and my own possibilities for deep reflection.

This perspective on deep evaluation and human agency, and the connections among language, criticism, and desire that it reveals brings out the extent to which deep reflection takes the form of articulation rather than simple description, the extent to which it is the result of criticism rather than simply sensation. To examine our deepest evaluations, those that are constitutive of our personal identity, is not simply a process of describing something that is an independent object, preexistent to our account of it. In articulating our deepest evaluations, we are attempting to clarify precisely that part of our self that is inchoate, unclear, repressed, and vague. To make that which is inarticulate articulate, to clarify what is unclear, to make the repressed expressed, is to give new shape and force to that which was previously undifferentiated and perhaps formless. It is to bring the inchoate, ambivalent, and unclear into a language that embodies standards of rationality and criticism. In the process of reflection that is most completely realized in deep evaluation, "One's desire to act in certain ways becomes something one may reflect upon, criticize, and abandon, because of the criticism, and not merely something that one has, as one has a sensation. Desires do not only occur; they may be formed, and formed as the outcome of the process of criticism" (Hampshire 1971, 38).

Given this constitutive relationship between articulations and experience, we are morally accountable in two ways. First, because our experience and possibilities for understanding are circumscribed by our deepest evaluations and prior experience; and because how we experience our evaluations is shaped by the articulations we give them, the failure to appreciate the depth, morality, or ethics of an issue or desire can be said to be a failure of our prior articulations, a failure of our willingness to cultivate an understanding in terms of depth, morality, or ethics when appropriate. In effect, the inability to appreciate the deeper or moral or ethical insight can be construed as a failure of moral character. In short, we hold a person responsible for his evaluations and desires not because he chooses them but for his failure to have critically engaged them (Hampshire 1971). There is perhaps no better example of this than the Eichmann trial. In an important sense, the Nazi S.S. officer's defense that he did not believe that he was involved in anything immoral was his condemnation.

In addition, because our deep evaluations are never complete but are continuing attempts to articulate a sense of the noble, sensitive, honorable, etc., they are open to challenge, reevaluation, and reconsideration. Consequently, we are responsible for their reconsideration whenever our interpretation of them seems inadequate or when alternatives present new challenges. "Responsibility falls to us in the sense that it is always possible that fresh insight might alter my evaluations and hence even myself for the better. So within the limits of my capacity to change myself by fresh insight, within the limits of the first direction of causal influence, I am responsible in the full, direct, modern sense for my evaluations" (Taylor 1985, 39).[5] We could not, of course, be expected to be constantly evaluating our deepest evaluations, our sense of who we are and what we hold important. But in so far as the possibility is open to us, and perhaps more open to us at some moments rather than others, we can be held responsible for the evaluations that help constitute our personal identity.

On this account of the self, then, to be a human agent in the fullest sense is to be capable of deep reflection of the type that goes to my very identity and questions (within limits) the type of life I wish to endorse or pursue. This, in turn, implies a dual, complementary moral responsibility as to the types of evaluations I am capable of understanding and the cultivation of a reflective stance toward the most fundamental articulations of my identity. The significance of this argument is that if correct, an essential part of being a human agent requires that one is morally responsible for the examination of the deep evaluations that are constitutive of the self, for the capacity to be sensitive to the moral, ethical, or honorable dimensions of an issue or question. Indeed, on this reading, moral responsibility is constitutive of our deepest possibilities for human agency.

A second implication emerges from the account of human agency for political and social theory. When this potential for deep evaluation is transferred to the social and public sphere, we have the possiblity of the practice of citizenship that goes beyond the mere registering of preferences or the pursuit of given interests. Rather, this account of the possibilities of deep evaluation and its connection to moral responsibility and human agency seems to identify the possibilities for citizens who can critically address practical issues in the classical sense, issues about how we collectively ought to live our lives. Moreover, one can make the case that if we are most completely human agents when we evaluate the deepest, constitutive elements of our personal identity, then we are most completely citizens when, in politics, we collectively address the fundamental evaluations that make possible and at the same time constrain our possibilities for political life. Indeed, from this perspective, politics at its best comes into being when we engage in the type of deep reflection that allows us to confront the limits of our political existence.

The crucial upshot of this is that the critical-expressivist version of political theory sees the possibility for democratizing our political life in ways that go beyond the registration of preferences in the process of elections. It seeks to incorporate the moral, reflective dimension into political life and the study of politics. Consequently, standards of evaluation of a set of political arrangements will, in large part, consist of the extent to which it encourages and enables this reflection to take place and the extent to which it lives up to the reflective standards that are constitutive of the personal and public identity of citizens. In other words, the legitimacy of any set of political arrangements will be determined by the extent to which it is the result of and enables the deep evaluation of citizens; and, in so far as the political arrangements reflect the deep evaluation of citizens, they can be said to be responsible for these arrangements.[6]

III. Genealogy: Power, Knowledge, and the Subject

Like much of his work, Foucault's critique of interpretive theory has changed significantly over the course of his separate works. His earliest critique dealt primarily with the level of epistemology. Interpretive theory, he argued, focused on the never-ending explication of a hidden meaning that did not exist, in search of a truth that was never to be had (Foucault 1975, pp. xv–xvi). But, as Foucault's own project moved from archaeology to genealogy and as his primary concerns became more focused, the critique of interpretive theory emerging from the genealogical perspective similarly shifted. I will begin by summarizing Foucault's notion of genealogy and then go on to examine the genealogical critique of interpretive theory before responding to Foucault's criticism.[7]

Perhaps the best way to approach the summary of genealogy is to contrast it with that view of knowledge and power that pervades the Enlightenment and which genealogy most explicitly seeks to undermine. According to the Enlightenment, there is an antithesis between knowledge and power. Though knowledge can be instrumental in the exercise of power, and although greater knowledge can promise humanity greater control over its affairs, truth can only flourish in an atmosphere insulated from political pressures and political authority. To the extent that power influences the development of knowledge, that knowledge is to be considered suspect, tainted, or compromised. Hence, the picture that is painted for us by the Enlightenment and its contemporary heirs (for example, Habermas) is that, on the one side, we have truth and knowledge and, on the other, power and authority. To the extent that the latter infect the former, the scientific enterprise is jeopardized. Moreover, knowledge itself, according to many Enlightenment heirs (though not Habermas), is neutral with respect to political and moral alternatives. Pure scientific knowledge endorses no particular set of political relations.

This view of the connection among knowledge, truth, and power is incorrect in Foucault's view. In fact, he claims, the development of any particular discourse of knowledge and truth makes possible a particular set of power relations, and the existence of any particular set of power relations makes some discourses of truth possible while excluding others. Foucault describes the connection between truth and power this way:

> . . . in a society such as ours, but basically in any society, there are manifold relations of power which permeate, characterize, and constitute the social body, and these relations of power cannot themselves be established, consolidated, nor implemented without the production, accumulation, circulation, and functioning of a discourse. There can be no possible exercise of power without a certain economy of discourses of truth which operate through and are the basis of this association. We are subjected to the production of truth through power and we cannot exercise power except through the production of truth (Foucault 1977a, 93).

In short, there can be no discourse of truth outside relations of power, and relations of power, in turn, can be established and perpetuated only through the production of discourses of truth. Consequently, any given discourse of truth comes to predominate not because it is actually more truthful or accurate or reflective of reality than other, competing discourses of truth, but rather because of its relationship to power relations.

One of the requirements and effects of the growth of any particular configuration of power-knowledge relations is the subjugation of other discourses and knowledges. These subjugated discourses take two forms. First, there are the erudite, historical knowledges that have been colonized by the totalizing, hegemonic knowledges. Second, there are the local knowledges, "a whole set of knowledges that have been disqualified as inadequate to their task, or insufficiently elaborated: naive knowledges, located low down on the hierarchy, beneath the required level of cognition or scientificity . . . a scientificity established by hegemonic regimes of thought" (Foucault 1977a, 82). Hence, as one discourse of knowledge becomes more systematized and gains hegemony, other discourses of truth are necessarily excluded. But, this exclusion is based not on the fact that they are any less objective, according to Foucault, but only on the fact that they are infiltrated, dominated, compromised, or disqualified by the systematic, totalizing, hierarchically organized knowledges that predominate.

Foucault admits that his description of the relation between power and knowledge is not peculiar to modernity. But in modernity there are several specific characteristics of the power-knowledge network that Foucault finds threatening or dangerous. First, in modern society, the production of truth, and hence the extension of power, is relentless. Speaking of the omnipresence of the power-knowledge connection and the distinct features it has in our society, Foucault says,

> This is the case for every society, but . . . I believe that in ours the relationship between power, right and truth is organized in a highly specific fashion. If I were to characterize not its mechanism itself, but its intensity and inconstancy, I would say that we are forced to produce the truth of power that our society demands, of which it has need, in order to function: we *must* speak the truth; we are constrained or condemned to confess or to discover the truth. Power never ceases its interrogation, its inquisition, its registration of truth: it institutionalizes and professionalizes and rewards its pursuit. In the last analysis we must produce truth as we must produce wealth, indeed we must produce truth in order to produce wealth in the first place (Foucault 1977a, pp. 93, 94).

One implication of this claim is that the very goal of an enlightened society, one in which there are no shadows in which 'untruth' can hide, is itself the will to extend power.

Second, in addition to its relentlessness, power-knowledge in modern society, particularly as manifested in the human sciences, takes the form of a disciplinary or normalizing power in a carceral society. The specific historical course of the human sciences, at least, was made possible only because of their connection to certain power-knowledge relations, both those that they made possible and those from which they grew:

I am not saying that the human sciences emerged from the prison. But, if they have been able to be formed and to produce so many profound changes in the episteme, it is because they have been conveyed by a specific and new modality of power: a certain policy of the body, a certain rendering of the group of men docile and useful. This policy required the involvement of definite relations of knowledge in relations of power: It called for a technique of overlapping subjection and objectification; it brought with it new procedures of individuation. The carceral network constituted one of the armatures of this power-knowledge that has made the human sciences historically possible. Knowable man (soul, individuality, consciousness, conduct, whatever it is called) is the object-effect of this analytical investment, of this domination observation (Foucault 1977b, 305).

Central to Foucault's thesis concerning the connections between modern forms of power-knowledge and the disciplinary society is the claim that it is the notion of the subject that has made modern discipline possible. This modern self is the self that is haunted by a hidden self, its double, the Other, that must be identified, revealed, uncovered and made to speak: "the whole of modern thought is imbued with the necessity of thinking the unthought, of reflecting the contents of the In-itself in the form of the For-itself, of ending man's alienation by reconciling him with his own essence, . . . of lifting the veil of the Unconscious, of becoming absorbed in its silence, or of straining to catch its endless murmur" (Foucault 1970, 327). In sum, what characterizes modernity is the growth of networks of power-knowledge that enable a disciplinary matrix dependent and focused upon forms of subjectivity that require the continued search for the deep self. Indeed, this is the imperative of modern thought; it is the only imperative, argues Foucault, that modern thought can produce: the interrogation of the Other that is, in fact, a construct of modern power-knowledge for which the self is then held responsible. The modern subject that is at the center of man and his doubles, who is the object of examination by the human sciences, is also the object of the disciplinary society. Speaking of the form that modern power takes, Foucault says: "This form of power applies itself to immediate everyday life which categorizes the individual, marks him by his own individuality, attaches him to his own identity, imposes a law of truth on him which he must recognize and which others have to recognize in him. It is a form of power that makes individuals subjects" (Foucault 1977b, 305). Modern power, then, is characterized by its relentless creation of speaking, confessing subjects who are brought into being by the coincidence of modern disciplinary techniques and modern discourses of human knowledge.

Third, the disciplinary power-knowledge that operates within and constitutes modernity narrows the range of possibilities of human being. For example, Foucault argues that, before the nineteenth century, sex was experienced in a more undifferentiated, unclassified, less specific manner than it is currently experienced. With the development of modern discourses on sexuality and with the discourse of normality that emerges with the medicalization of sexuality, the range of acceptable behavior was narrowed. This narrowing has consequences not only for those whose behavior falls clearly outside the range of acceptable behavior, but for those whose behavior apparently falls within the acceptable boundaries of normalcy as well. Specifically, as the development of discourses of sexuality proceed, the scrutinizing of peoples' sexual lives, both those labeled deviants and those labeled normal, is extended. This is not to say that a greater amount of behavior is now repressed. In fact, just the opposite is the case. According to Foucault, repression is not the most important form of sexual control. Rather, what happens is that there is an excitement conferred upon discourse concerning sexuality; the modern individual is required to speak about, to confess, to reveal, to produce the truth of the deepest secrets of his or her sexuality whether that individual falls squarely within the category of the normal or the non-normal or perverse. In effect, the individual is created as a subject which must be interrogated to obtain the truth of the individual or the self.

To counter this modern tendency toward drawing the bonds of discipline ever tighter and the tendency among modern forms of knowledge to disqualify alternative forms of experience and compromise alternatives that challenge it directly, a genealogy must begin with the insurrection of subjugated knowledges. It must be local in character, operate at the margins of established regimes of thought, refusing to accept established standards of truth, reason, and knowledge:

> Genealogies are therefore not positivistic returns to a more careful or exact form of science. They are precisely anti-sciences . . . . We are concerned, rather, with an insurrection of knowledges that are opposed primarily not to the contents, methods, of science, but to the effects of the centralizing powers which are linked to the institutions and functioning of an organized scientific discourse within a society such as ours . . . it is really against the power of a discourse that is considered to be scientific that a genealogy must wage its struggle (Foucault 1977a, pp. 83–84).

And again elswhere:

> a genealogy should be seen as a kind of attempt to emancipate historical knowledges from the subjection, to render them, that is, capable of opposition and of struggle against the coercion of a theoretical, unitary discourse, formal and scientific discourse. It is based on the reactiviza-

tion of local knowledges . . . in opposition to the scientific hierarchiza-
tion of knowledges and the effects intrinsic to their power (Foucault
1977a, 85).

The point of Foucault's strategy is not to replace one system, unity, or
totalizing matrix of power-knowledge in toto; by insisting on a form of
criticism founded in localized and historical knowledges, Foucault hopes
to be able to demonstrate the conventionality and fragility of modern
conceptions of truth, power, reason, knowledge, and the self. In doing
so, he seeks to rearrange the matrix of hegemonic power-knowledge; it is
an attempt to rearrange the existing order of things by an attack on its
most remote outposts or its most immediately experienced forms of
power, truth, and individualization.

IV. The Genealogical Critique of Critical-Expressivism

From this genealogical perspective a whole series of criticisms of interpretive theory emerges. The most basic problem with interpretive
theory and, in particular, with the version outlined earlier is that, in its
debate with so-called scientific approaches to the study of social life, it
attempts to replace one system or regime of thought with another. It does
this in two ways. First, interpretive political theory claims a more solid
epistemological foundation than alternative forms of social inquiry.
Hans-Georg Gadamer, for instance, claims to offer an alternative to the
understanding of understanding, claims to offer a more accurate account
of what is actually taking place in the act of gaining knowledge than is
commonly offered by contemporary philosophers and social theorists
(Gadamer 1976). He claims, in short, to be correcting the self-
misunderstanding of philosophers and social and political theorists as to
what happens, regardless of the method they employ, when they embark
on an examination of the social world. Similarly, both Charles Taylor
and William Connolly claim to offer a more fruitful approach to the
study of political life. They claim not simply to correct the self-
misunderstanding of social theorists; in addition, both argue that the empirical or positivist approach to the study of political life is fundamentally flawed and must be replaced by a form of political inquiry that is
primarily hermeneutic (Taylor 1971; Connolly 1981).[8]

Finally, the interpretive approach does not seek only to correct or
displace the existing self-understanding of political theorists and their
approach to the study of social political life. In addition to reorienting
philosophy and political theory, each of these interpretive thinkers attempts to reorient our thinking about our way of life itself. This is most

clearly demonstrated in the work of Taylor and Connolly. In the process of articulating alternatives forms of political inquiry, Taylor and Connolly offer, in addition, unique interpretations of contemporary politics. Indeed, both insist that the epistemological reorientation that they advocate requires a significant revision of our understanding of politics, social life, and the range of possible alternatives to political life. Taylor, for instance, offers us an alternative account of legitimacy that, if correct, would raise the possibility of a legitimation crisis in advanced, industrial societies, specifically the United States. Similarly, Connolly argues that no modern polity can persist without at least tacit notions of a politics of the common good and civic virtue, if political life is to avoid the extensive forms of repression that characterize totalitarian societies. Finally, both Gadamer and Winch have offered alternative interpretations of authority and its connections with reason and freedom which, if correct, require a radical reinterpretation of political life, the possibilities for modern politics, and perhaps the source of crisis in modern politics. In short, one of the central claims of critical-expressivist interpretive political theory is that the challenges it poses at the epistemological level have implications for substantive political theory and the practice of politics.

From the genealogical perspective, it is precisely the scope of the claims of interpretive political theory, with its substantive and practical implications, that is its failing. As I noted earlier, a distinctive feature of contemporary power-knowledge relations is their totalizing tendency and the claim that, although modern alternatives may differ somewhat in the substance of their claims, they follow similar patterns in their arrangement of knowledge, power, reason, and the self. The very attempt of interpretive theory to displace or reform hegemonic regimes of thought and practice is interpretive theory's first mistake:

> I think that to imagine another system is to extend our participation in the present system . . . . We readily believe that the least we can expect from our experience, action, and strategies is that they take account of the 'whole of society' . . . . The 'whole of society' is precisely that which should not be considered (Foucault 1977b, pp. 230, 233).

In aspiring to supplant empiricist approaches to the study of political life and in offering alternative accounts of political life, the self, deep evaluation, citizenship, and legitimacy, interpretive theory tries to replace one totalizing matrix of politics, knowledge, and morality with another. Hence, rather than supplanting the disciplinary society itself, interpretive theory would, at most, simply rearrange that disciplinary society. For, like the approach to the study of political life that it seeks to replace, it would disqualify some knowledge while privileging others, and would support a new constellation of morality, reason, and politics that would privilege some forms of political criticism at the expense of others. Moreover, its claim that the intersubjectivity of language and established ways of life are the foundation of deep forms of human agency, coupled with the claim that notions of deep reflection and moral responsibility are essential parts of the self, are seen by Foucault as drawing the self into a disciplinary matrix. For these claims tie the possibilities for criticism to established regimes of thought and hegemonic discourses. Indeed, its attempt to reconnect political discourse with moral discourse might even, if successful, draw the disciplinary matrix somewhat tighter.[9]

Precisely how interpretive theory remains trapped in the disciplinary society can be demonstrated by examining where its concern with deep evaluation, human agency, moral responsibility, and citizenship locate it with respect to hegemonic political discourses. Modern politics, claims Foucault, has been dominated by two primary types of political discourse. "Modern society . . . from the nineteenth century up to our own day, has been characterized, on one hand, by a legislation, a discourse, an organization based on public right, whose principal articulation is the social body and the delegative right of each citizen; and on the other hand, by a closely linked grid of disciplinary coercions whose purpose is in fact to assure the cohesion of this same social body" (Foucault 1977a, 106). These two heterogenous discourses are the limits of political discourse within modernity. Although heterogenous, they are not independent of each other. "The judicial systems — and this applies to both their codification and their thought — have enabled sovereignty to be democratized through the constitution of public right articulated upon collective sovereignty while at the same time this democratization of sovereignty was fundamentally determined by and grounded in mechanisms of disciplinary coercion" (Foucault 1977a, 105). This juridical discourse has functioned primarily to conceal the operation of normalizing power; it directs attention away from the more important operations and uses of power. But, in addition, Foucault maintains that the very idea of the democratization of modern sovereignty was founded upon disciplinary techniques. Hence, the juridical discourse accompanying the disciplinary society does not provide the basis of cirticism of the politics of normalization. Juridical discourse, its theory of sovereignty and accompanying notions of legitimacy, human agency, and citizenship, "have allowed a system of right to be superimposed upon the mechanisms of discipline in such a way as to conceal its actual procedures, the element of domination inherent in its techniques, and to guarantee to everyone, by virtue of the sovereignty of the State, the exercise of his proper sovereign right" (Foucault 1977a, 107). In short, normalizing discourses and disciplinary practices require the existence of some type of juridical discourse in order to mask the functioning of more extensive forms of power.

This relationship between the two types of modern political discourse is not reducible to simple dependency. The two discourses are distinct and in this distinction lies the possibility of conflict. To the extent that these discourses and their accompanying practices and structures of power do conflict, the human sciences have been the primary agents of adjudication:

> . . . it is not through some advancement in the rationality of the exact sciences that the human sciences have been gradually constituted. I believe that the process which has really rendered the discourse of the human sciences possible is the juxtaposition, the encounter, between two lines of approach, two mechanisms, two absolutely heterogenous types of discourse: on the one hand there is the reorganization of right that invests sovereignty, and on the other, the mechanisms of power of the coercive forces whose exercise takes a disciplinary form. And I believe that in our own times, power is exercised simultaneously through this right and these techniques and that these techniques and these discourses, to which the disciplines give rise, invade the area of right so that procedures of normalization come to be ever more constantly engaged in the colonization of law. I believe that all this can explain the global functioning of what I would call a society of normalization (Foucault 1977a, 107).

From Foucault's perspective, the concerns of interpretive theorists with the notions of human agency, deep evaluation, moral responsibility, citizenship, and legitimacy must be seen as resulting in the rearrangement or reconstitution of the juridical discourse and theory of sovereignty; it appears, from the genealogical perspective, as a rearticulation of a new disciplinary discourse of the self, sovereignty, and right imposed upon political life. In other words, it functions to replace one regime of truth and governmentality with another. To focus on the legitimacy of the modern state, its relationship to the personal identity of citizens, or the justification for political authority that these discourses imply, is to shift the focus away from the crucial functioning of normalizing power. "To pose the problem (of power) in terms of the state" and the related notion of citizenship that democratizes and justifies political arrangements "means to continue posing it in terms of the sovereign and sovereignty . . . . What I want to say is that relations of power, and hence the analysis that must be made of them necessarily extend beyond the limits of the State . . . because the State can only operate on the basis of other, already existing relations of power" (Foucault 1977a, 123). Thus, interpretive political theory, like other contemporary approaches to political theory, and the political theory that preceded it, "(have) never ceased to be obsessed with the person of the sovereign. Such theories still continue today to busy themselves with the problem of sovereignty. What is needed, however, is a political philosophy that isn't erected around the problem of sovereignty, nor therefore around the problem of law and prohibition. We need to cut off the King's head: In political theory that has still to be done" (Foucault 1977a, 121). Because it refuses to discard the political discourse that has characterized modern society since the eighteenth century, interpretive theory seeks only to offer a different version of governmentality; it does not challenge the very idea of governmentality which is the function that the state performs in the disciplinary society. Interpretive theory, like all political theory since the eighteenth century, is a political discourse trapped in the triangle of sovereignty, discipline, and governmentality, as reflected by interpretive theorists' cor.erns with legitimacy, deep evaluation, moral reponsibility, and citizenship. And, it is the themes of sovereignty, discipline, and governmentality that typify political thought and action in the carceral society (Foucault 1979, 19).

There is a sense in which Foucault's critique of critical-expressivist interpretive theory requires us, minimally, to abandon political theory as we know it. The very failure of political discourse since the eighteenth century has been its focus on how to provide good government consistent with the rights of and dignity of man. In other words, the failure of modern political discourse is to be found in its continuing concern with governmentality, including the connections between the self and legitimate political arrangements. Interpretive theory's concerns with legitimacy, deep evaluation, citizenship, and moral responsibility reflect this same failure to escape the discourse of governmentality and sovereignty. Moreover, interpretive theory's epistemological concerns of providing a more stable foundation for human sciences — one that would inform not just political theory but political action as well — would seem to reflect what Foucault considers to be support by the human sciences for the discourse of sovereignty and government whose function is to mask the operation of disciplinary forms of power. The claim by interpretive theorists to be able to clarify the hidden, unarticulated, or imperfectly understood dimensions of political life which nonetheless inform the self-understanding and action of participants of that way of life actually encourages a form of reflection that requires the examination of the self and the connection between one's personal life and established ways of life. At best, it seems to mask or distort the most extensive forms of power in modernity; at worst, it might serve as the discourse that allows the infiltration of the discourse of sovereignty and governmentality by the discourse of normalization and discipline.[10]

V. Genealogy and the Politicization of the Self

As I noted earlier, Foucault perceives the attempt to directly inform existing matrices of power-knowledge as a trap. What needs to be done, he argues, it to undermine these matrices through courses of action that render them ineffective, ultimately leading to the breakdown of the existing practices of power-knowledge (and the subsequent emergence of new ones). To accomplish the rearrangement of social and political life and modern knowledge, Foucault has suggested, employed, or endorsed several strategies. In his most radical alternative, Foucault proposed the carnivalization of modern life. The social theorist, genealogist, or effective historian must attempt to loosen or explode the connections between dominant regimes of thought and disciplinary practice on the one hand and how people experience their lives on the other. Specifically, the genealogist attempts to destabilize existing forms of modern identity; he or she

> must dismiss those tendencies that encourage the consoling play of recognition. Knowledge, even under the banner of history, does not depend on 'rediscovery' and it emphatically excludes the rediscovery of ourselves. History becomes 'effective' to the degree that it introduces discontinuities into our very being — as it divides our emotions, dramatizes our instincts, multiplies our body and sets it against itself. 'Effective' history deprives the self of the reassuring stability of life and nature . . . (Foucault 1977b, 153–54).

The form that the destabilization of identity is to take is through the supply of an excessive choice of identity. The genealogist "will push the masquerade to its limit and prepare the great carnival of time where masks are constantly reappearing . . . . Genealogy is history in the form of a concerted carnival" (Foucault 1977c, 161). The parodic and the farcical are to be used to demonstrate that there are no constants, there is no real foundation for the identity and self-recognition that this modern (that is, carceral) society requires.

In his later work, this idea of history as a carnival gives way to a somewhat tamer approach to the attempt to loosen the connection among dominant discursive practices and disciplinary techniques, contemporary practices of knowledge and the self, and our everyday experiences. This tamer approach consists of contrasting our experience of reason, knowledge, sexuality, criminality, and the subject with how reason, knowledge, bodily desire, nonconformity and the self were experienced in other epochs and in other cultures.[11] In *Discipline and Punish*, for example, Foucault contrasts modern forms of punishment, military discipline, and the quarantine of contagious illness with somewhat different approaches to punishment, soldiering, and illness in previous historical periods. Similarly, in *The History of Sexuality*, Foucault contrasts *scientia sexualia*, the will to knowledge and power-knowledge relations that typify modern experience of desire, with the *ars erotica* of Far Eastern cultures. Finally, in his latest work — cut short by his untimely death — Foucault had begun to trace the different constitutions of the self, sex, desire, reason, and knowledge that are to be found in Western Civilization, going back to the Greek and Roman views on the connections among the self, knowledge, and desire (Foucault 1979, 1981).

In addition to the use of contrasts as a means of bringing attention to alternative conceptions of the self, desire, and reason, Foucault has most recently suggested the possibility of developing a new ethics based on treating one's life as a work of art. In an interview with Hubert Dreyfus and Paul Rabinow, Foucault claims that we need to stop thinking of ethics as being connected to other aspects of our social life (for example, family, democracy, the economy, etc.). Once we recognize that the connections between ethics and other social structures are simply 'historical coagulations,' once we recognize that there is no necesary relation between ethics and other structures, new possibilities emerge for ethics. Specifically, Foucault proposes the possibility of treating one's life as a work of art:

Q: So what kind of ethics can we build now, when we know that between ethics and other structures there are only historical coagulations and not a necessary relation?

A: What strikes me is the fact that in our society, art has become something that is related only to objects and not to individuals or to life. That art is something that is specialized or that is done by experts who are artists. But couldn't everyone's life become a work of art? Why should the lamp or the house be an art object, but not our life?

. . . we have to create ourselves as a work of art (Foucault 1983, pp. 236–37).

To treat one's life as a work of art in a manner similar to, albeit not identical with, that of the Greeks, would presumably help to loosen the connection between lived experience and the disciplinary techniques that Foucault claims constrain modern experience. Because modern institutions require modes of behavior that are consistent with established notions of reason, sexuality, and responsibility, to treat one's life as a work of art in the manner suggested by Foucault would be to introduce modes

of behavior that are not only inconsistent with established forms of identity but which also would reveal the artificiality of those forms of identity
and the notions of reason, sexuality, and responsibility that they require.
I think Foucault hoped it would lead to a general recognition of the
anomalies that exists between one's lived experience and the notions of
reason, sexuality, responsibility, and self-identity that are imposed by the
disciplinary society. In short, to treat one's life as a work of art would be
to politicize the modern self, but to do so obliquely, in a manner that
does not offer a totalizing alternative that would trap the genealogist into
swapping one matrix of power-knowledge for another. Most importantly, it would enable one to confront what are imposed as limits by our accepted standards of rationality and by our existing institutions.
Foucault's alternative, conceived as an approach to undermining the current normalizing arrangements among power, knowledge, and the self,
ought not be dismissed out of hand as frivolous.

VI Aesthetics, Politics, and Modernity

Foucault's suggestions that we treat our lives as a work of art is part
of a more general characteristic of neo-Nietzscheanism that attempts to introduce or uncover an aesthetic dimension to political thought and action. Foucault's particular arguments for the importance of art for notions of the self and ethics are among the more obviously political attempts to open up the alternatives to modern conceptions of the self and
to politicize the self. But this prescription is not without its own dilemmas. I now want to argue that Foucault's prescription has a set of pitfalls
that, itself, requires a form of reflection that is typified by the notions of
human agency and strong evaluation that characterize interpretive theory
and that these notions, in turn, lead us back to questions of political
philosophy as it has taken form in modernity. Hence, Foucault has not
eluded the problem of the moral subject and governmentality in his own
conception of the self, and the notion of treating oneself as a work of art
implies the type of deep evaluation and moral responsibility that I have
argued is the foundation of human agency.

My main criticism of Foucault's rejection of the project of critical-
expressivist political theory involves the idea of making one's life a work
of art and the type of critical evaluation that such a project entails.
Foucault recognizes that political thought and action involve a certain
amount of risk. This is no less true of the alternative of treating one's life
as a work of art. Of the various ways in which one might approach treating
one's life as a work of art, only one is consistent with Foucault's view, as I
understand it. The others could trap one in what Foucault would consider a modernist-aesthetic version of the normalizing society.

The Aesthetic View

An aesthetic approach to making one's life a work of art would involve making oneself into an object of art; it would require the objectification of one's life. For example, one might buy into the "beautiful life" — that is, the right home, a physically attractive but insipid spouse one may or may not love, the trendy automobile — in short, a world of mere physical and material appearances. As such, it is not inconsistent with most established disciplinary techniques and might actually be the type of posture toward one's life that would be most consistent with a consumer-oriented society that is part of the current disciplinary-normalizing matrix.

Art and Truth

A second possibility of the merger of art, the self, and politics comes from a Heideggerian viewpoint. This approach to treating one's life as a work of art posits the possibility of a truth that is revealed in art that is not found in technocratic or scientific conceptions of truth. Though it is in some respects a preview of the Foucauldian idea that truth is simultaneously revealing and concealing, it differs from Foucault's project in that it insists that the truth that is revealed in art is more fundamental than, a complement to, or an alternative to the truth of science and technology. From Foucault's standpoint, this conception of art is still too closely bound to the modern episteme. It presumes the possibility of producing a truth about one's life, even if that truth is not a scientifically established truth.

The Aestheticization of Politics

A third conception of the connection between art and the self involves the aestheticization of politics that typified fascism. Directing the attention of its citizens away from the traditional themes of politics, including right and the question of property rights, fascism, as Walter Benjamin has argued, attempted to turn politics into the realm of expression. (Benjamin 1969, pp. 241–42). Though this is not the type of fusion of politics and art that Foucault endorses, it remains a possibility in the constellation of politics, the self, and art that Foucault would want to avoid.

Expressivism and Politics

A fifth possibility of the connection among art, the self, and politics lies in the idea, central to critical-expressivist, interpretive political theory, that language (political language in particular) is an expression of a mode of being in the world. This view of the connection between expressivism and politics attempts to appreciate the aesthetic dimension of political life without denying the importance of a moral dimension to politics nor the integrity of political life on its own account. It tends to see greater contestability and ambiguity within modern politics than Foucault seems to recognize, and it sees the connections among politics, morality, and aesthetics as constituting a triad of contestability. Accordingly, art might be that which expresses obliquely what cannot be expressed directly either because of political constraints or, more interestingly, because the vocabulary required is unavailable or what is available is insufficient for articulating the feelings, desires, etc. that one seeks to express. This view of the connection among politics, art, morality, and the self is also inconsistent with Foucault's conception of treating one's life as a work of art, for it implicates art in the hermeneutic inquiry, thereby compromising the aesthetic; the latter becomes another focus of examination and interrogation. Moreover, it tends to see connections among the self, politics, art, and morality that Foucault would want to deny.

The Nietzschean Alternative

The final possibility of making one's life a work of art is the Nietzschean conception that Foucault adopts. It rests on the idea that one can give style to one's life in a manner such that one's vulnerability to existing structures of the disciplinary society is reduced. Treating one's life as a work of art in this manner means questioning how one is created, questioning the limits that are imposed on modern experience. In other words, treating one's life as a work of art will be part of what Foucault sees as the most important accomplishment of the Enlightenment (one with which he does identify), that is, the critical onotology of the self which he describes as "an attitude, an ethos, a philosophical life in which the critique of what we are is at one and the same time the historical analysis of the limits that are imposed on us as an experiment with the possibility of going beyond them" (Foucault 1984, 50).

I do *not* want to argue that this last view of the connection among art, the self, and politics necessarily slides into one of the other constellations of the self, art, and politics, although that is a possibility. What I do want to say is that each of the alternatives outlined represents a possible direction for the aestheticization of the self and political life, for treating one's life as a work of art. Yet, only the last, according to Foucault, would escape the constraints of the normalizing, disciplinary society. The question is, how does the genealogist hope to avoid the derailment into objectivist, phenomenological, Romanticist, fascist, or expressivist versions of the fusion of the self, art, and politics? What are the form and standards of evaluation and of reflection that will allow one to critically examine and identify derailments, dead ends, and dangerous detours?

THE SUBJECT, THE SELF, AND REFLECTION. One of the primary casualities of genealogy, and neo-Nietzscheanism in general, has been the notion of the subject. Revealed as a mere construction that is supported by a variety of institutional pressures, normalizing discourses, and disciplinary techniques, the subject seems to be on the verge of being washed away like a drawing in the sand by the tide of post-modernity. But, before we bury this poor soul at sea, I would like to fish him out, momentarily at least, to be sure that news of his demise is not premature.

In thinking of the subject and reflexivity, we can distinguish between two models of deep reflection. The first model rests the notion of a deep self, a hidden other, for example the unconscious or the real me, that is the location of some constellation of one's real interests, beliefs, feelings, or concerns. This version of the subject is clearly the target of genealogy and much post-structuralism in general.

There is a second type of deep reflection, one in which my desires, beliefs, and feelings are located between two poles. On the one hand, there are desires, beliefs, and feelings such that I reflectively choose and (more or less) understand the conditions of their existence or emergence. On the other hand, there are those desires, beliefs, and feelings that are formed under mistaken assumptions, tied to wrong objects, or are the result, in some mechanical sense, of external effects.

These two models involve two subtly different types of self-reflection. The first seems to require a reflection of correspondence or representation. Its problem can be formulated as the following: How am I able to get my conscious self, interests, ideas, etc., to correspond to or represent my real interests? The truth of my conscious interests rests on their correspondence to an objective set of real or genuine interests. Or, my conscious drives, feelings, etc., must be understood simply as manifestations of my hidden, unconscious, incompletely understood feelings. The second type of reflection involves a somewhat different type of self-reflection. There, the process is one more closely resembling self-clarification and articulation. The questions that emerge are: How have I come to have the feelings, desires, and interests that I have? Are they the types of feelings, etc., that I want to have, given the opportunity to choose between alternatives, or are they the outcome of some previously unrecognized processes of which I have little or no control?

Now, what I want to claim is that some form of the latter type of self-reflection is an ineliminable feature of human life as we can conceive and pursue it. As long as a person can be said to have desires, wants, feelings, etc. — however they are characterized and whatever discourse is used to describe them — then the possibility of reflecting upon and evaluating those desires, etc., remains, even if that reflection takes different historical forms. A person may want to be one kind of person rather than another, have one set of ideas, beliefs or feelings rather than another, or be able to choose and cultivate one way of life and to smother another (for example, the complex problem of treating one's life as a work of art at the expense of a disciplinary society). This type of reflection is ineliminable for anyone who wishes to have a critical perspective on one's life.[12]

What is particularly important about this conception of human reflection is that it encompasses what Foucault has identified as the real value of modernity and the Enlightenment, a comportment or ethos that he claims is characteristic of his own project. This Foucauldian-Enlightenment ethos demands of us that we challenge what appear to be or are presented as necessary limits to our autonomy. "The point, in brief, is to transform the critique conducted in the form of necessary limitation into a practical critique that takes the form of a possible transgression" (Foucault 1984, 45).

Moreover, to be concerned with this type of reflection is to be concerned with the conditions under which one can more easily engage in this type of reflection and, subsequently, to be concerned with the conditions under which critical reflection flourishes. This in turn leads one to consider the social and political arrangements that encourage that type of reflection and allows the questions of political reflection and the problems of political philosophy to emerge. In short, those concerned with the question of human reflection are led to question the conditions of reflection, of political reflection — and thus, to questions of political philosophy, including those problems that Foucault classifies under the rubric of governmentality. If the argument to this point has been correct, then it seems that Foucault, because he is concerned with the question of treating one's life as a work of art, and because that project is a complex one calling for critical reflection upon historically imposed limits, is led back to the question of the conditions that help support reflection as well as those that tend to inhibit it.

At times, Foucault seems to recognize this. He says, at one point, "The . . . problem of our days is not to try to liberate the individual from the state . . . but to liberate us both from the state and from the type of individuation which is linked to the state. We have to promote new forms of subjectivity through the refusal of this kind of individuality which has been imposed on us for several centuries" (Foucault 1983, 216). And again elsewhere,

> Q. But aren't there relations of discipline which are not necessarily relations of domination?
>
> M.F. Of course, there are consensual disciplines. I have tried to indicate the limits of what I wanted to achieve, that is, the analysis of a specific historical figure, of a precise technique of government of individuals

and so forth. Consequently, these analyses can in no way, to my mind, be equated with a general analytics of every possible power relation (Foucault 1984, 340).

If this is the case, the odyssey of genealogy through interpretation is a genealogical circle that leads Foucault back to some version of *modern* political theory and issues concerning the nature of deep evaluation and the conditions that encourage it. These questions, the question of deep human evaluation and the political arrangements that encourage rather than constrain it, help constitute the ethos of the Enlightenment and modernity. Because these questions are still imperfectly formulated, and certainly imperfectly answered, they are of ongoing concern for social and political theorists. Consequently, modernity and the Enlightenment can be said to be an unfinished project, unfinished for Foucault and other Nietzscheans and for critical-expressivists alike.

Notes

1. One exception to this is Howard (1983) who distinguishes among three types of hermeneutics based on their intellectual roots and historical origins. While this type of approach is quite legitimate, I think a more fruitful approach for the purposes of political theory would be to distinguish among the different approaches to understanding and interpretation based on the relationship each see between thought and action.

2. See, for example Gadamer (1976); Winch (1958); Charles Taylor, "Language and Human Nature" (in Taylor 1985, 215–247); and Hampshire, (1959).

3. Needless to say, there are important disagreements among these thinkers concerning the interpretation of political life and the importance of notions such as legitimacy and authority. What I emphasize here is their agreement on the connections among the intersubjectivity of language and its implications for political life and self-reflection.

4. This account of human agency and its relationship to language, desire, and deep evaluation borrows heavily from Taylor (1985) and Hampshire (1971.)

5. Although not all interpretive theorists would commit themselves to as strong and unambiguous a connection among language, deep evaluation, responsibility, moral agency, and citizenship as I draw out here, virtually all, I think, would defend some version of this position.

6. This conception of deep evaluation and citizenship is admittedly schematic and leaves a number of questions open to argument. For example, it says nothing about what type of institutional arrangements most likely encourage moral responsibility on the part of citizens (for example, participatory or

representative). Similarly, space does not allow me to develop the complex relationship between the personal identity of citizens and the political arrangements that they are immersed in. For example, I would argue that an implication of the interpretive position is that there is unlikely to ever be complete correspondence between the personal identity of citizens and their social-political arrangements. Concerning this latter issue, see Connolly (1981).

7. Perhaps it is appropriate here to point out that Foucault never explicitly developed the implications of his critique of modern thought and the disciplinary society as it applies to hermeneutics-interpretive theory. This is due, I would argue, to Foucault's own style. He seldom confronts specific schools of thought in more than brief, isolated remarks. But it is clear, I think, that in *The Order of Things* among those whom he has in mind in developing his critique of modern thought are theorists who take an interpretive approach to the social sciences. Hence, my account of the Foucauldian critique of interpretive theory is in large part an extrapolation of how Foucault's critique of modernity applies to interpretive political theory.

8. This theme is also present in the work of Gadamer, Winch, and Hampshire.

9. For an examination of this issue, see Connolly (1983b).

10. This would, from Foucault's perspective, be particularly true of a notion of the common good and civic virtue. These notions are tacitly present in Taylor's account of legitimacy; they are more extensively developed in Connolly's account of the necessity of a politics of the common good. The point of Foucault's criticism would be that a virtuous citizenry requires that individuals exercise self-discipline, required by authorities when public policies conflict with their specific wants or interest. To the extent that people refuse to adjust their pursuit of their specific desires in the name of a common way of life, a range of more explicit forms of discipline and coercion are made possible and supported in the name of the common good.

11. See Foucault (1977a) and (1981). There are similarities here with interpretive theory that most commentators seem not to have noticed. Specifically, the claim that one can develop an awareness of the conventionality of accepted set standards of reason, the self, and politics through contact with other cultures or one's past or the history of one's own culture is partly what is at issue in the debate between Winch and the rationalists. Perhaps more importantly, Foucault's own claim that it is those variations of the connections among language, reason, politics, and the self from one's own cultural past that provide the best promise for a critical perspective on the present comes close to the interpretivist claim that the most important criticism available to a way of life is an internal critique.

12. I am indebted to the work of William Connolly, Charles Taylor, Stuart Hampshire, and Bruno Bettelheim for this distinction.

References

Ball, Terence, ed. 1977. *Political Theory and Praxis: New Perspectives*. Minneapolis: University of Minnesota Press.

Benjamin, Walter. 1969. *Illuminations*. New York: Schocken Books.

Connolly, William E. 1981. *Appearance and Reality in Politics*. New York: Cambridge University Press.

———. 1983a. *The Terms of Political Discourse*. Princeton: Princeton University Press.

———. 1983b. "The Dilemma of Legitimacy." In *What Should Political Theory Be Now*? edited by John Nelson. Albany: SUNY Press.

Dallmayr, Fred, and Thomas McCarthy, eds. 1977. *Understanding and Social Inquiry*. Notre Dame: University of Notre Dame Press.

Fay, Brian. 1977. "How People Change Themselves: The Relationship Between Critical Theory and Its Audience." In Ball, 1977, 200–233.

Foucault, Michel. 1970. *The Order of Things*. New York: Vintage Books.

———. 1975. *The Birth of the Clinic*. New York: Random House.

———. 1977a. *Discipline and Punish*. New York: Random House.

———. 1977b. *Language, Counter-memory, and Practice*. Ithaca: Cornell University Press.

———. 1979. "Governmentality." *Ideology and Consciousness*, 6: 5–21.

———. 1980. *Power/Knowledge*. Colin Gordon, ed. New York: Pantheon Books.

———. 1981. *The History of Sexuality*. New York: Pantheon Books.

———. 1983. "The Subject and Power," in Hubert Dreyfus and Paul Rabinow, *Michael Foucault: Beyond Structuralism and Hermeneutics*, 2nd ed. Chicago: University of Chicago Press.

———. 1984. *The Foucault Reader*. Paul Rabinow, ed. New York: Pantheon Books.

Gadamer, Hans-Georg. 1976. *Truth and Method*. New York: Seabury Press.

Habermas, Jürgen. 1977. "A Review of Gadamer's *Truth and Method*." In Dallmayr and McCarthy, 1977, 335–363.

Hampshire, Stuart. 1959. *Thought and Action*. New York: Viking Press.

———. 1971. *Freedom of the Individual*. Princeton: Princeton University Press.

Howard, Roy. 1983. *Three Faces of Hermeneutics*. Berkeley: U. of California Press.

Taylor, Charles. 1971. "Interpretation and Human Sciences." *Review of Metaphysics*, 25: 3–51.

———. 1985. *Human Agency and Language: Philosophical Papers Volume I*. Cambridge: Cambridge University Press.

Winch, Peter. 1958. *The Idea of a Social Science*. New York: Humanities Press.

———. 1967. "On Authority." In *Political Philosophy*, edited by Anthony Quinton. New York: Oxford University Press.

Part III _____

Beyond Empiricism And Hermeneutics

Fred Dallmayr

7

Political Inquiry: Beyond Empiricism And Hermeneutics

The following essay seeks to make some headway in the thicket of behavioralism, anti-behavioralism, and post-behavioralism. In a first section, I intend to sketch some initial moves beyond the behavioralist paradigm—concentrating particularly on Habermas's (and my own) endeavors to supplement empirical analysis with interpretive or hermeneutical understanding. Against the backdrop of this bifurcation, the second section turns to critical discussions of epistemology and methodology, discussions inspired primarily by post-empiricist and "anti-foundationalist" trends in recent philosophy of science. Dissatisfied with the simple thesis that there is "no difference" between the natural and the social sciences (as articulated, for example, by Richard Rorty), in the concluding section I seek to delineate a differentiated approach to political inquiry relying on the notion of political "structuration" — an approach which, without effacing the explanation-understanding distinction, nevertheless points beyond empiricism and hermeneutics.

I

Although heralded by earlier initiatives from Herbert Spencer to Charles Merriam, behavioralism held sway over political inquiry primarily during the two or three decades following World War II. While not devoid of diverse accents, practitioners subscribed basically to a one-dimensional outlook or frame of analysis — a frame marked by empiricist epistemology and the "nomological" method of explanation and prediction. Objections to this one-dimensional mold soon arose from diverse quarters, ranging from neo-classicism to phenomenology to critical theory; for present purposes, I intend to focus chiefly on the last perspective (with a few side-glances at phenomenology). Attention to the diversity of social and political research had been a hallmark of the Frankfurt Institute from the beginning. Adapting the older dichotomy of natural and human disciplines (*Natur- und Geisteswissenschaften*), Max Horkheimer in 1937 had differentiated between two central modes of inquiry — labeled "traditional" and "critical," respectively — with the first restricted to the passive observation of empirical data and the second concerned with the intentional-historical genesis of social conditions (Horkheimer 1972, 188–243). Some three decades later, in *Knowledge and Human Interests*, Habermas (1971) further sharpened and radicalized Horkheimer's initiative by carrying the distinction of approaches to the very heart of "critical" social science itself.[1]

Designed as an attack on positivist one-dimensionality, *Knowledge and Human Interests* attempted to uncover both a broad-scale, philosophically grounded epistemology and the premises of methodological diversity. In pursuing this goal, Habermas relied, at least partially, on the guidance of two *fin-de-siècle* thinkers whose works had transgressed the positivist paradigm at crucial junctures: Charles S. Peirce and Wilhelm Dilthey. Concentrating mainly on natural-scientific inquiry, Peirce located the parameters of research not so much in empirical data-gathering as in the practices of a "community of investigators" and the experimental learning experiences occuring in this community. Roughly at the same time, Dilthey exposed positivism's shortcomings in the domain of cultural or human disciplines: while natural processes, in his view, were amenable to abstract-nomological models of explanation, cultural and historical life could be grasped only through interpretive understanding of intended meanings, an understanding involving the concrete mediation of particular phenomena with general contexts. Building upon and moving beyond the insights of these two mentors, *Knowledge and Human Interests* delineated a complex "quasi-transcendental" infrastructure underlying knowledge claims of all kinds, an infrastructure anchored in the operation of a limited number of cognitive dispositions or "interests." Defining cognitive interests as "those basic orientations which are rooted in certain fundamental conditions of the possible reproduction and self-constitution of mankind," Habermas's study proceeded to pinpoint three central types of cognitive endeavors, termed "technical," "practical," and "emancipatory," respectively — endeavors which, in turn, gave rise to different methodological strategies and, in a broad sense, were linked with three forms of inquiry or knowledge: namely, empirical science, hermeneutics, and critical social science (Habermas 1971, 196).[2]

"The hermeneutical disciplines," Habermas wrote at the time, "are embedded in ordinary-language interactions in the same way as are empirical-analytic sciences in the framework of instrumental behavior: both are governed by *cognitive interests* rooted, respectively, in the life contexts of communicative and instrumental action. Whereas empirical-analytic methods aim at disclosing and comprehending reality under the transcendental viewpoint of possible technical control, hermeneutical methods seek to secure the intersubjectivity of mutual understanding in ordinary-language communication and in action according to common norms." Regarding critical social science or "critique of ideology" Habermas found the guiding exemplar in Freudian psychoanalysis. Proceeding beyond the plane of consensual interaction, the Freudian model, in his portrayal, sought to unravel not only consciously intended meanings but also subconscious inhibitions and "systematically distorted" patterns of communication. To accomplish its twin goals of depth analysis and therapeutic recovery, the Freudian model had to correlate or combine otherwise conflicting cognitive orientations and methodologies, in the sense that the explanation of pathological symptoms was designed to promote deepened self-understanding and the emancipation from psychic constraints. According to *Knowledge and Human Interests*, the cognitive and methodological blend characterzing psychoanalysis could be transferred with benefit to the domain of critical social science. Aiming at the removal of social inhibitions and modes of repression as well as the undistorted self-realization of participants, critical social inquiry likewise had to combine the empirical explanation of prevailing social structures with the hermeneutical decoding of intentional goals and ambitions. Despite the asserted merger, however, the peculiarity of critical science could be elucidated only through reference to the competing strategies of the empirical and cultural disciplines, that is, causal analysis and hermeneutical interpretation.[3]

The distinction and correlation of empiricism and hermeneutics is a recurrent theme in all of Habermas's writings — including those not specifically devoted to issues of social science epistemology. *Legitimation Crisis* (published some five years after *Knowledge and Human Interests*) differentiated between "system" and "life-world" as two competing models or "paradigms" of social-scientific investigation: while life-worlds were "symbolically structured" frameworks amenable to interpretive scrutiny, systems basically denoted empirical processes of instrumental-cybernetic self-maintenance. In a more elaborate and nuanced fashion, the same distinction still serves as a backbone in *The Theory of Communicative Action* (Habermas 1981). Concentrating on the evolution of social and cognitive structures, the study explicitly portrays the process of modernization and rationalization as the progressive "uncoupling" of system and life-world — a process complemented by the separation of two modes of reasoning: namely, "instrumental (or technical) rationality" dedicated to environmental control, and "communicative rationality" devoted to the maintenance of a viable intersubjective life-world. Pursuing intimations contained in *Legitimation Crisis*, the recent work also profiles the implications of the dichotomy for social scientific research: "If we grasp the integration of society exclusively as 'social integration'," we read, "we opt for a methodology which, relying on communicative action, construes society as a life-world. Tied to the internal perspective of members of social groups, this approach requires the hermeneutical mediation of the analyst's and the participants' understanding . . . . If, on the other hand, we define integration as 'system integration', we opt for a conception of society patterned on the model of a self-regulating system; in this case social analysis is governed by the external perspective of an empirical observer (Habermas 1975, 4-5)."[4]

The bifurcation of approaches and methods is not the exclusive province of critical theory (from Horkheimer to Habermas); a similar intent or strategy can also be detected in the phenomenological movement. In a string of publications from *Ideas* to *The Crisis of European Sciences*, Husserl attacked the unreflectiveness of the positivist construal of science — but without trying to exorcise empirical research entirely in favor of phenomenological analysis. Somewhat later, in a forceful essay contained in *Signs* (1964a), Merleau-Ponty advocated a judicious balance and mutual interpenetration of empirical sociology and phenomenological reflection, a balance expected to be broadly beneficial to all the human sciences or "sciences of man." Drawing on both critical and phenomenological initiatives, some of my earlier writings sought to vindicate the same kind of balance or correlation in the field of political inquiry. Incorporating the legacy of the "two cultures" within the study of politics itself, I distinguished at the time between empirical or "behavioral political science" and "practical-hermeneutical inquiry" — the first being characterized by "observation and analysis of political phenomena in accordance with general principles of explanation," and the second designed "to assist in the elucidation of intentional human conduct and concrete social (and political) meaning patterns" through interpretive understanding. Rounding out the structure of the discipline, I specified as a third strategy "critical-dialectical political analysis," assigning to it the task of linking "the empirical explanations of law-like, social or behavioral processes with the exploration of intentional aspirations — in other words, the domain of natural or quasi-natural necessity with the dimension of human freedom (Merleau-Ponty 1964a, 98–113; 1964b, 43–95; Dallmayr 1981, 41–42).

II

Although plausible at a first glance, the division of approaches sketched above is flawed or problematical on several levels. A basic quandary arises in the confines of recent philosophy of science. If — as "post-empiricists" are wont to stress — science invariably presupposes a theoretical framework which, in turn, is based on interchanges in a 'community of investigators,' then behavioral political research cannot neatly be segregated from hermeneutical exegesis of meaning. Behind this methodological quandary, however, a host of further, more unsettling issues await. Clearly, the blurring of empiricism and hermeneutics implicates and throws into disarray a number of time-honored distinctions and antinomies, including those between "nature" and "spirit," freedom and causal necessity — antinomies which, for a long time, have buttressed the segregation of natural and cultural sciences. The erosion of these oppositions, furthermore, cannot leave untouched the underlying metaphysical or anthropological matrix — in Habermas's case, the infrastructure of cognitive interests, rational dispositions, and "world" orientations.

Among "post-empiricist" analytical philosophers, none has been more eloquent or vehement in denouncing the separation of approaches than Richard Rorty. His *Philosophy and the Mirror of Nature* (1979) launched a frontal attack on the division between science and hermeneutics seen as the outgrowth of a mind-nature dualism. "The notion," Rorty wrote, "that the empirical self could be turned over to the sciences of nature, but that the transcendental self, which constitutes the phenomenal world and (perhaps) functions as a moral agent, could not, has indeed done as much as anything else to make the spirit-nature distinction meaningful. So this metaphysical distinction lurks in the background of every discussion of the relations between the *Geistes*-and the *Naturwissenschaften*." In lieu of the older division, the study proposed a complete reformulation or recasting of "hermeneutics," in the sense that the term denotes simply an unusual, abnormal or 'incommensurable' type of discourse in contrast to the normalcy of empirical-epistemological inquiry. "If one draws the hermeneutics-epistemology distinction as I want to draw it," we read, "there is no requirement that people should be more difficult to understand than things; it is merely that hermeneutics is only needed in the case of incommensurable discourses, and that people discourse whereas things do not. What makes the difference is not discourse versus silence, but incommensurable discourses versus commensurable discourses" (Rorty 1979, pp. 343–44, 347).

The attack on methodological (and metaphysical) dualism was continued and reinforced a year later in a symposium devoted to the topic of
"Holism and Hermeneutics." Relying on his own concept of
hermeneutics as incommensurable discourse or "conversation," Rorty
insisted at the time on "the uselessness of the Diltheyan notion of a
'method of the human sciences'." As he pointed out, the explanation-
understanding bifurcation had been eroded not only by European
philosophical trends (from Heidegger to Wittgenstein) but also by post-
empiricist arguments in philosophy of science stressing the need for
holistic frameworks. In line with these arguments, Rorty concurred that
"the demise of logical empiricism means that there is no interesting split
between the *Natur-* and the *Geisteswissenschaften*." In his portrayal, the
split was ultimately attributable to Western metaphysics and, especially,
to the "correspondence theory" of truth and the postulate of grasping
external-empirical reality in "subject-independent" terms. Under the
auspices of traditional epistemology, mind was forced either to abandon
itself in the quest of external reality or to retreat into its innate ideas—a
dilemma evident in the "oscillation between philosophical manifestoes"
of empiricism and rationalism: "We shall alternately be urged to respect
the austere coldness of the atoms and to flee from them to the warm,
heimische Lebenswelt. So I think that the issue about whether we want a
distinction between natural and human science, and perhaps even between the 'method' of one and the 'method' of the other, boils down to
whether we want to hang on to the notion of truth as correspondence"
(Rorty 1980, pp. 39, 43).

Although adamant in his rejection of past antinomies, Rorty's
posture was itself not free of ambiguities and metaphysical overtones. In
supporting the post-empiricist plea for interpretive holism, his comments
endorsed a "universal hermeneutics" vaguely reminiscent of
Gadamerian philosophy and functioning as a substitute for the empiricist
unification of disciplines. More important, the affinity with Gadamer
tended to blur Rorty's notion of incommensurable discourse,
assimilating it more closely to the Continental conception of
hermeneutics as textual or existential "understanding" (opposed to
scientific explanation) and, at points, even to an interpretive-
metaphysical subjectivism. The latter assimilation was manifest in
remarks like the following: "Getting clear on the issue of whether there
can be 'an account of the world as it is independently of the meanings it
might have for human subjects' is, perhaps, the key to getting clear
about whether the distinctions between 'subject' and 'object' and between 'man' and 'nature' are worth preserving . . . . I do not think we
have any idea of what it would be like to 'account for the world in absolute terms'; we can only make sense of accounting for it in terms useful
for this or that human purpose" (Rorty 1980, 39–40, 44, 46).[6]

At the same symposium, a position starkly at odds with Rorty's was articulated by Charles Taylor. While sensitive to post-empiricist or holistic arguments, Taylor sought to vindicate the division of methods and sciences through appeal to their respective degree of objectivity (or objectivism). Post-empiricist initiatives, he conceded, had brought about a curious reversal of fortunes or battle lines: "There is now abroad a new thesis of the unity (or at least nonduality) of science, espoused by critics of logical empiricism." Under holistic auspices, natural and human sciences "turn out to be methodologically at one, not for the positivist reason that there is no rational place for hermeneutics, but for the radically opposed reason that all sciences are equally hermeneutic." In Taylor's account, however, this "reign of universal hermeneutics" was at best a "pleasing fancy" and epistemologically plainly "wrong" — for the simple reason that understanding plays a different role in the natural and human sciences. Although all disciplines were, admittedly, predicated on implicit "pre-understandings," concrete epistemological goals were radically divergent in the two instances. Going beyond implicit intuitions, the human sciences required a special kind of 'human understanding,' namely, the kind needed "to grasp desirability-characterizations" or to comprehend "the way in which relevant courses of action can be desirable or undesirable." Departing still more resolutely from implicit knowledge, the natural or strict empirical sciences, by contrast, were geared toward objective or 'absolute' descriptions, that is, toward "an account of the world as it is independently of the meanings it might have for human subjects" or independently of "subject-related properties." Since desirability criteria could not easily be dismissed in the first case, the "nub of the hermeneutic claim" was basically that "this kind of understanding is essential to human science, and therefore a distinction must be drawn with natural science" (Taylor 1980, pp. 26, 30–32).

As Taylor readily acknowledged, efforts had been afoot in the humanities for some time to purge their vocabulary of qualitative-experiential terms, or at least to segregate such terms from objective explanations; the latter segregation was, in fact, the hallmark of behavioralism. The attempt, he wrote, to split statements "into absolute descriptions and colorless reaction terms is very widespread in the sciences of man. For instance, the focus on 'behavior' in political science is an attempt to characterize human action in neutral terms, in language purged of desirability-characterizations; it is naturally complemented by what one could call a subjectivist view of culture, which is dominant in sociology and political science" (Taylor 1980, 32). The pitfall of behavioralism, however, was precisely its disregard of the distinction between disciplines, that is, its failure to realize that what may be feasible and even appropriate in the natural-empirical sciences tends to be lethal in the domain of human or cultural sciences, mainly because the "redescription of what men desire or seek in conformity with the canonical split" leaves out "something crucial" to a satisfactory account of human action. While critical of the behavioral separation of neutral descriptions and subjective reactions, Taylor's comments (it seems fair to observe) in the end reflected a similar bifurcation: his division of sciences in terms of "subject-related" and "subject-independent" vocabularies, in particular, paid tribute to traditional "subject-object" and "mind-nature" polarities (Taylor 1980, 36–37).

At the aforementioned symposium, opposition to Rorty was not restricted to Taylor's refurbished version of *Natur- und Geisteswissenschaften*. Mediating between the former's "no difference" thesis and the latter's restorative view, Hubert Dreyfus defended the distinctness of disciplines in terms of different modes of "holism." While post-empiricists stressed theoretical frameworks and thus subscribed to a uniform "theoretical holism," the uniqueness of the human and social sciences resided in their rootedness in human praxis — which required an interpretive-hermeneutical approach guided by practical-holistic criteria. "*Practical* understanding is holistic in an entirely different way from theoretical understanding," Dreyfus noted. "Although practical understanding — everyday coping with things and people — involves explicit beliefs and hypotheses, these can only be meaningful in specific contexts and against a background of shared practices." He added, "Heidegger, Merleau-Ponty, and Wittgenstein suggest that this inherited background of practices cannot be spelled out in a theory because (1) the background is so pervasive that we cannot make it an object of analysis, and (2) the practices involve skills." What unified any web of social and cultural practices, in Dreyfus's view, was not a theoretical account or a comprehensive belief system but a practical-holistic manner of living: "What makes up the background is not beliefs, either explicit or implicit, but habits and customs, embodied in the sort of subtle skills which we exhibit in our everyday interaction with things and people" (Dreyfus 1980, 7–8, 10, 12).

Because of its complexity, I will bypass the details of Dreyfus's argument except to note that his distinction between theoretical and practical types of holism served to buttress the differentiation between the natural and human sciences and, by implication, between empiricism and hermeneutics. As in the case of post-empiricist arguments, the differentiation was complicated by the fact that both kinds of sciences were predicated on background practices which operated in a manner akin to background assumptions. Replicating Taylor's argument on a more practical level, however, Dreyfus emphasized the possibility of bracketing or 'decontextualizing' implicit practices in natural science —

while rejecting this option in the human and social disciplines: "The important point for the natural sciences is that natural science is successful precisely to the extent that those background practices which make science possible *can be taken for granted and ignored by the science*" (Dreyfus 1980, 16–17).[7]

III

As the preceding review indicates, efforts to move beyond the empiricism-hermeneutics bifurcation are difficult and hazardous, just as much as are endeavors to preserve this dichotomy and, more broadly, the division between natural and human sciences. Prompted by strong "antifoundational" motives, Rorty attacks the explanation-understanding division as a residue of traditional mind-nature antinomies; yet, reluctant to clarify metaphysical premises (including his own), his pragmatic "no difference" thesis tends to pay homage to a metaphysical subjectivism, or at least to a "universal hermeneutics" wedded to the exegesis of intended meanings. What is more an unacknowledged byproduct in Rorty's case is a deliberate postulate in Taylor's presentation — evident in his distinction of sciences and approaches in terms of "subject-related" and "subject-independent" vocabularies. Some tentative steps into more uncharted (post-metaphysical) terrain are undertaken in Dreyfus's comments on practical holism and everyday practices; however, the division between theory and practice is just as much presupposed and taken for granted in his account as is Taylor's subject-object correlation.

It seems to me that a minimal requirement for making some headway in this domain is a reflective reconsideration of traditional terms or categories. Thus, to the extent that objective-empirical data are pitted against subjectively interpreted meanings, the status of the subject-object polarity is clearly at issue; if the two categories (subject and object) are both assumed to be real or to have "being" of some kind, their relationship is no longer self-evidently antithetical and demands inquiry into underlying ontological and historical premises. In a similar fashion, once the accent is placed on human praxis (as is appropriate in the human and social sciences), the status and meaning of praxis cannot simply be left unexamined — especially in view of the long-standing association of the term with intentional activity or subjectively meaningful behavior. In this respect, Heidegger's warning at the beginning of his 1947 *Letter on Humanism* still deserves to be heeded, namely, that "we still do not ponder the essence of action seriously enough. One knows action only as the production of effects whose effectiveness is measured in terms of utility." As Heidegger tried to remind his readers at the time, action or praxis is not equivalent to a mechanical chain of cause and effect, nor to a subjective production or engineering of effects. Rather, action carries its sense or essence within itself, namely, by virtue of its rootedness in "being" or an ongoing ontological happening in which it participates (Heidegger 1977, 193).

To put matters differently, positivism is not unequivocally overcome or vanquished through a simple turn to subjective meanings, or through a juxtaposition of empiricism and hermeneutics. Clearly, texts and symbolic meanings can also be treated as objective or "positive" phenomena amenable to phenomenological inspection (seen as a higher kind of positivism). Similarly, intentional actions or subjectively meaningful behavior can be viewed as positive occurrences accessible to objective sociological analysis. Thus, to exit from positivism involves more than a move from data to meanings — namely, a more radical shift toward "negativity" or, rather, toward the interplay of "being" and "nothingness," presence and absence, visibility and invisibility. Seen in this light, Heidegger's 1929 lecture on "What Is Metaphysics?" with its central focus on "nothing," constituted the most radical and uncompromising assault on positivism — as he realized when he said that "(positive) science wants to know nothing of 'nothing'." From Heidegger's perspective, however, the interplay of presence and absence was not a fixed 'foundational' premise, but rather itself part of an ongoing event or ontological happening which he called the "history of being" — a history which, in turn, molded and structured the status of basic metaphysical categories and distinctions. The history of being, we read in the *Letter on Humanism*, "sustains and defines every *condition et situation humaine*," that is, every conception of human nature, including notions of cognitive subjectivity (or an anthropology of knowledge). Going beyond this suggestive remark, I believe that Heidegger's comments on the history of being and the history of Western metaphysics can be construed as a move beyond empiricism and hermeneutics — namely, a move into a domain in which this distinction is itself constituted, just as are other metaphysical divisions and antinomies (Heidegger 1977, 98, 194).

To be sure, Heidegger has never explicitly elaborated the epistemological and methodological implications of his ontology, especially with regard to the human or social sciences. Yet, his intiatives have recently been emulated and further pursued by a number of social and political theorists, including Michel Foucault and Jacques Derrida. In a string of publications ranging from *The Order of Things* to *Discipline and Punish*, Foucault has sought to uncover the discursive and non-discursive practices underlying different cognitive orientations and approaches; "practices," in his usage, denoted not so much intentional activities inaugurated by individuals or "communities of investigators" but rather paradigmatic, quasi-ontological contexts structuring or conditioning the status of subjects, subjective communities, and objective data. Moreover, in Foucault's treatment, the status of these categories and their mutual correlation was not invariant but subject to historical change — a change reflecting not an inner "logic" or a continuous teleology of meaning but a discontinuous "genealogy" involving the interplay of meaning and non-meaning, presence and absence. As Foucault stated at one point: "We must rid ourselves of the constituting subject, rid ourselves of the subject itself, which is to arrive at an analysis which can account for the constitution of the subject within a historical framework" — which also means accounting for the status of relevant objects. In view of this paradigmatic endeavor, Dreyfus and Rabinow in their study on Foucault describe his work as a step "beyond (empirical) structuralism and hermeneutics," noting: "In sum, Foucault is seeking to construct a mode of analysis of those cultural practices in our culture which have been instrumental in forming the modern individual as both subject and object."[8]

Proceeding from a more linguistically inspired perspective, Derrida likewise has insisted on the need to explore the paradigmatic matrix underlying distinct metaphysical categories and cognitive orientations. Seeking to correct the deficiencies of both an invariant (logical-empirical) structuralism and historicist hermeneutics, his writings adumbrate a "structuration of structure" operating in accordance neither with mechanical laws nor a subjective intentionality but with a more amorphous, de-centered "play" of "difference," that is, the interplay of absence and presence. As he wrote in one of his essays specifically devoted to the status of the "human sciences": "Play is always the play of absence and presence; but if it is to be thought radically, play must be conceived of prior to the alternative of presence and absence. Being must be conceived as presence or absence on the basis of the possibility of play and not the other way around." In Derrida's presentation, the notion of structuration is closely linked with the erosion or weakening of traditional metaphysical dichotomies, including the mind-nature and nature-culture doublets. Pointing to recent anthropological research (and especially to Lévi-Strauss's studies on the prohibition of incest), Derrida registered the progressive obfuscation of the traditional dichotomy between nature and culture — and, by implication, of the division of *Natur- und Geisteswissenschaften*: "One could perhaps say that the entire philosophical-conceptual arsenal, which is systematically linked with the nature-culture polarity, is designed to leave unthought or unthematized the domain that makes this conceptualization possible in the first place."[9]

In the confines of Anglo-American social theory, Foucault's and Derrida's overtures are paralleled on a more systematic level in the writings of Anthony Giddens. His *Central Problems in Social Theory*

(1979) relies explicitly on Derrida (and kindred French thinkers) for the purpose of developing a sociological concept of "structuration" or a "theory of the structuration of social systems," while linking this concept more closely than Derrida with the notion of social or cultural "practices." As presented in *Central Problems*, "structuration" denotes basically the reproduction and transformation of social "structures"; the latter term stands for a paradigmatic or virtual matrix, an "absent set of differences, temporally (and spatially) 'present' only in their instantiation, in the constituting moments of social systems." In the process of structuration, the "duality" of social structures is said to come to the fore, that is, the fact that structures are both the result and the precondition of social action or praxis. Most importantly, structuration accounts for the constitution of social agents as well as their relevant objective environments: "According to this conception, the same structural characteristics participate in the subject (the actor) as in the object (society). Structure forms 'personality' and 'society' simultaneously — but in neither case exhaustively, because of the significance of unintended consequences of action, and because of unacknowledged conditions of action (Giddens 1979, 30, 45–46, 64, 69–70)."[10] In a more detailed fashion, the theory of structuration has been elaborated by Giddens recently in *The Constitution of Society* (1984). The study takes its point of departure explicitly from the division between empiricism (exemplified by functionalism and empiricist structuralism), on the one hand, and hermeneutics or "interpretative sociology," on the other. While empiricist approaches are said to express "a naturalistic standpoint" and to tend "towards objectivism," hermeneutics emphasizes the discrepancy between "the social and natural sciences" and "the gulf between subject and social object," with "subjectivity" being seen as the "preconstituted center of culture and history" and as the "basic foundation of the social or human sciences." As Giddens observes, accentuating the difference: "Whereas for those schools of thought which tend towards naturalism subjectivity has been regarded as something of a mystery, or almost a residual phenomenon, for hermeneutics it is the world of nature which is opaque — which, unlike human activity, can be grasped only from the outside (Giddens 1984, 1–2)." The central goal of the study is to bypass this bifurcation of approaches, by trying to uncover the matrix of structuring practices. "If interpretative sociologies are founded, as it were, upon an imperialism of the subject," we read, "functionalism and structuralism propose an imperialism of the social object. One of my principal ambitions in the formulation of structuration theory is to put an end to each of these empire-building endeavors. The basic domain of study of the social sciences, according to the theory of structuration, is neither the experience of the individual actor, nor the existence of any form of societal totality, but social practices ordered across space and time" (Giddens 1984, 17).[11]

Instead of pursuing further the details of Giddens's argument, I want to return to my own starting point: the domain of political inquiry. Although originating mainly in linguistic and sociological investigations, the "structuring of structures" (in my view) can be transferred without difficulty to the study of politics. Actually, seen as a virtual order involved in the generation of time-space contexts, structuration has an eminently political cast — where "politics" stands not for the exercise of domination but for the constitution of a public space conducive to the display and reconciliation of human differences. Construed as a mode of political inquiry, structuration implies a step beyond behavioralist and subjective-hermeneutical frameworks, a step revealing the "structured" or historically conditioned character of this distinction and, more generally, of traditional subject-object or mind-nature polarities. Structural or genealogical analysis in this sense — I want to emphasize, however — does not simply entail the obliteration or fusion of approaches or a bland endorsement of the "no-difference" thesis. Rather, given the prominence of subjectivity in modern Western society and the sway of sophisticated techniques, empiricism and hermeneutics are bound to occupy a central and distinctive place in contemporary political research — although a place devoid of "foundational" support and unable to account for itself (in either empiricist or hermeneutical terms). In this respect, again, Giddens's work contains helpful guideposts: especially his acceptance of a contingent differentiation of disciplines in terms of "simple" versus "double hermeneutics" (Giddens 1976, 158).[12]

In concrete terms, structural or genealogical analysis means the readmission of history or a historical dimension into political research — where "history" does not denote a linear evolutionary scheme nor a purposive-intentional project but rather a succession of partially discontinuous frameworks or temporal and spatial world-contexts. Akin to the sequence of paradigms in scientific inquiry, genealogy probes not only the functioning of existing structures or settings but also the processes "constituting" or engendering (non-subjectively) new political arrangements and institutions. From the perspective of genealogy, historical periods are differentiated not only by distinct cultural "ideas" or values, but also and more importantly by different conceptions of the meaning and status of political agents and their corresponding "worlds." Thus, the citizen of ancient Greece can not be equated with the burgher of medieval Europe; nor does the latter coincide with the bourgeois citizen of the French Revolution or with the consumer citizen of contemporary society (seen as recipient of administrative and economic decisions). Similarly, the just ruler of classical and medieval times is worlds apart from the modern sovereign construed along rationalist lines and still further from the plebiscitarian-charismatic leaders of democratic or quasi-democratic societies. Most importantly, the Greek polis is segregated not merely in detail but intrinsically from preceding empires, feudal kingdoms, and from the nation-states dominating politics in recent centuries. The difference, one might say, resides not only in personal attitudes or political preferences, but in a difference between "worlds" and basic life forms. Although politics can be broadly defined as the perennial pursuit of the good life, the concrete manifestations of this pursuit undergo historical transformations which obey neither linear-evolutionary nor straightforward dialectical patterns — and which it is the task of structural genealogy to investigate.[13]

Structuration, I want to add, is not simply a neutral methodological device, especially when employed in contemporary political inquiry. In an age of global contacts and cultural confrontations at different levels of "development," structuration is liable to have a strong practical-political impact: namely, by exposing the contingency of modern Western metaphysics and thereby the limitations of prevalent Western modes of social and political analysis. Given their rootedness in a contingent type of subject-object correlation, these modes of analysis cannot claim undisputed universal validity, nor function as the invariant telos of more embryonic or undeveloped forms of investigation. From this angle, the "structuration of structures" has a potentially liberating or emancipatory effect, both for intellectuals in non-Western countries and for Western social and political scientists unreconciled to the prevalence of empiricist and subjective-interpretive methods.

Notes

1. For a discussion of the distinction between natural and human disciplines (*Natur- und Geisteswissenschaften*) and its impact on political inquiry, see "Political Science and the 'Two Cultures'," in Dallmayr (1981).

2. For a more detailed discussion see Dallmayr (1981, pp. 220–69).

3. See, in particular, Habermas (1971, pp. 133, 175–76, 185, 216–217, 270); I have altered the translation slightly.

4. Compare also (1984, 10); (1981, vol. 1, 28; and vol. 2, pp. 226–27). Particularly revealing, from a methodological viewpoint, are the chapters on "The Problem of Understanding Meaning in the Social Sciences" (vol. 1) and "The Concept of the Life-World and the Hermeneutical Idealism of Interpretive Sociology" and "The Uncoupling of System and Life-World" (vol. 2).

5. Compare also Dallmayr (1981, pp. 41–42).

6. The same kind of metaphysical subjectivism surfaces in Rorty's comments (p. 52) on Heidegger's phrase, "only a God can save us now": "Dewey, it seems to me, is saying: No, neither something like the Nazis, nor something like the descent of the spirit, but *just* conversation (i.e., can save us). That is, just us on our own."

7. In the concluding section of his essay, Dreyfus accuses Rorty (as well as Derrida and even Gadamer) of "nihilism" (pp. 20–21) — a charge which seems heavy and far-fetched, especially given the unclarified status of the term.

8. See Dreyfus and Rabinow (1982, pp. 120–22). Dreyfus and Rabinow characterize Foucault's approach — his alternative to structuralism and hermeneutics — as an "interpretive analytics."

9. See Derrida (1978, 283–84, 292); translation slightly altered.

10. Giddens criticizes Derrida for his lack of social concreteness (1979, 45–46). See, further, Dallmayr (1982).

11. For critical comments on Foucault's notion of "timing and spacing," see Giddens (1984, 145–158). For concrete research implications of structuration theory, see (1984, 327–34).

12. The "double hermeneutic"in political science could be rephrased, perhaps more appropriately, as a "double practice" — that is, an investigative practice about political practices. Habermas endorses the notion of a "double" hermeneutic, though not quite for the reasons given by Giddens (Habermas 1984, 110).

13. For examples of structural genealogy compare Foucault (1979) and (1980).

References

Dallmayr, Fred. 1971. *Beyond Dogma and Despair: Toward a Critical Phenomenology of Politics.* Notre Dame, Ind.: University of Notre Dame Press.

———. 1981. *Twilight of Subjectivity: Contributions to a Post-Individualist Theory of Politics.* Amherst, Mass.: University of Massachusetts Press.

———. 1982. "Agency and Structure." *Philosophy of the Social Sciences,* 12: 427–38.

Derrida, Jacques. 1978. *Writing and Difference.* Translated by Alan Bass. Chicago: University of Chicago Press.

Dreyfus, Hubert L. 1980. "Holism and Hermeneutics." *Review of Metaphysics,* 34: 1–21.

——— and Paul Rabinow. 1982. *Michel Foucault: Beyond Structuralism and Hermeneutics.* Chicago: University of Chicago Press.

Foucault, Michel. 1979. *Discipline and Punish: The Birth of the Prison.* Translated by Alan Sheridan. New York: Vintage Books.

———. 1980. *History of Sexuality,* vol. I: *An Introduction.* Translated by Robert Hurley. New York: Vintage Books.

Giddens, Anthony. 1976. *New Rules of Sociological Method.* New York: Basic Books.

———. 1979. *Central Problems in Social Theory.* Berkeley and Los Angeles: University of California Press.

———. 1984. *The Constitution of Society: Outline of the Theory of Structuration.* Berkeley and Los Angeles: University of California Press.

Habermas, Jürgen. 1971. *Knowledge and Human Interests.* Translated by Jeremy J. Shapiro. First German edn. 1968, Boston: Beacon Press.

———. 1975. *Legitimation Crisis.* Translated by Thomas McCarthy. Boston: Beacon Press.

———. 1981. *Theorie des kommunikativen Handelns,* 2 vols. Frankfurt: Suhrkamp.

———. 1984. *The Theory of Communicative Action.* Translated by Thomas McCarthy. Boston: Beacon Press.

Heidegger, Martin. 1977. *Martin Heidegger: Basic Writings.* Edited by David L. Krell. New York: Harper and Row.

Horkheimer, Max. 1972. *Critical Theory: Selected Essays.* Translated by Matthew J. O'Connell. New York: Herder and Herder.

Merleau-Ponty, Maurice. 1964a. *Signs.* Translated by Richard C. McCleary, Evanston, Ill.: Northwestern University Press.

———. 1964b. *The Primacy of Perception and Other Essays.* Edited by James M. Edie. Evanston, Ill.: Northwestern University Press.

Rorty, Richard. 1979. *Philosophy and the Mirror of Nature.* Princeton, N.J.: Princeton University Press.

———. 1980. "A Reply to Dreyfus and Taylor." *Review of Metaphysics*, 34.

Taylor, Charles. 1980. "Understanding in Human Science." *Review of Metaphysics*, 34.

Jeffrey C. Isaac

8

After Empiricism: The Realist Alternative

The aspiration to become a science has played an important role as a regulative ideal in modern political inquiry. In contemporary American political science, at least since the 1950s, the governing ideal of scientific practice has been broadly empiricist. Empiricism is the doctrine that the aim of science is to discover empirical uniformities of the form "whenever A, then B" on the basis of which one can explain and predict future events. Empiricism is a philosophy with many difficulties, particularly when transposed from the study of nature to the study of human society. In response to these all-too-evident difficulties, some students of politics have sought to distance themselves from the ideal of science altogether. There has thus emerged a rough division of labor between, on the one hand, those self-styled "political scientists" who attempt to develop empirically predictive theories and, on the other, those "political theorists" who concentrate on those interpretative questions, regarding the meaning and significance of human conduct and its intersubjective framework, which they believe are properly at the center of social study.

Here I will sketch the outlines of a "realist" alternative to these nonviable options. The version of realism I will outline is a philosophy of science which holds that the task of scientific explanation is the discovery of those enduring mechanisms which cause the occurrence of empirically observable events. Realism, as developed here, is to be distinguished from two other views also labelled "realist." The first is the doctrine of *Realpolitik* of the Kissinger–Morgenthau variety, according to which hard-headed "practicality" in a world of incessant struggle is recommended (Berki 1981). Realism, as a theory of scientific explanation, has nothing to do with this particular perspective on international politics.

The second version of realism is a view within the philosophy of science, which holds that scientific theories converge upon a rough "correspondence" with reality (Putnam 1978; van Fraasen 1980; Popper 1982). this view is often associated with the version of realism I will outline, and there are some genealogical affinities, particularly as regards their common criticism of positivism. However, this version of realism, in the view of many philosophers, obscures the significance of the social practice of science and severely underestimates both the complexity of scientific language and judgment and the discontinuity which characterizes the actual history of science. The view I will outline, then, recognizes a necessary tension between the real objects of scientific explanation and theoretical explanation itself, and it posits no necessary correspondence between our understanding of the world and the way the world really works.

After briefly sketching out the major claims of realist philosophy, I will suggest its relevance to contemporary problems of political inquiry. First, I argue that realism enables us to understand and transcend recent debates surrounding the concept of power. Second, I suggest that a realist perspective is a necessary precondition of the contemporary revival of the concept of the state. And finally, I suggest that realism offers a way to bridge the gap between political science and political theory through the non-reductionist study of ideology.

1. Empiricism, Realism, and Social Science

In philosophy, empiricism is usually associated with the idea that sensory experience is the foundation of knowledge. This epistemological claim, first stated in its classical form by David Hume and later asserted with a vengeance by logical positivists, has now fallen into philosophical disrepute (Brown 1977). But Hume, in making this argument about knowledge, also made an ontological claim about the nature of reality itself. He argued that the only meaning that could be given to the notion of causality was that of a constant conjunction of events. As he wrote, causal knowledge "arises entirely from experience, when we find that any particular objects are constantly conjoined with each other" (1975, 27). This idea is at the root of empiricism, which takes the empirical world of experienced occurrences to be the object of scientific investigation and eschews any appeal to underlying causes as unscientific "metaphysics" (Bhaskar 1978, 16). This view is widely accepted by philosophers and social scientists who are otherwise critical of Hume. Thus Karl Popper, arguably the most important post-positivist philosopher of science, describes science as "methodological nominalism":

Methodoligical essentialism, i.e., the theory that it is the aim of science to reveal essences and to describe them by means of definitions, can be better understood when contrasted with its opposite, methodological nominalism. Instead of aiming at finding out what a thing really is, and at defining its true nature, methodological nominalism aims at describing how a thing behaves in various circumstances, and especially, whether there are any regularities in its behavior (1966, 32).

Like Hume, Popper associates any attempt to provide real definitions (for example, "the state is a structure which tends to suppress conflict") with medieval scholasticism and modern pseudo-science. And, like Hume, he contends that the only sense we can give to causality is as empirical regularity. As Popper writes:

To give a causal explanation of an event means to deduce a statement which describes it, using as premises of the deduction one or more universal laws, together with certain singular statements, the initial conditions . . . The initial conditions describe what is usually called the 'cause' of the event in question (1959, pp. 59–60).

The task of scientific explanation thus becomes what Carl Hempel has called "deductive-nomological" — the formulation of generalizations about empirical regularities which enable us to predict that "whenever A, then B" (1965, p. 173–79).

This remains the dominant view of causality and scientific explanation in political science. As one very influential book on research method asserts: "Typically, the [scientific] hypothesis involves a predicted relationship between at least two variables and takes the general form of 'If A, then B' " (Holt and Turner 1970, 6). This is what students of American politics and comparative politics learn in graduate school, and the generation and testing of such hypotheses through regression analysis is considered a rite of passage into the world of truly "scientific" inquiry. This view is a legacy of the 'behavioral movement' that swept American political science in the 1950s. As one early prescriptive tract, produced by the influential Social Science Research Council, proposed: "[we favor] a decision to explore the feasibility of developing a new approach to the study of political behavior . . . with the object of formulating and testing hypotheses concerning uniformities of behavior" (Dahl 1961, 764). And as David Easton wrote, in defense of a truly "scientific" political analysis, a theory "is any kind of generalization or proposition that asserts that two or more things, activities, or events, covary under specific conditions" (1965, 7).

In its extreme, positivist form, behavioralism went so far as to deny the relevance of certain sorts of political inquiry — particularly those moral or "normative" inquiries associated with the history of ideas — as insufficiently systematic and "scientific" (Easton 1951). But, even in its less imperialistic form, it practiced a policy of containment, suggesting that, whatever possible relevance conventional political philosophy had, causal and explanatory analysis must be behavioral (Dahl 1976). This claim to explanatory hegemony was soon countered, however, by those whom Giddens (1976) has usefully labeled "interpretative theorists." They argued that: (1) the social world, unlike the world of nature, must be understood as the skilled creation of active human subjects; (2) the constitution of this world as meaningful depends upon language, regarded not simply as a system of signs but as a medium of practical and intentional activity; and (3) generating descriptions of social conduct depends upon the hermeneutic task of "penetrating the frames of meaning which lay actors themselves draw upon in constituting and reconstituting the social world" (Giddens 1976, 155). In advancing this argument, interpretivists properly rejected the predictivist view of science offered by empiricism. But they also — and improperly — rejected the project of causal and explanatory theory, claiming that proper social study should limit itself to grasping the self-understandings of human beings in their ordinary lives. This interpretative approach has become something of a counter-orthodoxy in political science, particularly among those who consider themselves "theorists" but reject the implications of behavioralist "scientific" theory. This explains the preoccupation of contemporary political theory with questions regarding the nature of language and subjectivity (Taylor 1971 and 1980; Connolly 1981) and the history of political thought (see Section 4 below). However, it should be clear that the interpretivist rejection of social science rests upon their implicit acceptance of the empiricist view of science. There is, then, a rough consensus that causality is the conjunction of events, and scientific explanation the documentation and prediction of these conjunctions. The only dissension is over whether or not students of society should practice a science thus understood.

Contemporary realist philosophy of science rejects the empiricist account of science and, in particular, its understanding of causality as regular sequences of events. Realism defends the concept of natural necessity, that scientific theories explain the properties and dispositions of things which are not in turn reducible to their empirical effects. The physical properties of copper, for example (malleability, fusibility, ductility, electrical conductivity), are not contingent effects caused by antecedent events; they are the enduring properties of copper as a metal, which can be accounted for by its atomic structure. On this view, causality is understood as the actualization of the properties of natural entities endowed with "causal powers" (Harré and Madden 1975). Scientists devise theories which explain the phenomena of experience (like the fact that copper conducts electricity while string does not) via appeal to the structures which generate them.

On the realist view, the world is not so constituted that its phenomena can be explained by subsuming events under 'covering laws' of the form 'whenever A, then B.' Rather, it is composed of a complex of what Harré calls "powerful particulars," or causal mechanisms, which operate in an unpredictable, but not undetermined, manner. As Roy Bhaskar writes in *A Realist Theory of Science*:

> The world consists of things, not events . . . On this conception of science it is concerned essentially with what kinds of things there are and with what they tend to do; it is only derivatively concerned with predicting what is actually going to happen. It is only rarely, and normally under conditions which are artificially produced and controlled, that scientists can do the latter. And, when they do, its significance lies precisely in the light that it casts upon the enduring natures and ways of acting of independently existing and transfactually active things (1978, 1).

This understanding of science does not eschew empirical evidence. But it construes this evidence as the means by which scientists come to explain underlying causes. On the realist view, this understanding is implicit in what scientists actually do, in their classificatory schemas, in their experimentation, and in their development of causal concepts. As Stephen Toulmin has written of the scientist:

> He *begins* with the conviction that things are not just happening (not even just-happening-regularly) but rather that some fixed set of laws or patterns or mechanisms accounts for Nature's following the course that it does, and that his understanding of these should guide his expectations. Furthermore, he has the beginnings of an idea what these laws and mechanisms are . . . [and] he is looking for evidence which will show him how to trim and shape his ideas further . . . This is what makes 'phenomena' important for him (1961, 75).

For the realist, then, science is "essentialist" in Popper's invidious sense — it operates on the basis of a distinction between empirical appearances and the underlying realities which cause them. But it does not, therefore, presume any immutability or teleology about the world, nor does it presume that underlying causes can be unproblematically perceived. Rather, it presumes that the world exists independently of human experience, that it has certain enduring properties, and that science, through the development and criticism of theories, can come to have some (however imperfect) knowledge of it. No greater testimony can be provided on behalf of this view than that of Albert Einstein who, in a 1931 letter to the positivist Moritz Schlick, wrote:

> In general your presentation fails to correspond to my conceptual style insofar as I find your whole orientation so to speak much too positivistic . . . I tell you straight out: Physics is the attempt at the conceptual construction of a model of the real world and its lawful structure . . . In short, I suffer under the (unsharp) separation of Reality of Experience and Reality of Being . . . You will be astonished about the 'metaphysicist' Einstein. But every four- and two-legged animal is de facto this metaphysicist (quoted in Holton 1968).

On the realist view, social science would be similarly concerned with the construction of models of the social world and its lawful structure.[1] Not behavioral regularities, but the relatively enduring relationships (e.g., husband/wife, capitalist/worker, state official/citizen) which structure them, would be the primary object of theoretical analysis. However, in proposing this I am not advocating a form of hyper-determinism which reifies social structure. As realists have recently developed the concept of social structure, it is based upon a categorical rejection of any bifurcation of structure and human agency (Manicas 1980). Anthony Giddens (1976) has argued that there is a "duality of structure." He proposes that social structures are both the medium and effect of human action. As such, they do not exist apart from the activities which they govern and human agents' conceptions of these activities. Giddens uses the analogy of language to illustrate this — there would be no language without speakers speaking, and yet language is, at the same time, the medium of speech, a pre-given system of symbols which agents draw upon in order to perform communicative acts.

The major point of this approach is that purposive human activity has among its social preconditions those historical relations which complexly constitute any given society. Individuals and groups participate in these relations, reproducing and transforming them in the course of their ordinary lives, usually in quite unintended ways. Thus, individual men and women do not marry in order to reproduce the nuclear family, but that is the structural consequence of marrying. As interpretive theory rightly recognizes, a proper understanding of the practice of mariage requires grasping those norms and purposes ("love," "masculinity" and "femininity," the breadwinner ethic, etc.) which constitute this practice as intersubjectively meaningful. But it also requires understanding certain structural conditions (the nuclear family, patriarchy, the family wage system) which are causally effective even if they are usually opaque to those who sustain them. Therefore, as Giddens writes: "in respect of sociology, the crucial task of nomological [i.e., general-theoretical] analysis is to be found in the explanation of the properties of social structures" (1976, 160).

Social science, like natural science, then, explains the natures of causal mechanisms. However, the mechanisms of social life, social structures, are in fact nothing more than the ways in which people tend to behave and the relatively enduring relations within which they act. A social science of this kind is empirical and causal. But it is very different in orientation from what political scientists normally call behavioral research. To see how and why this is so, I turn now to the long-lived controversy over the concept of power.

2. Realism and the Concept of Power

It should not be surprising that behavioralist notions of science have played an important role in conceptual analysis, as they are often invoked precisely to this end. In the case of the concept of power, this has had the consequence of severely limiting the scope of debate, which has often been called the "three faces of power controversy."

The origins of this debate lie in the gestation period of behavioralism in political science. Floyd Hunter, in his case study of community power in Atlanta (1953), and C. Wright Mills, in *The Power Elite* (1956), were two of a number of critical analysts who wrote about the "structure of power" in American society in ways which seemed to indict the system and its professed democratic norms. This precipitated a counter-attack by behavioral political scientists. Led by Robert Dahl and his student Nelson Polsby, this counter-attack was levelled not so much at the substantive arguments of these so-called "elite" theorists, but at the "unscientific method" which they were presumed to have applied (Dahl 1958). Thus, Dahl proposed that a truly "scientific," *behavioral* political science, required a formal and operational concept of power (1957):

> For the assertion 'C has power over R' we can substitute the assertion 'C's behavior causes R's behavior' . . . the language of cause, like the language of power, is used to interpret situations in which there is a possibility that some event will intervene to change the order of other events (1968, 418).

This notion of power rests on a Newtonian analogy. We are all naturally at rest or at constant velocity, until our movement is altered by an external force. Power is that force whereby social agents alter the behavior of other agents or, as Dahl puts it, get them to do what they would not otherwise do. And, true to his empiricism, Dahl insists that there are no necessary relationships between the (behaviors) of agents: "The only meaning that is strictly causal in the notion of power is one of regular sequence: that is, a regular sequence such that when A does something, what follows, or what probably follows, is an action by B" (1965, 94).

Polsby went so far as to assert, in his influential and recently reissued *Community Power and Political Theory*, that any talk about the distribution of power which failed to document such empirical regularities of stimulus and response failed "to mean anything in a scientific sense" (1980, pp. 5-6).

This analysis of the concept of power did not go uncontested. But what is interesting is that most of the criticisms of it did not challenge its major premise — that, for talk of power to be properly 'scientific', it must refer to empirical regularities. As Lukes (1974) points out, Bachrach and Baratz's "second face of power" (1970) is little different from Dahl's "first face." And as Lukes summarizes the entire debate, the various arguments "can be seen as alternative interpretations and applications of one and the same underlying concept of power, according to which A exercises power over B when A affects B in a manner contrary to B's interest" (p. 27). The differences between these alternative interpretations are not insignificant. But the degree of consensus is more significant still. All the contestants in the debate agree that power is a causal relation between the behavior of A and the response of B. All agree that power is best understood through the Newtonian analogy that A gets B to do something B would not otherwise have done, that power is a contingent outcome of behavioral interaction. And all employ an 'exercise' rather than a 'capacity' concept of power, treating power as something exhausted by its exercise, and providing, in place of a real definition of the concept an 'operational' definition of 'A exercises power over B.'

As I have argued elsewhere (Isaac 1987b, 1987c), this consensus is grounded in the shared premises of behavioralism, particularly the idea that all talk of capacities involves what Nagel has called "objectionable metaphysical implications" (1975, 36). But, from a realist perspective, it makes perfect sense to talk about capacities and to thus develop the concept of power in a linguistically and theoretically more plausible way (Ball 1975). According to the realist philosophy outlined above, powers are a central subject matter of natural science. As Harré writes: "To ascribe a power to a thing or material is to say something about what it will or can do . . . in virtue of its intrinsic nature" (1970). Thus, to assert that conductivity is a power of copper is to claim that copper possesses the enduring capacity to conduct electricity in virtue of its intrinsic nature, in this case its atomic structure. Social science should be similarly concerned with the ascription of powers to social agents and the explanatory reference to agents' intrinsic natures. But by their intrinsic natures, we mean not their unique characteristics as individuals but their social identities as participants in enduring structural relations.

On the realist view, social power can be defined as *the capacities to act possessed by social agents in virtue of the enduring relations in which they participate.* On this view, power is not the contingent outcome of behavioral interaction. It is implicated in the very constitution of social life, providing a set of capacities and resources upon which agents draw and which they exercise in the course of their everyday lives. This alternative concept of power opens up many possibilities denied in principle by empiricism. First, it enables us to talk about the structuring of power and of structural relations of domination and subordination. The relationship between a capitalist and a worker, for example, is a relationship of power.[2] But the power of the capitalist is not simply the wholly contingent regularity with which he prevails over the worker. It is a necessary feature of the enduring relation between these classes in a capitalist society that the capitalist possess certain powers — of investment, of supervision, etc.—which put him in an asymmetrical relationship of domination with the worker. In fact, the capitalist does not always prevail over the worker, but this does not negate his power; it only means that he has failed to successfully *exercise* it on these occasions, a distinction lost to empiricism. Second, it enables us to talk about the powers possessed by subordinate groups, whose behavior is not simply heteronomously caused by the actions of the dominant. Workers, for instance, possess labor power. The power that the capitalist has over the worker does not reside in the regularity with which he gets the worker to do what he says. The capitalist's behavior does not 'cause' the worker's behavior in this sense; and the worker's behavior is not simply a 'response' to the capitalist's 'stimulus'. Rather, the capitalist/worker relationship provides the capitalist with the *power to* control the work process, and the worker the *power to* perform actual labor. The relationship is the material cause of interaction, the specific ways the capitalist *and* the worker decide to act the efficient cause.

Finally, this view enables us to conceptualize the endemic reciprocity, contestation, and negotiation which is constitutive of all social relations of power (Giddens 1979). And it enables us to think theoretically about strategic calculation and bargaining not as those decisions from which power springs *ex nihlo*, but as those definitions of reality, brought to bear by all parties to social relationships and which, in turn, determine the way power is exercised within structural limits.

A realist understanding of power thus opens up many possibilities for research into the structuring of social and political life.[3] And it enables us to acknowledge that much of the research that is already being done — about patriarchy and gender relations (Barret 1980), about class relations (Wright 1978 and 1980), and about the state — is scientific and explanatory despite the fact that it fails to conform to the canons of empiricism.

3. Realism and Theories of the State

The concept of the state has been a central category of modern political thought. Yet the advent of behavioralism in political science led to the decline of the state as an object of theoretical inquiry. This is doubly ironic given the fact that, corresponding to this conceptual eclipse, the real state grew into, among other things, a massive financial supporter of behavioral research. Yet, despite (or perhaps, precisely because of) this fact, the concept of the state was an early casualty of "scientific rigor." As Lasswell and Kaplan wrote in *Power and Society:*

> In recent decades a thoroughgoing empiricist philosophy of the sciences has been elaborated . . . concurring in an insistence on the importance of relating scientific ideas to materials ultimately accessible to direct observation. Adopting this standpoint, the present work analyzes such political abstractions as 'state' and 'sovereignty' in terms of concrete interpersonal relationships of influence and control (1950, p. xiv).

"As science," they continue, political theory "finds its subject matter in interpersonal relations, not abstract institutions or organizations" (xxiv). David Easton, in *The Political System* (1953) and other works, unleashed an assault on the "metaphysical" connotations of the concept of the state, preferring instead the concept of the political system as one more amenable to the development of empirically deductive theories. This move was part of the more general surge in popularity of structural-functional modes of political research, which had the consequence of sacrificing a concern with political structure to a preoccupation with general theories of process (See LaPalombara, in Holt and Turner 1970).

In response to the recent revival of interest in the theory of the state, Easton has recently reiterated his behavioralist critique. His specific target was the late Greek Marxist Nicos Poulantzas, but the enemy was really the concept of the state (the title of the article is "The Political System Besieged by the State"; and, once again, it is ironic that Easton is not as concerned with the real state's besieging of society as he is with the challenge the concept of it poses to his theory). As Easton argued, either the state is the empirical behaviors of government officials, "or it is some kind of undefined and undefinable essence, a 'ghost in the machine,' knowable only through its variable manifestations" (1981, 316). As should be obvious, Easton is here drawing upon empiricism's characteristic denial that there are enduring causal mechanisms. As the language of "ghost in the machine" is meant to suggest, all of this talk of the state is really nothing but "metaphysics," the debates about the state's relative autonomy being no different from medieval scholastic debates about how many angels can dance on the head of a pin.

But what Easton fails to see is that *all* science is based upon reasoning from empirical phenomena to their causal mechanisms. The concept of the state is no different in this respect[4] from the concept of a magnetic field — we cannot observe a field, and yet the concept of it has definite meaning and denotes a (hypothetically) real structure with real effects. Contemporary political theorists are agreed that the concept of the state is necessary in precisely this sense — that it explains the unity of government institutions and policies, a unity which is real but which is present only in its effects, the most important of which is centralized territorial control or sovereignty (Carnoy 1984). There is, of course, little agreement among contemporary theorists about the nature of the state. The degree of its autonomy from other social relationships (Poulantzas 1975 and 1980; Nordlinger 1981), the question of its own independent interests (Skocpol 1979), the causes of "systems overload" and fiscal crisis (O'Connor 1973; Offe 1984), and the determinants of foreign and military policy (Barnet 1973; Halliday 1983) are all live theoretical controversies. No philosophy of science can resolve them. But the sort of questions being asked, about the *nature* of the state and its determinants, presuppose a realist perspective. In Popper's (pejorative) terms, the inquiries are 'essentialist' insofar as they aim at "finding out what a thing really is, and at defining its true nature." Realism does not license any particular substantive conclusions about the nature of the state. But it does enable researchers to treat the state as a causal structure, and to inquire into its nature, free of the stigma of "metaphysics."

Theorists of the state have begun to recognize that these philosophical issues are central to their own research. Thus, Bob Jessop, in *The Capitalist State* (1982), discusses the state as a set of structural relationships which distribute power to government officials. As he writes: "the state is a set of institutions that cannot, *qua* institutional ensemble, exercise power" (221). Rather, the powers of the state are exercised separately, by specific officials, occupying specific institutional roles. But, he insists, a theory of this power must be a theory of the structural relations which organize and distribute the power so exercised. In making this argument, about the state as an underlying structure, he cites the work of Roy Bhaskar and other realist philosophers of science.

4. Realism and the Study of Political Ideology

As I suggested earlier, the consequence of the hegemony of behavioralism in political science was a retreat from causal analysis on the part of many political theorists. In place of the attempt to discover predictive generalizations about human behavior, theorists emphasized the significance of language and its role in constituting political conduct. In place of survey research and correlational analysis, which seemed to be the only "scientifically" approved mode of studying "political culture," theorists emphasized the idiographic characteristics of speech and action, paying close attention to questions of particular intentions and local usages.

The most influential form this turn in political theory has taken is the "new history" of political thought, spawned by the work of Quentin Skinner (1969 and 1974), John Dunn (1968 and 1978), and J.G.A. Pocock (1972 and 1980). They have insisted that the primary task of political theory is interpretative, that of grasping the self-understandings of agents as they engage in political speech. Skinner, in an early article, criticized the causal analysis of political ideas, equating it with deterministic and predictivist explanations which treat the ideas themselves as "epiphenomenal." He concluded that "the primary aim should not be to explain, but only in the fullest detail to describe" the various uses to which political ideas are put (1966, 214). Dunn, too, has argued for the "epistemological primacy of description" in the human sciences. And Pocock has insisted that political language can be understood on Kuhn's model of a paradigm — it provides a set of concepts, norms, and exemplars without which political conduct is meaningless.

There are significant differences in emphasis and approach between these authors. But they all share a common "conventionalism" — they insist that the only proper task of the study of ideology is the recovery of historically conventional beliefs. And they maintain that to attempt a causal and explanatory analysis is to implicitly reduce language and intentionality to some set of antecedent events, motives, or interests.

The philosophical contribution of the "new historians" to the non-reductionist study of politics has been enormous. And accompanying this contribution has been a number of exemplary histories — Skinner's *The Foundations of Modern Political Thought* (1978), Dunn's *The Political Thought of John Locke* (1969), and Pocock's *The Machiavellian Moment* (1975). But it should be clear that the "new history" accepts one of the major premises of empiricism — namely, that causal explanation consists of the documentation of empirical regularities and that the causal analysis of political ideology would reduce it to the mere effect of an external cause.

On a contrasting realist view of social science, however, theoretical explanation would concentrate not on predictive generalizations but on the analysis of social-structural causes. Further, on the realist view, social practices cannot be understood apart from the norms and beliefs which constitute them. So the causal analysis of political speech and belief need not reduce particular speech acts and interventions, nor the more general languages and beliefs which they draw upon, to some extra-linguistic substratum. The sort of close attention to the concepts and intentions of historically situated agents recommended by the new historians is perfectly compatible with a realist account of reasons as causes of action (Bhaskar 1978, ch. 3). But it is also compatible with more structural accounts of the enduring relations and norms which are reflected and reproduced in ideological expression.

The new history is correct in insisting that language and speech are irreducible features of political life. But, it is wrong in suggesting that narrative-descriptive accounts exhaust the study of ideology. To take an earlier example, the utterance "I do" during a wedding ceremony is a performative act which can only be understood by locating its particular context. The act of getting married is (partly) constituted by this utterance, and the understanding of this act must take account of the language which makes it meaningful. But there is no reason to suppose that the language employed here — involving the concepts of free choice, of loving/honoring/cherishing, of lifetime fidelity — and the belief about marriage which it expresses is all that is taking place. In saying "I do," I express my intention to marry a particular woman and avow my feelings for her. But I am also reproducing the social relations of the nuclear family, a set of relations constituted, in part, by the language of the wedding ceremony, but also by a set of power relations which are probably completely unacknowledged by its participants.

On the realist view, the analysis of political ideas must be a part of the more general analysis of social structures and belief systems and their historical transformations. As Shapiro has written:

> For the conventionalist the intentions of authors are the principal concern, and the actual function of their ideas are not seen as part of the subject-matter proper of the history of political theory. For the realist the ways in which political theorists' ideas in fact function in the world is of principle concern in the history of *ideologies*, and the intentions of authors should always be explained with reference to this real context (1982, 573).

For example, there is no reason to limit the analysis of John Locke's theory of property in the *Second Treatise* to the author's intentions in invoking a neo-Thomist conception of human nature (as Tully 1980, proposes); and, it is possible to interpret this text as a justification, however unintended, of an emerging capitalist mode of production (Isaac 1987a). Similarly, Shapiro (1986) has shown, for example, that the language of toleration in late seventeenth century English politics, invoked in a very specific context regarding the succession of Charles II, also served to articulate certain more generally liberal notions of the limited state and the priority of private life. And Manicas has argued that the anomolous character of England in Montesquieu's *De l'Esprit des Lois* was due to the limitations of his historic vision: "because Montesquieu was not omniscient but was a great theorist writing during a period of crucial tran-

sition, events at the end of the century will make his book even more influential even as his central classification is made anachronistic" (1981,
313). In these examples, the analysis of political texts and political ideas
begins with specific idioms employed by their authors, but proceeds to
set these interventions in a broader historical context.

Richard Ashcraft, in a recent article on the future of political
theory, suggests that the gap between causal explanation and interpretive
analysis must be bridged in order for both tasks to better accomplish
their objectives:

> A particular political theory could thus be related to these particular
> conventions of meaning and to the organization of practical interests
> which, together, comprise the social context. The interpretation of
> social action . . . is, therefore, implicitly or explicitly, made in terms of a
> theory of social relationships: i.e., how society is structured (1983, 543).

A realist perspective can support this project, by accomodating the interpretative objections to behavioralism while insisting upon the necessity
of causal and structural analysis.

5. Conclusion: A Realistic Appraisal of
What Realism Can Do

One of the unfortunate consequences of behavioralism in political
science has been a preoccupation with methodological questions and a
belief that methodological arguments could substitute for actual social
scientific investigation and criticism. It would be more that a little ironic
if a critique of behavioralism were to end on the same note.

Methodological inquiry is not without value. It forces us outside of
the sometimes narrow boundaries of empirical research and compels us
to engage broader philosophical questions. And, given the enormous
significance which the honorific label of science has acquired in social
study, inquiries such as this essay have a necessary remedial function, of
clearing away intellectual rubbish and paving the way for substantive
theoretical analysis. Although the analogy is a bit dramatic, the
methodologist is a bit like an academic Moses — he can lead the way to
the promised land, but he cannot, *qua* methodologist, enter it.[5] This is a
peculiar analogy with which to suggest the necessary modesty of
methodological analysis. But it is important to recognize the limits of all
methodological approaches, including that of realism. Realism opens up
a number of important possibilities in political theory. It illuminates controversies surrounding the study of power, the state, and ideology. But it
is no more a substitute for the study of these things than the concept of
cause is a substitute for the study of physics. To paraphrase Marx, realist
philosophy has merely interpreted the nature of social science. The point,
however, is to practice it.

Notes

I would like to thank Terence Ball for his helpful comments.

1. This does not mean that there are no differences between natural and social science. There are, particularly as regards the normative and critical possibilities of the latter (Bhaskar 1979). The point is only that social scientific explanation should take the same, realist, form that natural science takes.

2. I only provide this as an illustrative example of a relationship of power. Its point does not require that one accept the truth of Marxian class analysis.

3. Once again, realist philosophy does not provide a formula for a uniquely adequate social scientific theory. It is a metatheoretical perspective which opens up many different theoretical possibilities.

4. To say that the concept is no different *in this respect* does not mean that there are no differences. One difference is that the concept of the state has a much more tortuous and contested history. Another is that this concept, unlike the concept of a magnetic field, is partly constitutive of the reality to which it refers. Magnetic fields exist whether we have ideas about them or not. But states, as social structures, exist (in part) in virtue of the *beliefs* people have about them.

5. Terence Ball has suggested another way of seeing the analogy: any good theorist must, like Moses, see through the sham of worshipping the Golden Calf of methodology.

References

Ashcraft, Richard. 1983. "One Step Backward, Two Steps Forward: Reflections Upon Contemporary Political Theory." In *What Should Political Theory Be Now?*, edited by John S. Nelson. New York: SUNY Press.

Bachrach, Peter, and Morton Baratz. 1970. *Power and Poverty*. New York: Oxford University Press.

Ball, Terence. 1975. "Power, Causation, and Explanation." *Polity*, 2, 189–214.

Barnet, Richard. 1973. *The Roots of War*. Baltimore: Penguin.

Barret, Michele. 1980. *Women's Oppression Today: Problems in Marxist Feminist Analysis*. London: Verso.

Berki, R.N. 1981. *On Political Realism*. London: J.M. Dent & Sons.

Bhaskar, Roy. 1978. *A Realist Theory of Science*, 2d. ed. Sussex and New Jersey: Harvester and Humanities.

———. 1979. *The Possibility of Naturalism: A Philosophical Critique of the Contemporary Human Science*. New Jersey: Humanities.

Brown, Harold I. 1977. *Perception, Theory, and Commitment: The New Philosophy of Science*. Chicago: University of Chicago Press.

Carnoy, Martin. 1984. *The State and Political Theory*. Princeton: Princeton University Press.

Connolly, William. 1981. *Appearance and Reality in Politics*. Cambridge: Cambridge University Press.

Dahl, Robert A. 1957. "The Concept of Power." *Behavioral Science*, 2, 201–15.

———. 1958. "A Critique of the Ruling Elite Model." *American Political Science Review*, 58, 463–69.

———. 1961. "The Behavioral Approach in Political Science: Epitaph for a Monument to a Successful Protest." *American Political Science Review*, 55, 763–72.

———. 1965. "Cause and Effect in the Study of Politics." In *Cause and Effect*, edited by Daniel Lerner. New York: The Free Press.

———. 1968. "Power." *International Encyclopedia of the Social Sciences*. New York: The Free Press.

———. 1976. *Modern Political Analysis*, 3d. ed. New Jersey: Prentice-Hall.

Dunn, John 1968. "The Identity of the History of Ideas." *Philosophy*, 43, 85–116.

———. 1969. *The Political Thought of John Locke*. Cambridge: Cambridge University Press.

————. 1978. "Practicing History and Social Science on 'Realist' Assumptions." In *Action and Interpretation: Studies in the Philosophy of the Social Sciences*, edited by C. Hookway and P. Pettit. Cambridge: Cambridge University Press.

Easton, David. 1951. "The Decline of Modern Political Theory."*Journal of Politics*, 13, 36–58.

————. 1953. *The Political System*. New York: Knopf.

————. 1965. *A Systems Analysis of Political Life*. New York: Wiley and Sons.

————. 1981. "The Political System Beseiged by the State." *Political Theory*, 9.

Giddens, Anthony. 1976. *New Rules of Sociological Method*. New York: Basic Books.

————. 1979. *Central Problems in Social Theory*. Berkeley: University of California Press.

Halliday, Fred. 1983. *The Making of the Second Cold War*. London: Verso.

Harré, Rom. 1970. "Powers." *British Journal of the Philosophy of Science*, 21.

———— and E.H. Madden. 1973. *Causal Powers*. New Jersey: Rowman and Littlefield.

Hempel, Carl. 1965. *Aspects of Scientific Explanation*. New York: The Free Press.

Holt, Robert T., and John E. Turner. 1970. *The Methodology of Comparative Research*. New York: The Free Press.

Holton, Gerald 1968. "Mach, Einstein, and the Search for Reality." *Daedelus*, 97.

Hume, David. 1975. "Enquiry Concerning Human Understanding." In *Enquiries Concerning Human Understanding and Concerning the Principles of Morals*, edited by L.A. Selby-Bigge. Oxford: Oxford University Press.

Hunter, Floyd. 1953. *Community Power Structure*. North Carolina: University of North Carolina Press.

Issac, Jeffrey C. 1982. "On Benton's 'Objective Interests and the Sociology of Power:' A Critique." *Sociology*, no. 16, 440–42.

————. 1983. "Realism and Social Scientific Theory: A Critique of Porpora." *Journal for the Theory of Social Behaviour*, 13, 301–308.

————. 1987a. "Was John Locke a Bourgeois Theorist?: A Critical Appraisal of Macpherson and Tully." *Canadian Journal of Political and Social Theory*, in press.

————. 1987b. "Beyond the Three Faces of Power: A Realist Critique." *Polity*, in press.

————. 1987c. *Power and Marxist Theory: A Realist View.* Ithaca, N.Y.: Cornell University Press, in press.

Jessop, Bob. 1982. *The Capitalist State.* New York: New York University Press.

Lukes, Steven. 1974. *Power: A Radical View.* London: Macmillan.

Lasswell, Harold D. and Abraham Kaplan. 1950. *Power and Society.* New Haven, Conn.: Yale University Press.

Manicas, Peter. 1980. "On the Concept of Social Structure." *Journal for the Theory of Social Behaviour,* 10, 65–82.

————. 1981. "Montesquieu and the Eighteenth Century Vision of the State." *History of Political Thought,* 2, 313–47.

———— and C. Wright Mills. 1956. *The Power Elite.* London: Oxford University Press.

Mills, C. Wright. 1956. *The Power Elite.* London: Oxford University Press.

Nagel, Jack H. 1975. *The Descriptive Analysis of Power.* New Haven, Conn.: Yale University Press.

Nordlinger, Eric A. 1981. *On the Autonomy of the Democratic State.* Cambridge, Mass.: Harvard University Press.

O'Connor, James. 1973. *The Fiscal Crisis of the State.* New York: St. Martin's Press.

Offe, Claus. 1984. *Contradictions of the Welfare State* Cambridge, Mass.: M.I.T. Press.

Pocock, J.G.A. 1972. "The History of Political Thought: A Methodological Inquiry." In *Philosophy, Politics, and Society,* 2d. series, edited by W.G. Runciman. Oxford: Basil Blackwell.

————. 1975. *The Machiavellian Moment.* Princeton: Princeton University Press.

————. 1980. "Political Ideas as Historical Events: Political Philosophers as Historical Actors." In *Political Theory and Political Education,* edited by M. Richter. Princeton: Princeton University Press.

Polsby, Nelson S. 1980. *Community Power and Political Theory,* 2d. ed. New Haven, Conn.: Yale University Press.

Popper, Karl R. 1959. *The Logic of Scientific Discovery.* New York: Harper and Row.

————. 1966. *The Open Society and its Enemies,* vol. I. Princeton: Princeton University Press.

————. 1982. *Realism and the Aim of Science.* Ottawa: Rowman and Littlefield.

Poulantzas, Nicos. 1975. *Political Power and Social Classes*. London: Verso.

———. 1980. *State, Power, Socialism*. London: Verso.

Putnam, Hilary. 1978. *Meaning and the Moral Sciences*. Boston: Routledge & Kegan Paul.

Shapiro, Ian. 1982. "Realism in the Study of the History of Ideas." *History of Political Thought*, 3, 535–78.

———. 1986. *The Evolution of Rights Liberal in Theory*. Cambridge: Cambridge University Press.

Skinner, Quentin. 1966. "The Limits of Historical Explanations." *Philosophy*, 41.

———. 1969. "Meaning and Understanding in the History of Ideas." *History and Theory*, 8.

———. 1974. "Some Problems in the Analysis of Political Thought and Action." *Political Theory*, 2.

———. 1978. *Foundations of Modern Political Thought*, 2 vols. Cambridge: Cambridge University Press.

Skocpol, Theda. 1979. *States and Social Revolutions*. Cambridge: Cambridge University Press.

Taylor, Charles. 1971. "Interpretation and the Science of Man." *Review of Metaphysics*, 3, 1–45.

———. 1980. "Understanding in Human Science," *Review of Metaphysics*, 34, 23–38.

Toulmin, Stephen. 1961. *Foresight and Understanding*. New York: Harper.

Tully, James. 1980. *A Discourse on Property: John Locke and his Adversaries*. Cambridge: Cambridge University Press.

van Fraasen, Bas C. 1980. *The Scientific Image*. Oxford: Clarendon Press.

Wright, Erik Olin. 1978. *Class, Crisis, and the State*. London: Verso.

———. 1980. "Varieties of Marxist Conceptions of Class Structure." *Politics and Society*, 9.

Part IV

Political Science and Political Discourse

Kathy E. Ferguson

9

Male-Ordered Politics: Feminism and Political Science

To examine the discipline of political science from a feminist viewpoint is to be confronted immediately with two larger sets of questions about knowledge and about power. A central claim of contemporary feminism is that a political discourse generated from women's experiences of the world is different in significant ways from that created by men, and is capable of transforming the male-ordered public world in important ways. By discourse I mean the characteristic ways of thinking and speaking that both constitute and reflect our experiences by illuminating certain roles, rules, and events while leaving others unnamed. A dialogue between feminists (some of whom are political scientists) and political scientists (some of whom are feminists) could open up the discourses on politics to a larger and more heterodox community of inquiry. It could, if taken seriously, point our collective conversations in fresh directions by loosening the hold of the established discourse in favor of a more fluid way of thinking and acting.

The claim for a feminist discourse is usually met with considerable skepticism from the men who study politics, when in fact the study of the history of politics in the West over the past three centuries would suggest that such a theoretical and practical challenge to the established discourse might well appear at this point in time, and from women. One thinks of parallels to past emergent discourses in the modern Western world: that of modernity itself, bringing into a medieval society filled with signs and meanings the instrumental and disciplinary discourse of the modern age, and creating/reflecting the creation of the modern subject, the individual-as-responsible-agent; or of classical liberalism, articulating and reflecting the experience of middle class males in emergent market society; or of Marxism, similarly describing/creating the experience of the male working class in later, developed market society. The position of women across classes, races, and ethnic groups has changed rather radically in the last century and in complex ways. Why not, then, expect a discourse from women, reflecting and at the same time helping to create women's experience as the grounds for an alternative set of claims to knowledge? Feminist discourse is a vehicle for making sense of women's changing experiences, clarifying and differentiating them, and suggesting possible directions for further thought and action.

The women and (some) men who are involved with or attuned to the creation of feminist discourse, in political science and other academic disciplines as well as outside the academy, face a number of crucial questions. The creation of a discourse is essentially the creation of a web of meaning through which to define and apprehend the discontinuous flux of collective life. It is a net cast across the "bloomin' buzzin' confusion" of which William James spoke. Since every new voice emerges from some specific point in history, its starting point and direction are, to some extent, laid out by the previous patterns of discursive and institutional practices. So, feminist discourse needs both an appreciation of the contributions that the other discourses of the past and present have made to it, and a wariness of the institutional and discursive dangers they entail. For example, feminism itself is part of the modern episteme or structure of discourse, and it is difficult to imagine how its theories and practices could have emerged absent the pervasive norms of subjectivity and agency that permeate modern life. Liberalism and Marxism continue to be sources of various dialogues within feminism, and questions of reform and revolution continue to hold central practical concern. But our connections to these earlier discourses and our inheritance of much from each raises difficult questions about knowledge and power. Liberalism, Marxism, and modernity itself claim universality for their perspectives on the world; feminists, in response, have always replied, with Simone de Beauvoir, that men "describe the world from their own point of view, which they confuse with absolute truth" (1952, 133). Rightfully wary of such universalistic claims, feminists tend to seek to avoid them; but what, then, are the grounds for our own claims to knowledge? Thus, the most central questions of epistemology and ontology are brought into full play, revealing feminist discourse to be as rich, varied, and problematic as any other complex and layered field of meaning.

Feminist discourse is an emergent perspective on the world, a submerged discourse which is still not fully articulated. In some senses, feminism needs to remain as a submerged discourse, if the mainstream of academic life stays as it is. But there are sources within the dominant discursive and institutional practices that the discourse draws upon, while at the same time standing against the dominant discourse as a voice of oppositon. There are forerunners of feminist discourse, other ideas and practices akin to those that feminism espouses. For example, Joan Tronto argues that the moral theory of the Scottish enlightenment thinkers anticipates feminist notions of moral reasoning examined by Carol Gilligan and others (Tronto forthcoming; Gilligan 1982). Mary Dietz, Nancy Hartsock, and Jean Elshtain have offered differing interpretations of ancient Greek dramas that call upon feminist themes (Dietz 1985; Hartsock 1983; Elshtain 1983). Hanna Pitkin sees a vision of participatory citizenship paralleling feminist notions of community even in that most gynophobic of thinkers, Machiavelli (Pitkin 1984). And much of feminist organizational practice reflects longstanding anarchist themes of decentralization and participation (Mansbridge 1984).

Like questions of knowledge, questions of power are part of the larger context within which the relation of feminism and political science should be considered. This is true for two reasons. First, political science as an academic discipline is situated within the patriarchal arrangements of contemporary Western (primarily American) society. "The discipline" — as it is revealing termed — thus participates in patriarchal power relations in its theories and its practices. It is part of what Foucault calls "the institutional regime of the production of truth" (1972, 133). Real change in the direction of political science inquiry requires radical change in the larger social order as well. Second, as feminists have been at pains to point out, claims to knowledge about the world have their very conditions of possibility in power relations, including gender relations: truth, in other words, is power (MacKinnon 1983). But, political science is hostile to both the epistemological and the political lines of questioning that feminist discourse raises. The discipline has, in Foucault's words, a "radical deafness" on such issues. Through comprehending the nature of this hostility, we may be able both to envision an alternative form of political inquiry and to imagine what differences such an alternative might make.

The Radical Deafness of Political Science

The lack of entry for feminism into political science can be accounted for by reference to two related dimensions of the discipline: its dominant epistemology (which carries a subtle and pervasive politics) and its professional politics (which reflects implicit claims about legitimate knowledge). Political science is certainly not alone in possessing these traits; all of the academic disciplines carry the baggage of patriarchy in more or less overt fashion. Of all the social sciences, political science is particularly inhospitable to feminist concerns, reflecting the longstanding equation of public life with masculinity in the West. For example, Donald Freeman refers to the discipline as a "fraternity" in *Foundations of Political Science*; the twenty-two essays in the book are all by men, and feminism is conspicuous by its absence (1977). Similarly, *Political Science: The State of the Discipline* mentions women and briefly mentions feminism in only one of its seventeen articles; the four articles by women are as much exercises in and apologetics for positivism as are the remaining essays in this book and in the Freeman reader as well (Finifter 1983). Like economics, political science is particularly tied to that hard-headed world of *Realpolitik*, where so-called "laws" of macrolevel behavior are said to operate and where only that which is "pragmatic" and "realistic" (that is, which conforms to the existing contours of power) is considered legitimate. An unpacking of the epistemological and political contexts of the discipline can help one to understand its restrictions more fully.

In its approach to inquiry, political science is still ensnared in the limitations of positivism. The post–World War II victory of behavioralism drove a wedge between the "normative" and the "empirical" dimensions of knowledge. Behavioralism makes an implicit connection between metatheoretical assumptions and gender difference. That is, it divides language into empirically meaningful and nonsensical propositions; propositions of the former kind refer to objects in the world and are thus seen as verifiable or at least falsifiable. Such claims are admitted to the field of rational discourse about politics. Nonsensical statements, those which are said not to relate to this factual world, are labeled as unverifiable, emotive, or axiomatic. They do not have the same claim, and are sometimes given no claim to any standing as legitimate knowledge about the political world; their status in the world of "rational" discourse is highly questionable. Alternately conceived of as the correspondence theory of truth or the designative conception of language, this view posits an essentially unproblematic relationship between things in the world and the words/sentences that describe and explain these things (Rorty 1979; Taylor 1985).

It is of course no surprise that political science contains some widely accepted criteria for distinguishing rational or legitimate claims from nonrational and illegitimate ones. As Peter Winch points out, such a criterion is necessary to any language: "Where there is language it must make a difference what is said and this is only possible where the saying of one thing rules out, on pain of failure to communicate, the saying of something else" (1977, 177). But, the knowledge claims of positivism and its behavioral offspring reflect a particularly masculine (and, more generally, a particularly Western) set of experiences in the world.

Women's experiences in our society are qualitatively different from those of men in several ways: women, on the whole, are more embedded in (and more aware of their embeddedness in) social relations than are men; women, as a group, are more inclined toward a morality of responsibility and caretaking, while men, as a group, give more allegiance to an ethic of rights and obligations; women's experience tends to incline them toward greater appreciation of the concrete and the relational, while men give greater credence to that which is abstract and disembodied.[1] Winch and others have pointed out that the dominant metatheory in the social sciences, by giving epistemological primacy to Western notions of rationality, renders many non–Western cultures well-nigh incomprehensible; similar barriers to understanding are thrown up between characteristically masculine and characteristically feminine experience and with similar results. In each case, it is the outsider's claims to truth that are discredited and the outsider's discourses that are submerged.

The ghost of positivism/behavioralism haunts political science in at least two other ways: it splits the mainstream of political science away from the more open-ended enterprise of political theory; and it generates an impatience with points of view that are emergent, not fully articulated, and indirect in their approach to knowledge. The split with theory has, as Joni Lovenduski points out, pulled the discipline away from "the resources inherent in its manifold origins" (1981, 83). Political science has, she argues, tended to borrow techniques from its cognate disciplines but to eschew the innovative theoretical developments they might also offer. In standing apart from theory (or pretending to do so, since, of course, positivism is itself a theory), political science has also divorced itself from its own history, resulting in "a general erosion of the traditional integration of applied politics specialists and the more explicitly normative political philosophers and theorists" (Lovenduski 1981, 84). The split of the mainstream from theory has been a kind of backhanded advantage for political theorists, since there is somewhat greater latitude among theorists for eccentrics, renegades, and radicals. When the mainstream is inhospitable and dangerous, the fringe is often a better place to be. But, even in the somewhat more open ranks of political theorists, feminism exists largely in the margins of the enterprise. For example, a recent issue of *Political Theory* carrying the title "Political Theory in the 1980s: Prospects and Topics" contains one article by a woman and no mention of feminism (1981). An all-male American Political Science Association panel at the 1984 meetings on the future direction of political theory made no mention of feminism (although several members of the audience did so). John Nelson's *What Should Political Theory Be Now?* contains essays by sixteen contributors, all men. Nelson himself notes and decries, in a rather smug footnote, the absence of a feminist standpoint from the other articles in the volume, then proceeds to ignore it in his own essay as well (1983, 216–217n). Freeman and Robertson's edited volume *The Frontiers of Political Theory: Essays in a Revitalized Discipline* contains nine essays, all by men; theory's revitalization seems not to include feminism, since no mention is made of it (1980). One would think that theorists who live in glass houses would be less willing to throw stones.

The impatience of mainstream political science with modes of inquiry that are emergent and tentative also follows from its positivist commitments. The discipline's definition of the properly scientific calls for sharp edges — quantitative measures, "hard-headed" conceptualization, clear-cut causal relations. (Might this obsession with that which is *hard* — hard facts, hard data, hard-headed concepts — reflect a peculiarly phallocentric worry?) The discipline reflects a predisposition toward what one feminist terms "the desire to control reality with the idea, and to describe reality as always predictable" (Griffin 1981, 279). Feminism's frequent appeals to emergent insights and intuitions, to barely grasped ideas, to fragments of a buried past or a nearly-forgotten twist of history, are received with great impatience by those trained to be like "Prussian soldier[s] in the world of the intellect" (Griffin 1981, 279).

Following close on the heels of the discipline's positivist commitments are its professional ambitions. An overall post-World War II trend has been toward increased specialization, cutting political science off more and more from the humanities and other social sciences. Lovenduski attributes the narrowing of the discipline's field of inquiry to American dominance over its activities, suggesting that our well-known concern for "pragmatism" and "practical" matters of governance is the cause (1981, 83).[2] While this is probably part of the problem, the impetus toward professionalization lies much deeper, in the institutional tendency for bureaucracies to survive and grow by becoming resources for other bureaucracies. Political science has, or claims to have, knowledge useful to those in power. By setting up reciprocal arrangements with local, state, and federal governments, political science departments can assure themselves of a constant flow of students (with jobs, or at least connections to jobs, waiting for them), of grant monies, of lucrative consulting contracts, and the like. Political scientists, like those in criminal justice, social work, and other state-serving disciplines, are increasingly pressured to offer for "sale" only what the state wants to buy. It comes as no surprise, then, that the decline of political theory has been accompanied by the rise of public administration and public policy (nor is it surprising to find frustrated political theorists hiding in the ranks of the latter).

The consequence of increasing professionalization for feminism has been a complicated one. For those women scholars who are able to embrace, or at least tolerate,the constraints of positivism, professionalization offers a certain opportunity; by tying reward to merit (as defined within this context, of course), professionalization allows individual women some appeal against sexist practices in recruitment and promotion. But the greater impact on feminism as a whole is toward increasing marginality, because feminism brings an explicitly engaged stance to inquiry, rejecting positivism's pretensions to disinterested objectivity as both impossible and undesirable: impossible, in that all knowledge is seen as having its conditions of possibility in power relations, and undesirable, in that most feminists bring (some version of) a commitment to changing the world to their study of that world. From its engaged perspective, feminist discourse views claims to professional neutrality as naive and bogus. Feminist discourse is explicitly tied to the feminist movement, both inside and outside of the academy. This connection is one of the great sources of vitality for feminist theory and practice; it gives feminist theorists something that most other political theorists and political scientists lack: an audience outside the university. It also stands as a rejection of both the knowledge claims of positivism and the staid politics of the profession, and is thus usually rejected as being "too political."

My characterization of the political and epistemological bases for political science's hostility to feminism implicitly raises some serious questions about the nature of feminist discourse. I have argued that political science ignores women, disqualifies and devalues women's experience. I have also suggested that feminist discourse, grounded in the characteristic experiences of women, can offer an alternative perspective on political and social life. But, given the colonizing impetus of mainstream political science, what would become of feminism if it were to be integrated into such a profession? Political science is a discipline, in the Foucauldian sense of the word, and it does just that — it *disciplines.* That is, it classifies, orders, and distributes knowledge claims. It is "a principle of control over the production of knowledge" (Foucault 1981, 61). Feminism, as a part of a struggle for liberation, has no desire to discipline; yet all knowledge, in its way, participates in the disciplining of experience.

Further, if the creation of feminist discourse is, as I have characterized it, the articulation of a conceptual net to cast across the vast, undifferentiated and processual field of experience, what distinguishes feminism from the conceptual net of its positivist opponents? All knowledge, in this view, is an imposition, an active ordering of the world that forces the experienced world to "fit." From genealogical theorists, such as Nietzsche and Foucault, we can understand something about this ordering process and about the will to truth that it entails. Following their lead, all knowing consists in articulating some particular perspec tive on the world. Objectivity, then, is not equated with disinterested contemplation but, in Nietzsche's words, with "having one's pros and cons in one's command" (1956, 255). Our views of the world consist of nets cast across a discontinuous temporal flux, necessary but inevitably partial efforts to capture that which is always in motion and to order that which never truly and completely fits. Feminists have become increasingly aware of the dangers to our own project that our epistemology entails. Consider, for example, the following passage from feminist theorist and poet Susan Griffin:

> But when a theory is transformed into an ideology, it begins to destroy the self and self-knowledge. Originally born of feeling, it pretends to float above and around feeling. Above sensation. It organizes experience according to itself, without touching experience. By virtue of being itself, it is supposed to know. To invoke the name of this ideology is to confer truthfulness. No one can tell it anything new. Experience ceases to surprise it, inform it, transform it. It is annoyed by any detail which does not fit into its worldview. Begun as a way to restore one's sense of reality, now it attempts to discipline real people, to remake natural beings after its own image. All that it fails to explain it records as dangerous. Begun as a theory of liberation, it is threatened by new theories of liberation; slowly, it builds a prison for the mind (1981, 280).

To draw upon feminist discourse for a critique of and an alternative to male-ordered political science, without losing sight of this Nietzschean warning about the will to truth, is the goal of the remainder of this essay.[3]

Constructing an Alternative Discourse

Feminist revision of political inquiry goes on at two different levels, each connected to — and in some ways dependent on but in tension with — the other. The first level consists of a process of adding to the existing body of knowledge: for example, exposing sexist biases in the literature of political socialization, political participation, voting studies, and so forth, or collecting non-sexist data bases for the conduct of similar types of studies (Lovenduski 1981, 93). Public policy analyses of issue areas relating to women — equal pay for equal work, pay equity, and comparable worth; pregnancy and child care policies; rape, wife beating, child beating, incest, and pornography — have become increasingly common and have added substantially to the theoretically threadbare subfield of public policy (Diamond 1983; Boneparth 1982). Other studies have asked "What were the women doing while the men were doing _____?" and have in this way filled in enormous gaps in our history, examining, for example, women's role in the labor force and the military in times of war, women's role in the trade union movement and the civil rights movement, women's role as clerical workers, women's role as clients (Evans 1979; Freeman 1984). In political theory, feminists have examined the treatment of women, reproduction, and the family in the writings of well-known political theorists (Clark and Lange 1979; Okin 1979).

The second level entails a radical rethinking of the traditional categories of analysis from the perspective that women's experiences can offer. Recognizing that women's place in our world is shaped by patterns of racial and class power as well as by gender, feminist analysis, at this level, seeks to understand and appreciate the important differences among women while at the same time articulating the common threads of women's lives in our society. Here the tacking back and forth between diversity and commonality in women's lives gives feminism enormous richness and complexity; it also provides an arena in which struggles among feminists over issues of racism, homophobia, and class bias take place (Hooks 1981; Koedt, Levine, and Rapone 1973). It is at this level that feminist discourse has begun to emerge; nascent voices offer accounts of the world from women's perspectives and while they sometimes seem to be more a cacophony than a well-tuned orchestra, they nonetheless offer a suggestive and vivid challenge to dominant, male-ordered accounts of the world.

It is difficult to exaggerate the resistance to both these levels of inquiry from the mainstream of political science. Beyond the continuing silence on the subject of women from most political scientists, Susan Bourque and Jean Grossholtz describe four types of difficulties with the literature: (1) the practice of "fudging the footnotes" by removing the careful qualifications when citing studies about women, such as Maurice Duverger's much-maligned *The Political Role of Women*; (2) the assumption of male dominance that many researchers bring with them to their material, which inclines them to see, for example, father dominance in the family as unproblematic and as reflective of women's own preferences for subordination; (3) the corresponding belief in the eternal feminine, that is, the faith that women are naturally the loving and willing subordinates of men; and (4) the definition of rational and relevant political behavior in purely masculine terms (1974, pp. 227–28). The first of these is a perennial problem in scholarship, reflecting both laziness and a desire to see only what one expects to see. The second and third, while still common, may be abating somewhat as male political scientists are berated for these practices by their (few) female colleagues. But the fourth has a tenacity all its own: the definition of politics in exclusively masculine terms, and the disqualification of any other perspective or activity, suggests an enormous psychological and institutional commitment to male dominance. Bourque and Grossholt's conclusion in their 1974 article is still right on the mark; they argue that within political science

> politics is defined as masculine activity. The basis for assertions of male
> political dominance and the unwillingness to take female participation
> seriously, derives from this definition of politics. Those characteristics
> and enthusiasms which supposedly sway men (war, controversy, elec-
> toral manipulation) are defined as specifically political, while those
> characteristics and enthusiasms which supposedly sway women (human
> needs for food, clothing and shelter, adherence to consistent moral prin-
> ciples, the pre-emption of national by human concerns, a rejection of
> war as rational) are simply not considered political. When women are
> being 'political' they are being more like men, and in fact, most women
> have learned to be just that (1974, 258).

It is the contested definition of politics that provides the most fertile
ground for the evolution of feminist discourse, as well as for revealing
the important but problematic relationship between the two levels of
feminist debate. Removing sexist assumptions and practices from existing models of inquiry and then applying those models more equitably
fails to challenge the basic presuppositions of the dominant mode of inquiry. At this level, feminists aim at "a revised standard version of the
political science of women, instead of at the development of a radical,
altogether innovative feminist Political Science" (Lovenduski 1981, 96).
It is understandable why this level of inquiry would prevail over the
other: it is somewhat easier to introduce into the mainstream, and it at
least allows feminists to get a foot in the door. It is also a lot easier to do.
As Nannerl Keohane has noted, "In women's studies, a good piece of
conventional wisdom holds that it is simply not enough to 'add women
and stir'. In political science, women are just now being added, and the
field has hardly begun to stir" (1981).

Adding women into established political inquiry can, then, result in
a capitulation to the limits and constraints of that inquiry. It can be a
form of what Foucault calls "misplaced resistance," a kind that appeals
to established doctrines for more equitable treatment and thus participates in the perpetuation of those very doctrines. Feminists who accept the constraints of positivism/behavioralism in their methods, and of
professionalism in their practice, present no real challenge to male-
ordered politics and sometimes get in the way of other's efforts to present such a challenge. At the same time, the demands to "let us in" can
sometimes shade into the more radical rethinking of politics and
knowledge that feminist discourse seeks. Efforts to "fill in the blanks,"
as it were, can eventually recast the enterprise itself, as the weaving in of
new and different "parts" reconstitutes the whole. For example, Jean
Elshtain's *Public Man, Private Woman* both relates what some major
political theorists in the Western tradition have said about families and
suggests an innovative reweaving of the relation between public and
private life (1981). Wendy Brown's article on reproductive freedom takes

up the longstanding "right to life" versus "right to choice" positions and develops from them a creative feminist analysis of the nature of rights within patriarchal capitalism (1983). Ann Douglas's *The Feminization of American Culture* both fills in some pieces of missing history about women in Victorian America and suggests a reinterpretation of that society, showing that history has to undergo radical revision in order to make room for "herstory" as well (1977).

To articulate fully the experiences and perspectives of women, recognizing that such experiences contain multiple threads and are constantly emergent over time, leads to a stretching and challenging of the established discursive domain. Mainstream practitioners of political science might, conceivably, choose to welcome feminist discourse as a breath of fresh air or take it as an intellectual challenge or at least look at it with some curiosity. Most, however, have done none of these things. Political theorists, in particular, might see feminist discourse as a vehicle for both opening the discipline to theory and opening up theory itself. Some of the same questions that, for example, Peter Winch and others raise about understanding across cultural boundaries could be directed at understanding gender differences as well, although of course the two are by no means identical. In both cases, to encounter, seriously, another way of life and to seek to understand it on its own terms is a political act that modifies and expands the dominant discourse. As Winch says:

> We are seeking a way of looking at things which goes beyond our previous way in that it has in some way taken account of and incorporated the other way that members of S [the other group] have of looking at things. Seriously to study another way of life is necessarily to seek to extend our own — not simply to bring the other way within the already existing boundaries of our own, because the point about the latter in their present form, is that they *ex hypothesi* exclude the other (1977, 176).

If the imaginative reconstruction of discourse can be anticipated with regard to Western encounters with so-called "primitive societies," might not women's experiences (which are more available to the dominant discourse, although perhaps also more colonized by it) do so as well? Consider Winch's appeal for cross-cultural appreciation, recouched with reference to women:

> What we may learn by studying [women's experiences] are not merely possibilities of different ways of doing things, other techniques. More importantly we may learn different possibilities of making sense of human life, different ideas about the possible importance that the carrying out of certain activities may take on for a [woman], trying to contemplate the sense of [her] life as a whole (1977, 182).

Challenging the Power to Name

Changes in the unfolding web of language are amorphous, opaque, and many-directioned. Language is a process and thus never simply stands still; conscious efforts to fashion a fresh discourse, like more random alterations in practices of speech and thought, are never completely new because they must somehow hook into the existing web in order to be intelligible. Efforts to change the common language by showing that it is not so common after all, that there are submerged and disqualified strands of discourse which have their own claims to make on our lives, are full of surprises, potentialities, and unintended consequences. It is unclear just exactly what feminist discourse(s) will look like, both because it is still emergent and because women's experiences in the world are not all of a piece; expressing both the diversity and the commonality of female experience will surely give rise to a complex, shifting, and many-layered field of meaning, and will also probably replicate some of the perennial problems of political theory, while shedding fresh light on others.

Two of the perennial problems that are most clearly featured in the clash between feminist discourse and political science are those dealing with knowledge and with power. Both are what William Connolly and others have called "essentially contested concepts," or rather, clusters of concepts; each serves, in Nietzsche's characterization, as "a fat word taking the place of a vague question mark" (1956, 266). I would like to conclude this essay by offering some modest suggestions about a feminist reformulation of power and knowledge and some speculations about the difference it might make.

From the conventional perspective of political science inquiry, women are generally thought to be naive about power; the public world, being primarily male in both its recruitment and its institutional configuration, dismisses women's "soft" notions about social relations as more fitting for the kitchen, the nursery, or the bedroom. But women are not ignorant of power; like any oppressed group, we know power through being recipients of it. More accurately, we participate in the vast web of power relations embedded in our society on radically unequal terms, as subordinates to men; we also exercise certain kinds of power, both directly, and indirectly, both legitimately (as in regard to children, the elderly, the sick) and illegitimately. It is important to understand power not as an object but as a process. Following Foucault, we can see power as a name for certain sets of relations running through the social fabric. Women enter into, are defined by, and in turn define themselves in opposition to these power relations in many ways.

A feminist redefinition of power calls for, in Nancy Hartsock's words, "a relocation of theory onto the epistemological terrain defined by women's lives" (1983, 151). Women theorists writing on power, whether they were self-consciously feminist or not, have tended to "stress those aspects of power related to energy, capacity, and potential" (1983, 210). In contrast to the masculine notion of the self as a 'walled city', as radically separate from others toward whom it maintains an essentially hostile or at least aloof distance, the concept of the self most adequate to women's experience stresses continuity and connectedness with others and acknowledges reciprocity of needs. For such relational selves power could be, not the ability to make people do what they would not otherwise do, but the ability to enable people to do what they could not otherwise do. Power could be translated into empowerment, the ability to act with others to do together what one could not have done alone. Empowerment stresses the cooperative dimensions of human interactions and seeks to engage our imaginations, extend our potentialities, enable us as collective actors, ultimately to enrich our lives.

These ideas about power are generally dismissed by the discourse of *Realpolitik* as naive, idealistic, and irrelevant to "the real world." But the real world, for women, is one in which relations with others, and the need for and responsibility to care for those relations, are every bit as "real" as the "war of all against all" that shapes male-ordered politics. If we indeed accept that power is not a thing but rather a set of relations, then would not different sets of relations, such as those characterizing the world of women, give rise to and reflect a different shape of power? Leadership, then, would lose its essentially military meaning and instead become more of a pedagogical and facilitative activity; rather than standing at the top of the hierarchy, the leaders would be those who stand at the center of the web, who stimulate and coordinate the activities of the others and serve as a focus for marshalling the energies of the whole.

Different feminists have elaborated upon this concept of empowerment in many ways. Nancy Hartsock, for example, has suggested a reformulation of the notion of eros that takes it away from the negative form dominant in our society, which stresses domination of the other, denial of the body, and fascination with death, and toward a more life-giving form stressing intimacy, creativity, sensuality, and generation. She argues that

> such an understanding of power would recognize that relations with another may take a variety of forms, forms not structured fundamentally by alterity but by distinction. The body — its desires and needs, and its mortality — would not be denied as shameful but would be given a place of honor at the center of the theory. And creativity and generation would be incorporated in the form of directly valuing daily life activities — eroticizing the work of production and accepting the erotic nature of nurturance (1983, 259).

Other feminist theorists have taken different approaches, but have arrived at similar notions about empowerment as a relational capacity, an interactive competence in the world. My concern here is not to recapitulate these ideas, but rather to take them seriously and see what sorts of questions they might lead us to ask about power. If empowerment were put at the heart of a feminist community, and egalitarian, participatory institutions were created to generate and sustain this empowerment, where might it lead? One can imagine that, even under the best of all possible circumstances, power-as-empowerment would always be exclusionary. The community could not pursue all possible courses of action; some would have to be selected over others. Empowerment, like its dark twin power, expresses/creates a certain truth in the world, not all possible truths. Empowerment, then, contains a tragic dimension; it must close off some possibilities in order to open up others. Those who are the leaders, who are closer to the center of the web, would most acutely bear the burden of empowerment's tragic face. They might protect themselves by projecting a false arrogance, or a deep humility; they might shrink back from any action or take too much upon themselves. In any case, the weight of lost possibilities would weigh heavily upon them. For a feminist community, then, Plato's question "Who will guard the guardians?" might be rephrased as "Who will care for the caretakers?" Balancing and maintaining the relationships within the community would be a constant and ongoing process, not a once-and-for-all settlement. Empowerment, like power, is a process.

The feminist emphasis on taking care and on embodiment suggests a refocusing of emotion in relation both to power and to knowledge. Emotion has, of course, been discredited in mainstream political inquiry as an "irrational" influence that interferes with one's "objectivity." Emotion is often described as an uncontrollable force that overpowers reason, usually with disastrous results. A feminist understanding of knowledge would relocate emotion, not opposite reason but in tandem with it. Feeling, like sight or hearing, is one of the ways in which we know the world. A person who suppresses his emotions, who is out of touch with his feelings, is denied a crucial point of connection with both the social and natural worlds. Nietzsche's invocation of feeling and knowing comes very close to the mark: "all seeing is essentially perspective, and so is all knowing. The more emotions we allow to speak in a given matter, the more different eyes we can put on in order to view a given spectacle, the more complete will be our conception of it, the greater our 'objectivity' " (1956, 255). Emotion, then, both sustains and derails our understanding of the world; feeling is a mode of knowing, central to perception, yet vulnerable to distortion and deception like any other way of knowing would be. The naming and expressing of feelings serves both to place those feelings within a field of meaning and also, potentially, to transform the feelings themselves.

To give credence to feelings as epistemologically legitimate ways of knowing the world is to call sharply into question theories of mind and self that stress only the cognitive. Models of politics based on such impoverished views of knowing would have to be seen as woefully inadequate. Defenders of positivism/behavioralism are likely to argue that feeling should be separated from knowing because feeling is not intersubjectively transmissible or verifiable; in other words, I cannot feel what you feel in the same way that I can see what you see. From the "walled city" of the masculine self, this is probably true; for men, who are likely to define their autonomy in terms of their cut-off-ness from others and from the other in themselves, feelings are unreliable and dangerous, not like "facts." But for those whose life training has been aimed at cultivating intuitive knowledge and connection with others, and who are deeply aware (sometimes all too aware) of the other within themselves, the question "How do you feel?" is as central to full comprehension as "What do you think?" Political language that denies and degrades emotions — such as, for example, that which defines "national security" in a way that makes people feel less and less secure — is not "objective"; it is simply impoverished.

The validation of feeling as knowing might also make political inquiry more receptive to the nonorthodox knowledge claims that some make with regard to the world of nature and of spirit. The world-views of the American Indians, or of many Eastern philosophies, are rendered incomprehensible by positivism's rules. But surely these world-views are/were comprehensible to their own subjects, so doesn't it follow that there is something inadequate and less then universal about knowledge claims that simply disqualify them? Perhaps something within the "bloomin' buzzin' confusion" might speak back to us, if we could only learn to listen.

The Difference It Makes

I have argued that mainstream political science is propelled by a rather heavy-handed will to truth, a belief that there is, at bottom, a single truth to be discovered and that all the uncovered parts of knowledge will slide smoothly into place in a unified picture. The carriers of this truth make themselves into instruments of it, imposing their needed schemes upon the multiplicity of sensations in lived experience and conflating their own partial and constructed encounter with the world with a full and universal account. One of the goals of feminist discourse, should it make itself heard within political science is, in Foucault's words, to "call into question our will to truth, restore to discourse its character as an event" (1981, 66). Feminism might, if taken seriously, loosen up the discipline (in both senses of the word) of political science, politicize the given, unsettle the settled, acknowledge the plurality of meanings as well as the imposition of meaning. We might force political science to respond to Nietzsche's question, "What would our existence amount to were it not for this, that the will to truth has been forced to examine itself?" (1956, 217).

Joni Lovenduski argues that political science's responsiveness to a genuine challenge from feminism is dependent on four related factors. The first is its openness to interdisciplinary perspectives and to epistemological questions. One of the advantages of feminism in the Nietzschean struggle with our own will to truth is feminism's denial of disciplinary boundaries. Again, note both meanings of the word "discipline": because feminist scholarship ranges widely across academic fields, it facilitates rebellion against both the arbitrary and self-serving imposition of academic boundaries on knowledge and against the inscriptions of power that knowledge carves on its subjects. Feminist discourse draws heavily on poets, novelists, and artists and (uneasily for many of us) on those attuned to the spirit, and it is from such ranks that the demystifiers and resisters often come. In a moment of questionable optimism, Lovenduski asserts that "there is theoretically no reason why Political Science should not be open to what will inevitably be interdisciplinary research initiatives" (1981, 95). Unfortunately, there are at least two good reasons to expect this resistance to continue: the discipline's commitment to its own thin version of science, and the professional self-interests of those who sell their wares to the state.

The second factor Lovenduski considers is the discipline's attention to women's changing role in government. There has been perceptible change here in recent years, as women enter state and local offices in increasing numbers and occasionally appear at higher levels as well. Political scientists have begun to study these women and their experience, thus pursuing the first level of feminist discourse by "filling in the blanks." This work is to be welcomed. But, as Lovenduski herself recognizes, if this is all that happens, then not much will have changed. Such work should be seen as, in her words, "preliminary to a confrontation with and a challenge to the way in which knowledge has come to be constructed in the Political Science profession" (1981, 96). The definition of "the political" has to be stretched to include what women do and say in their own lives, not just to what they say and do when they are imitating or pleasing men.

The third factor that Lovenduski discusses is the impact of women and of feminists organizing within political science. In the last decade, the feminist presence within political science has become perceptible; few political science conferences are without panels dealing with women and/or with feminism; more and more political science departments boast "women and politics" courses; and the relevant published literature continues to grow. But these courses, panels, and publications are still ghettoized within the discipline; the mainstream of political science stands apart from them, seemingly fearing too-close contact. The women and men who present an organized feminist presence within political science are doing some of the most interesting work in the field (if panel attendance and enthusiasm is any measure) but they are very much on, or beyond, the fringe.

Lastly, Lovenduski cites the quality of the new scholarship as an important factor determining political science's responsiveness to feminism. I would like to believe that the quality of scholarship determines its acceptability, but a decade of attending conventions and reading respectable professional journals suggests otherwise. In fact, it is precisely the definition of "acceptable" scholarship that is at issue here. Epistemological commitments to positivism/behaviorism and organizational commitments to professionalism and its attendant "neutrality," it seems, weigh more heavily than intellectual or scholarly claims. As I suggested earlier, given the solid boundaries of orthodoxy in the discipline as a whole, the academic fringe is a much safer and more interesting place to be.

Whatever the ultimate impact of feminism on the discursive and institutional practices of political science, it helps to remember the feminist critique of the discipline, if for no other reason than to keep an eye on our own will to truth. All interpretation does a sort of violence to the world; it casts a partial net, from a particular point of view, across the vast, ongoing, discontinuous web of collective life. All knowing, including feminist knowing, is an imposition on the world; an affirmation of one submerged discourse, for example, might distort or silence others, since there is no clear and predetermined 'fit' between them. And any submerged discourse carries the risk of becoming a mirror image of its opponent. Acknowledging the limits and the necessary falsifications of language, offering interpretations that are informed by an acute awareness of the violence they do to the possible world, staying attuned to that which might be lost, or never spoken, so that one might come back around to it again — this is the tentative and perhaps paradoxical task that I see for feminist discourse. Understanding the limits of self-reflection, we might nonetheless force examination of ourselves. The paradoxes entailed in the project of creating new truths while simultaneously combatting the will to truth might better be seen as a riddle, a rich and profound reflection of our ambiguous affirmations. The tension within this riddle is best sustained through the raising and maintaining of dialogues within and between various communities of discourse. Seeing that our claims to knowledge involve both liberation/resistance and domination/power, we could seek a mode of affirmation that allows difference to emerge and ambiguity to persist.

Notes

My thanks to Bill Connolly and the members of the 1984 N.E.H. summer seminar on interpretation and genealogy in political theory, especially Tom Dumm, Alex Hooke, and Kathy Jones. Thanks also to Chris Robinson for lending his knowledge about the history of political science.

1. This argument seems particularly vulnerable to misinterpretation. For the record: I am not saying that all women are the same, or that all men are the same; I am not saying that race and class are less important than gender; nor am I saying that women's moral codes are embedded in nature, or that they are ahistorical or constant. I am drawing upon the arguments that I made in my book *The Feminist Case Against Bureaucracy* (1984) and, through that book, on ideas developed in recent feminist theory.

2. This usage of "pragmatism," while common, does great injustice to William James, George Herbert Mead, Charles Sanders Peirce, and John Dewey, whose theoretical breadth and depth are a match to the European traditions of thought. For an interesting discussion of this see Michael Weinstein (1982).

3. There are substantial differences among feminists on these epistemological questions. Those who draw most heavily on Marx tend to accept his assumptions about the progressive revelation of truth in history. See, for example, Nancy Hartsock's *Money, Sex and Power* (1983); this otherwise excellent book bows too heavily to Marx and too often uses slippery concepts such as "real" or "scientific" to conceal knowledge questions. Other feminists adopt some other teleological perspective, claiming to uncover some underlying foundation for women's experience in the body or in nature or in women's greater spiritual wholeness. Others dispute teleology from a genealogical viewpoint.

References

Boneparth, E., ed. 1982. *Women, Power and Policy*. N.Y. Pergamon Press.

Bourque, S.C. & J. Grossholtz. 1974. "Politics as Unnatural Practice: Political Science Looks at Female Participation." *Politics and Society*, Winter, 225–66.

Brown, W. 1983. "Reproductive Freedom and the Right to Privacy: A Paradox for Feminists." In *Families, Politics and Public Policy*, edited by I. Diamond. N.Y.: Longmans.

Clark, L. & L. Lange. 1979. *The Sexism of Social and Political Thought*. Toronto: University of Toronto Press.

de Beauvoir, S. 1952. *The Second Sex*. N.Y.: Alfred A. Knopf.

Diamond, I. 1983. *Families, Public Policy, and the State*. N.Y.: Longmans.

Dietz, M. 1985. "Citizenship with a Feminist Face: The Problem of Maternal Thinking." *Political Theory*, 13, 19–38.

Douglas, A. 1977. *The Femininization of American Culture*. N.Y.: Alfred A. Knopf.

Dumm, T. 1984. "Toward a Neo-Hobbesian Theory of Power: Foucault and the New Nominalist Moment." Paper presented at the American Political Science Association Meetings, August 29–September 2, Washington, D.C.

Elshtain, J. 1981. *Public Man, Private Women*. Princeton, N.J.: Princeton University Press.

———. 1983. "Antigone's Daughters." In *Families, Politics, and Public Policy*, edited by I. Diamond. N.Y.: Longmans.

1979. *Personal Politics*. N.Y.: Vintage.

Ferguson, K. 1984. *Feminist Case Against Bureaucracy*. Philadelphia, Penn.: Temple University Press.

Finifter, A.W. 1983. *Political Science: The State of the Discipline*. Washington, D.C.: The American Political Science Association.

Foucault, M. 1972. *Power/Knowledge: Selected Interviews and Other Writings*. N.Y.: Pantheon Books.

———. 1981. "The Order of Discourse." In *Untying the Text: A Post-Structuralist Reader*, edited by R. Young. London: Routledge and Kegan Paul.

Freeman, D.M. 1977. *Foundations of Political Science*. N.Y.: The Free Press.

Freeman, J. 1984. *Women: A Feminist Perspective*, 3d. ed. Palo Alto, Cal.: Mayfield Publishing Co.

Freeman, M. and D. Robertson. 1980. *The Frontiers of Political Theory: Essays in a Revitalized Discipline.* N.Y.: St. Martin's Press.

Gilligan, C. 1982. *In a Different Voice.* Cambridge, Mass.: Harvard University Press.

Griffin, S. 1981. "The Way of All Ideology." In *Feminist Theory,* edited by N.O. Keohane, M.Z. Rosaldo, & B.C. Gelpi. Chicago: University of Chicago Press.

Hartsock, N. 1983. *Money, Sex and Power.* N.Y.: Longmans.

Hooks, B. 1981. *Ain't I a Woman.* Boston, Mass.: South End Press.

Hunter College Women's Studies Collective, The. 1983. *Women's Realities, Women's Choices.* N.Y.: Oxford University.

Keohane, N.O. 1981. "Speaking from Science: Women and the Science of Politics." In *A Feminist Perspective in the Academy,* edited by E. Langland & W. Gove. Chicago: University of Chicago Press.

Koedt, A., E. Levine, & A. Rapone. 1973. *Radical Feminism.* N.Y.: Quadrangle Books.

Lovenduski, J. 1981. "Toward the Emasculation of Political Science: The Impact of Feminism." In *Men's Studies Modified,* edited by D. Spender. N.Y.: Pergamon Press.

MacKinnon, C. 1983. "Feminism, Marxism, Method and the State: Toward A Feminist Jurisprudence." *Signs,* 8, Summer, 635–58.

Mansbridge, J. 1984. "Feminism and the Forms of Freedom." In *Critical Studies in Organization and Bureaucracy,* edited by F. Fischer & C. Sirianni. Philadelphia, Penn.: Temple University Press.

Nelson, J. 1983. "Political Theory as Political Rhetoric." In *What Should Political Theory Be Now?,* edited by J. Nelson. Albany, N.Y.: State University of New York Press.

Nietzsche, F. 1956. *The Genealogy of Morals.* N.Y.: Doubleday Anchor.

Okin, S. 1979. *Women in Western Political Thought.* Princeton, N.J.: Princeton University Press.

"Political Theory in the 1980s: Prospects and Topics." *Political Theory,* August 1981.

Pitkin, H. 1984. *Fortune Is a Women: Gender and Politics in the Thought of Niccolo Machiavelli.* Berkeley, Cal.: University of California Press.

Rorty, R. 1979. *Philosophy and the Mirror of Nature.* Princeton, N.J.: Princeton University Press.

Taylor, C. 1985. "Language and Human Nature." *Philosophical Papers*. Cambridge: Cambridge University Press.

Tronto, J. Forthcoming. *From "Women's Morality" to Humane Politics: Contextual Morality and Political Theory*.

Weinstein, M.A. 1982. *The Wilderness and the City*. Amherst, Mass.: University of Massachusetts Press.

Winch, P. 1977. "Understanding a Primitive Society." In *Understanding and Social Inquiry*, edited by F. Dallmayr & T.A. McCarthy. Notre Dame, Ind.: University of Notre Dame Press.

J. Donald Moon

10

Political Science and Political Choice: Opacity, Freedom, and Knowledge

One of the most attractive political ideals in contemporary life is the vision of a society in which political and social arrangements would be "transparent" to their participants. Rooted in positive conceptions of freedom as self-determination, the ideal of transparency anticipates a form of society in which people do not suffer from illusions about their own lives and activities, but rather are fully able to understand themselves and others. Because such understanding would be general in this society, and not the preserve of a special class of savants or scientists, social science as a specialized form of knowledge would largely disappear. A role for specialized social knowledge might continue to exist, particularly in the implementation of political decisions. But this role would necessarily be very restricted; the knowledge necessary for significant matters of political choice would have to be widely shared.

It is unlikely that anyone considers a fully transparent social order to be a realistic goal for large, complex societies. There are obvious, practical difficulties that stand in the way, such as limits of time, attention, and capacity to absorb and process information. But the problems with this ideal are not merely practical because, ultimately, the notion of a fully transparent social order is incoherent, and the attempt to realize it would require the sacrifice of the very values — particularly freedom — which make it appealing. What is genuinely important about the idea of transparency is best captured by the more modest notion of a "well-ordered" society, and that is a form of society in which social science will have a more robust role than the ideal of transparency would allow.

231

1. The Ideal of Transparency

The ideal of a transparent social order is closely linked to the idea of freedom, particularly the positive freedom of self-determination or self government, for ignorance is one of the principal impediments to a person's ability to determine oneself, to live an authentic and autonomous life. This is especially true when it is ignorance of myself — of my needs, my aspirations, and my capacities — that is in question. To the extent that I am ignorant in these ways, I will be unable to understand the meaning of my own actions and I will find myself drawn into and responding to situations in ways that I neither comprehend nor control. It may be difficult for me to set projects for myself, as I may find myself too uncertain about what I want, or the prospects of making important choices may cause me great anxiety. Perhaps worse, I may find myself unable to carry out whatever projects I do adopt, unable to live according to the goals and values I profess.

In addition to self-knowledge, I must also have a reasonable understanding of my situation. Otherwise, I will be unable to set realistic goals for myself or to plan courses of action which I can direct and which will be responsive to my initiatives and choices. It is not simply that I may find myself frustrated if my projects are unrealistic. In fact, I may well choose to pursue goals that I realize cannot be attained or that I recognize will be very difficult and that will surely involve my experiencing great frustration and even complete failure. As long as these are matters of choice, however, that kind of frustration should not be seen as an impediment to freedom. But, when I choose in ignorance, there is a sense in which I do not choose at all. I may believe that I have a choice between doing A or doing B, and choose to do A. But, if it turns out that A and B were not actually available to me, that in reality I faced a choice between C and D, then my attempt to do what I thought of as A will not merely be frustrating: it will also indicate a lack of freedom. For, in an important sense, I would not really be choosing at all in attempting to do A. Because I am deluded about the choices I face, I cannot set my own course or be self-determining. Instead, events will be governing me. At best I will be reacting to things that occur, to situations that confront me. Thus, to the extent that I or my world is opaque to me, my freedom of self-determination is limited.

As a personal ideal, this image of freedom and its linkage to knowledge — both of self and of situation — is at least as old as Socrates. The unexamined life is not worth living precisely because it is not a life worthy of a person. Such a life denies the capacity for freedom, for choice and self-determination, that makes us human.

Because we are social and political beings who necessarily live in association with others, this idea of individual freedom necessarily gives rise to a political ideal. Given the intimate connection between freedom and knowledge, not just any kind of society is compatible with the ideal of freedom as self-determination. In particular, social orders which systematically foster illusion, whose existence depends upon their being opaque to their participants, are fundamentally incompatible with human freedom for the reasons sketched above. Thus, we can say that freedom requires a society in which social and political relationships are transparent or, at a minimum, not opaque to the members of the society. This means that the major practices and institutions of the society must not only be freely accepted by its members, but they must also be rationally grounded, and the members of the society must have some understanding of the justifications of these practices. Otherwise, their adherence to these practices could only be understood as some kind of habitual or conditioned behavior, and such behavior could hardly be said to be free.[1]

In a rational society, the political arena will make collective self-determination possible; politics will be the sphere of social life in which "we", collectively and deliberately, determine the conditions of our existence. In a rational society, the political becomes a sphere of human freedom in which we make our own history. And, to the extent that we self-consciously determine the conditions of our (collective) lives, there will be a coincidence of social reality and appearance. The alienation of the individual from the society which is characteristic of existing forms of social life will be overcome.[2]

This line of argument leads to a certain ambivalence about political and social science. On the one hand, the political and social sciences may be seen to be symptomatic of a society that is not free. Because a free society is transparent to its members, there is a sense in which political and social science would be unnecessary, for we do not need science to teach us what is obvious, what is on the surface of things. Moreover, to the extent that social and political knowledge is "scientific," to the extent that it is systematic and theoretically organized, it will require special training to master, and it will therefore be the province of a particular group within society. But, this means that a society in which social science is required for political choice would be one in which there would be significant limits on the capacity of its members collectively to determine the conditions of their own existence. Because some would have a monopoly of the required knowledge, others would be dependent upon them, and their ability to set their own directions will be constrained. Of course, citizens would still have various means to control experts and to evaluate their advice, but there remains a certain tension between the need for political and social science and the ideal of positive freedom and a politics of collective self-determination.

On the other hand, political science can be seen to be potentially emancipatory, by playing a role in helping to bring about a transparent society. To the extent that we come to have a better and more accurate understanding of ourselves and our situations, we satisfy one of the conditions of freedom. Further, political and social science may advance human freedom by discovering the kinds of institutions and practices that are required for a rational society and by pointing out what must be done in order to bring such a society into existence.

This ambivalent nature of social science has attracted some attention from advocates of social transparency. For example, in an essay entitled "Karl Marx and the Withering Away of Social Science," Gerald Cohen explicates the nature of this ambivalence and tries to show how it can be reduced, although not fully overcome. He begins by endorsing the desirability of "a society whose intelligibility does not depend upon [social science]" (1972, 182), an idea he traces to Marx, particularly to Marx's conception of science as revealing the essence of things. Given this conception, science enable us to overcome the illusions from which we suffer by being confined only to appearances. Cohen correctly criticizes Marx's view of science, pointing out that science does not always show that appearances are illusory. Sometimes, he argues, science "uncovers a reality unrepresented in appearance," but does not "discredit appearance" (201). For example, when science discovers that water is made up of two elements that are gases under normal conditions, it does not lead us to revise any of our common sense ideas about water, such as our belief that water puts out fires. On the other hand, when science discovers that the earth is not the center of the universe, but revolves around the sun and rotates on its own axis, it does cause us to revise common sense ideas based upon the ways things appear to us. Once we have accepted the Copernican account of the solar system, we will no longer believe that the sun rises, but that the earth turns, causing the angle of the sun to a fixed point on the earth to change. Calling science "subversive" when it discredits common sense appearance, and "neutral" when it does not, Cohen argues that a form of society is desirable in which "subversive theory will be unnecessary and . . . neutral theory will be generally accessible" (203).

Cohen prefers a maximally transparent society because it is only in such a society that alienation can be overcome. As Cohen argues,

> it is desirable for a person to understand himself without relying upon theory. For there is a sense, difficult to make clear, in which I am alienated from myself and from what I do to the extent that I need theory to reach myself and the reasons governing my actions (202).

Thus, he continues,

> The need for a theory of the social processes in which I participate
> reflects a similar alienation from those processes. (203)

While recognizing that this alienation can never fully be overcome,
Cohen sees its abolition — and with it the abolition of at least subversive
social science — as an ideal to which we should aspire.

2. The Well-Ordered Society

In opposition to the ideal of a society in which alienation is overcome — in which citizens' understanding of social processes does not
have to be mediated by social theory — I would like to defend Rawls'
idea of the well-ordered society. In Rawls' analysis, a society is well-
ordered only if it satisfies what he calls "the full publicity condition"
(1980, 538). This condition requires that the "basic structure of society"
satisfy, and is *known* (according to accepted canons of knowledge) to
satisfy, publicly recognized and accepted principles of justice (537–38).
This implies that the "maintenance of social order does not depend on
historically accidental or institutionalized delusions, or other mistaken
beliefs about how its institutions work" (539).

A well-ordered society will be similar to a fully transparent society in
that it does not depend upon illusions, in the sense that "nothing . . .
need be hidden" (539). The maintenance of the society should not be
undermined by its members' coming to a fuller and more accurate
understanding of its structures. However, a well-ordered society need not
be fully transparent; indeed, it is even compatible with the existence of
social institutions whose appearance systematically differs from their
reality, so that they have a tendency to give rise to false or misleading
beliefs on the part of social actors. Thus, not only neutral, but also
subversive social theory, may flourish in a well ordered society.

I should emphasize that not all practices that give rise to illusion are
compatible with a well-ordered society. In some cases the need for
subversive theory will be indicative of a social reality that is oppressive,
or in some other way undesirable. For example, if we accept the Marxian
analysis of capitalism, apparently equal exchange between capitalists and
workers masks a social reality of domination and exploitation. If this account were completely correct, a well-ordered society could not be a
capitalist society, because it would depend upon workers' succumbing to
the illusion that markets involved equal exchange, an illusion that, by
hypothesis, would be necessary for them to accept capitalism as just. Indeed, part of the purpose of Marxism, understood as a critical theory, is

to unmask this illusion so that workers can see the need for and the possibility of a revolutionary transformation of social relationships.

Now, it might be suggested that the presence of a gulf between social reality and appearance will always be indicative of some kind of oppression. If reality must assume a form in which it presents an illusory appearance, then it must be oppressive — why else should it present itself in this way? If a social reality gives rise to illusions, it seems plausible to suppose that those illusions will be in some way be related to the continuation of that reality. Surely, it might be argued, that particular form of social reality in question will be sustained in part because of the fact that actors suffer from the illusions it generates. And a structure that depends upon illusions must be condemned by those who love freedom.

Supposing this (implicitly functionalist) argument were true, the critical issue is what it means for the existence of a social structure to depend upon illusions. It may well be that part of the cause of a particular structure's persisting is that people perform actions on the basis of false beliefs, thereby perpetuating it. But the structure may not be *dependent* upon their holding false beliefs, for they may have reasons to perform those same actions even in the absence of illusions. If they came to be enlightened by the work of social scientists, they might continue to perform the same actions because there may be other reasons to do so, reasons that do not involve the holding of false or illusory beliefs. Indeed, they may not fully abandon their false beliefs under these circumstances, but continue to act and talk as if they were true — just as we continue to speak of sunrises and sunsets.

Take, for example, the Marxian analysis of capitalism that I referred to above. According to this analysis, the treatment of human labor (or labor power) as a commodity is the basis of the alienation of the workers and of their exploitation by the owners of capital. Workers fail to realize this in part because they suffer from the illusions generated by the capitalist system, including bourgeois notions of rights and property that supposedly offer a patina of justice, masking the reality of unequal power.

In recent years, two Hungarian social theorists have analyzed the state socialist societies of Eastern Europe using Marxist categories and principles. They have argued that the attempt to replace capitalism by the "social regulation of production upon a definite plan, according to the needs of the community and of each individual" (Engels 1892, 712; compare Marx 1887, 80), in actuality leads to the creation of a centralized bureaucratic system. In this system, the economic "surplus" — production in excess of that required to reproduce the means of production and to meet the subsistence needs of the workers — comes to be controlled by the intellectual elite that staffs state and party bureaucracies. Naturally, entrance to this elite is controlled by educational institutions which are also in the hands of the intellectuals. In this system, the "fundamental interest" of the class which controls the surplus is "that the administrative system of purchasing labor-power — which necessarily entails the enforced sale of labor — should not give way to a genuine labor-market in which the price of labor would become the subject of transactive bargaining between legally equal, autonomous contracting parties" (Konrad and Szelenyi 1979, 225). On the other hand, it

> is the most elemental interest of the workers to raise the price of labor, removing the determination of the surplus product from the sphere of politics and changing the ratio of wages to surplus, to the advantage of wages. In order to achieve that, the purely administrative 'sale' of labor must be turned into a transaction; the sale of labor-power under government compulsion must be done away with, so that workers gain the right to decide themselves whether or not to sell their labor . . . and [therefore gain] the right to make the price of their labor the subject of collective bargaining in a real labor-market (226).

In other words, given that the abolition of the labor market has led to a bureaucratic organization of production that is at least as oppressive as capitalism, the workers' interests lie in the commodification of labor power.

I do not wish to defend the accuracy of Konrad and Szelenyi's analysis of the state socialist regimes of Eastern Europe, not to mention its generalization to other cases. My point is that if a generalization of this account were correct, then we would have a situation in which there would be good reasons for workers to support a social structure — the labor market — which gives rise to illusions even after they have come to realize that their perceptions are illusory. They could admit that the apparently equal exchange between owners or controllers of capital and workers masks a reality in which the former group has the power to dispose of part of the surplus production of the latter. But they might nonetheless support the commodification of labor power and possibly other practices of capitalist society, because they see no alternative structures that would, on balance, be better. While the commodification of labor power and the labor market might give rise to illusions, these practices may not "depend upon" illusions in the sense that social actors would have adequate reasons to sustain these practices even after they have been enlightened.

In a society whose social practices present an appearance that is at variance with reality, there is a crucial role for social science. For such a society could be, in Rawls' terms, a "well-ordered" society only if its members came to have an adequate understanding of these practices and accepted them in spite of their tendency to generate illusions. But, this means that they would have to have an adequate, scientific understanding of these institutions — and of the alternatives to them. Otherwise, they would not have a basis for believing that the social order actually satisfied publicly accepted principles of justice.

This is a very important problem, going well beyond the inherently controversial examples I have just given. There is good reason to suppose that certain aspects of social life (or at least of any conceivable social life) will systematically give rise to a disjunction between reality and appearance. At the most obvious level, this results from the fact that we live in large, complex societies. Because one's own experience will necessarily be limited, much if not most of one's knowledge of society will be indirect, impressionistic, and colored by one's particular circumstances and experience. An important role for social science research is to correct misperceptions arising from our (necessarily) limited experience. For example, in *The American Soldier*, researchers presented evidence to suggest that many commonly held beliefs about the American military during World War II were false. One striking example was their finding that soldiers in units with low rates of promotion were more likely to be satisfied with the opportunities for promotion in the army than soldiers in units with high rates of promotion (Stouffer, 1949, 250ff.). More recently, a panel study of American families conducted by the University of Michigan's Institute for Social Research has exploded widely held, but false beliefs about the nature of poverty in America. It is widely believed, for example, that there is a fairly large, identifiable stratum of "poor" people in America, which we have come to identify as those families with incomes below the "poverty line." In recent years, the size of the stratum has appeared to stabilize at some 10%–15% of the population. But Duncan and his associates report that this static picture belies a more complex, dynamic process in which families are continually moving into and out of poverty. Indeed, they find that only 0.7% of American families had incomes below the poverty line in every year of the decade (1969–1978) that they studied (Duncan 1984, 41). One of the things that is striking about this finding is that it overturns a widely held belief—one which underlies many of our social policies — which was partly a result of social science research in the first place.

In both of these examples, it is easy to explain why distorted or false beliefs are apt to arise. In the first example, outsiders are likely to misperceive how the situation will appear to those who are part of it because they may be mistaken about the standards people will use in evaluating their situation. In the case at hand, soldiers appeared to assess their opportunities for promotion by comparing their achievements to those of others whom they took to be similar and who were in their own units. In units with low rates of promotion, there was less cause for dissatisfaction because those who were weren't promoted had lots of company, while those who did receive promotions had reason to feel "unusually rewarded." The reverse occured in units with high rates of promotion. In the example of poverty, the misperception arises from the use of metaphors such as "structure" or "stratum" in describing and explaining society, which give rise to an unduly static picture. The assumptions and conceptualizations that lead to these errors are not in any way irrational or wrong-headed; that they lead to errors in these and many other cases could not be discovered without systematic and controlled observation.

It might be argued that the progress and dissemination of social science could gradually overcome these problems. While any individuals's personal experience will obviously be limited, this need not lead people to hold false beliefs if their education includes an adequate exposure to social science, and if the findings of social science enter into the common stock of beliefs, concepts, and ideas which are in part constitutive of our social practices, rules, and institutions.

The incorporation of what we might loosely call "theoretical" knowledge of society into the ongoing, practical culture of a people is surely an important process—part of the celebrated "reflexivity" of social science. We might even hope that the immediate effect of the advance of social science is to cause people's perceptions to accord better with social reality over time, although it often does not work that way. Even when the concepts and theories of the social sciences have revealed important aspects of society, these same concepts and theories may also have obscured or misled us about others. The example I presented above, in which the "stratification" model of society has played a role in sustaining apparently false beliefs about the character of poverty, is a case in point.

Quite apart from these problems, the very reflexivity of social science virtually guarantees that the progress of social science will not lead to a convergence between social reality and appearance. As social actors come to accept theoretical accounts of social phenomena, these accounts will become part of the social world itself, altering, in unpredictable ways, the very institutions and practices that had originally been described. This may occur in several ways. The most obvious is when individuals adjust their own behavior in accordance with their new understandings of the reality of certain institutions; this kind of mechanism has often been used to explain how inflation can become entrenched in an economy. In a more subtle way, the socially understood and accepted meanings of a practice or an institution may be altered by a fuller understanding of it, so that it comes to have a fundamentally different character, or becomes a matter of deep political conflict in the manner described by Ball in this volume (Chapter 4). While it is certainly true that social science can help to overcome the gap between reality and appearance, it also contributes to the very dynamism of society which constantly tends to re-open that gap.

3. Transparency, Freedom, and Alienation

The argument presented to this point is intended to show that the ideal of a society that is transparent to its members is chimerical. This is certainly true in that actors will inevitably be ignorant of significant aspects of their social relationships. More importantly, a well-ordered society may contain social structures which tend to cause members of society to acquire illusory or false beliefs. Such mistaken beliefs are likely to be generated in large, complex, dynamic societies. And while the progress and dissemination of social knowledge may contribute to the overcoming of such delusions, it may also contribute to the dynamic forces which breed new and different sources of opacity.

What are we to make of this situation? Is this something we should regret, an unrelieved evil to which we may have to resign ourselves, but against which we should protest? It would be odd, even in this post–Enlightenment age, to celebrate darkness and delusion, and I have no intention of doing so. But I will argue that our situation is not a matter for despair. Indeed, the ideal of transparency is, in an important sense, incoherent and must be qualified in significant ways if we are to gain our moral bearings.

One obvious way in which the ideal of transparency must be qualified, at least as an ideal for society, results from its tension with negative liberty. The freedom of individuals to make important choices in certain areas of their lives in accordance with their own judgments, and without having to answer to others who have authority over them for what they decide, is a major source of opacity in a society. To the extent that individuals are free to make such choices and to act on them, significant areas of social life will exhibit an unplanned and uncontrolled process of development. Social outcomes will not reflect social decisions reached on the basis of reasons that have been widely discussed and have become generally shared in the society. Rather, they will reflect concatenations of individual choices; they will often be unintended and may sometimes be undesired, leading to calls for collective action to correct them.

Markets are often — too often — used as the only example of a social practice embodying negative liberty and leading to unplanned and unintended social outcomes. Not surprisingly, advocates of forms of society in which alienation is overcome, in which social relations are as transparent as possible to their participants, tend to be hostile to markets for precisely this reason. Even granting that the organization and direction of production is of fundamental importance, this concentration on markets is altogether too narrow. The scope of negative liberty goes well beyond the freedoms of the market (which are, in any event, significantly constrained everywhere) to include the organization of culture, education, family life, religion, scholarship, science, and communications. Although it is true that even in liberal societies the state has been drawn into these realms, their basic commitment continues to be that "the state should not be the architect of social order, but that most social functions should be performed through collective undertakings emerging spontaneously within the political community" (Anderson 1984, 15).

To the extent that these wide areas of social life are not subject to authoritative, collective choice, basic aspects of society will develop in unplanned and uncoordinated ways. Under these circumstances social policy will often be reactive and adaptive. In recent years, we have seen this occur in the area of education and, increasingly, in family life, as dissatisfactoin with educational attainments or the concern with increasing rates of illegitimacy have prompted calls (as yet largely unheeded) for public action. Similarly, we have seen major changes in the role of women in our society, particularly regarding participation in the workforce; these changes have prompted some alterations in public policy, such as the adoption of equal pay laws or pressure for the Equal Rights Amendment. To a very significant extent, however, public policy in this area has reacted to social changes rather than directing them.

To the extent that significant aspects of our society result from the kinds of processes I have been describing, our understanding of the social life in which we participate will have to be mediated by the work of social science. We will not be able to grasp these phenomena directly or, unaided by theory, to see the reasons for the arrangements that evolve from the largely uncoordinated and spontaneous interactions of individuals. The reason for this is that these activities and arrangements are the result of individuals responding to their own assessments of their particular situations in terms of their own values and beliefs. Moreover, given the arguments advanced in section two, it is likely that some of these arrangements will also involve a significant gap between reality and appearance, so that our immediate or common sense grasp of them will be mistaken. Some degree of social opacity, then, is a price we must pay for negative liberty. While it can be reduced through increased knowledge and, if necessary, conscious political intervention, it would not be possible nor, as I will now argue, desirable to eliminate it.

The connection between negative liberty and social opacity that I have been arguing presupposes the value of negative liberty, of a significant sphere of activity in which individuals are free from legal or physical restraint to choose their own courses of action. At the beginning of this essay, I explained how the ideal of transparency was rooted in a positive conception of freedom, and so it might be thought that criticizing transparency in the name of negative liberty would be to beg the question at issue. For do not adherents of positive liberty reject negative liberty — and vice versa?

Unfortunately, this view is all too commonly held. Negative liberty is often contrasted with "positive liberty" in a way that suggests that these two notions are diametrically opposed to each other. But this is surely an error. If, as Berlin writes, "The 'positive' sense of the word 'liberty' derives from the wish on the part of the individual to be his own master" (Berlin 1969, 131), it necessarily requires that there be a range of actions over which the individual may freely choose — that is, it necessarily requires a certain degree of negative liberty. Berlin's famous essay, in which the distinction between negative and positive liberty is presented so forcefully, is often read as a rejection of positive liberty and an affirmation of a purely negative liberty. But this is an error. As he explains,

> to be free to choose, and not to be chosen for, is an inalienable ingredient in what makes human beings human; and . . . this underlies both the positive demand to have a voice in the laws and practices of the society in which one lives, and to be accorded an area, artificially carved out if need be, in which one is one's own master, a 'negative' area in which a man is not obliged to account for his activities to any man so far as this is compatible with the existence of organized society (lx).

Berlin's purpose in contrasting positive and negative liberty is to explain why it is that the concept of positive liberty has leant itself to the justification of totalitarian political orders and movements which have involved the denial of freedom — both positive and negative. This historical experience justifies us in insisting upon the importance of negative liberty, but it does not in any way suggest that an adequate understanding of human freedom could neglect its positive dimension.

Charles Taylor has suggested that positive freedom might be thought of as an "exercise-concept" of freedom, in contrast to an "opportunity-concept" that is central to negative liberty. Positive freedom involves the exercise of certain abilities — "one is free only to the extent that one has effectively determined oneself and the shape of one's life (1979b, 177). Negative freedom, by contrast, involves one's having certain opportunities, "where being free is a matter of what we can do, of what it is open to us to do" (1979b, 177). The burden of Taylor's argument is that a pure "opportunity-concept" of freedom is inadequate; in part, it fails to capture the notion of individual self-realization that is such an important value in our culture. But his argument equally entails the inadequacy of a pure "exercise-concept" of freedom. For what sense can be given to the notion that "one has effectively determined oneself and the shape of one's life" if one lacked the opportunity, indeed the right, to make important choices about the shape of one's life — if one were not permitted to shape one's life differently?

The standard response to this line of argument is to question the identity of the "self" that is said to be free. For if one is sufficiently opaque to oneself, if one is deeply confused and mistaken about one's fundamental needs and aspirations, if one is a prisoner of arrested desires rooted in the past which one is unable to comprehend or even acknowledge, then one cannot be free no matter what opportunities one confronts. Under these circumstances, we could hardly say that enlarging a person's opportunities would significantly increase his or her freedom:

> A man who is driven by spite to jeopardize his most important relationships, in spite of himself, as it were, or who is prevented by unreasoning fear from taking up the career he truly wants, is not really made more free if one lifts the external obstacles to his venting his spite or acting on his fear. Or at best he is liberated into a very impoverished freedom (Taylor 1979b, 192).

The policy of deinstitutionalization of mental patients may provide a less hypothetical example. As a result of this policy, large numbers of mentally ill people have been released from psychiatric hospitals into the "community." Unable to take care of themselves, some have become part of a homeless population, living in the streets and soup kitchens, "free" to be abused, victimized, and exploited.

These examples raise difficult and distressing issues. But even granting the full force of this argument, it shows at best that some degree of self-clarity, some capacity for making rational choices and for directing one's activities, is a necessary condition for being free. But, equally, some significant range of opportunities for action is also a necessary condition of freedom. Even if we agree (and it is not obvious that we should) that deinstitutionalizaton has failed to increase the freedom of the people who would otherwise be confined to psychiatric institutions, locking these people up again would hardly increase their freedom. And it would be monstrous to invoke freedom to justify a program of reconditioning the man in Taylor's example who is driven by spite or fear to act in self-defeating ways (compare Taylor 1979b, 190).

I have been arguing that freedom must be seen as a unitary concept, that positive liberty and negative liberty are different aspects, rather than opposed kinds, of freedom. Viewing them in this way permits one to see that the demand for full transparency is incoherent. The demand for transparency in our social relations is rooted in the ideal of positive liberty; but positive liberty requires negative liberty, and negative liberty in turn necessarily limits the transparency of our social relationships. Thus, the demand for full transparency conflicts with the very values of freedom and self-realization that are its ground. Moreover, to the extent that social opacity requires that our understanding of the institutions and social relationships in which we participate be mediated by the theoretical knowledge provided by social science, the distance or estrangement we experience in our relationships to others and to our society is an essential part of the human condition. Finally, to the extent that social opacity inevitably limits our freedom as essentially social and political beings, we can say that freedom itself is, in a certain sense, a self-limiting concept.

Before leaving this topic, I would like to suggest that this tension between the requirements and possibilities of freedom is not confined simply to the level of our social relationships. I would like to suggest — and I can only suggest at this point — that even at the level of the individual a similar dialectic is at work. Self-realization or self-determination obviously requires self-knowledge. The unexamined life is necessarily an unfree life. But the process of self-examination is also a distancing process, for it requires that one come to be able to distinguish what is genuine or authentic about one's desires and aspirations and what is not. It requires that one come to recognize the ways in which one may be enslaved to one's past, in which one may be acting on the basis of deeply confused or mistaken purposes. For if it is possible to be confused or mistaken in this way (and who would deny it?), then we could not know this directly, through introspection. We could only discover this if we could somehow test our immediate knowledge of our own desires, beliefs, or purposes, against a larger interpretative framework. Such a framework is required to test our desires and beliefs for their coherence and distinguish among those which we can, on reflection, affirm and those which we will come to change or discard. This testing will require some general understanding of human psychology. For it is only in terms of such a general understanding that we could articulate the principles, or what Wollheim (1984) calls the "constraints," on such interpretations. Further, such an understanding is required if we are to know how self-deception and self-misunderstanding is possible, the mechanisms that produce it, and the signs through which it is manifested.[3]

This necessity of "theoretical" knowledge for self-understanding in many ways parallels the role of social science knowledge in our understanding of society. There are, of course, obvious differences, not the least of them being that self-understanding begins with introspection and tends to end with self-change, while one's knowledge of society and one's effort to effect social change always remain "external" to oneself in an important sense. In both cases, however, one's relationship to oneself or to one's society is mediated in an important way be theoretical knowledge, so that the achievement of understanding invariably requires a loss of immediacy and the creation of a kind of distancing or estrangement. Freedom understood as self-realization or self-determination can only be achieved against a background of an identity, of a self, that is in some ways given. We do not so much create or determine ourselves as discover ourselves. Even if we understand the desire to be self-creative as the desire "to make of [oneself] what it satisfies [one] to be" (Plamematz 1975, 334), we must learn what genuinely satisfies us, and that learning, as I have argued, requires some degree of theoretical understanding of human psychology. Both self-consciousness and freedom, to the extent that they are possible, depend upon coming to understand, accept, and affirm much of what we must take as given.[4]

Nothing that I have argued here should be used to support the view that opacity is desirable in itself. What I have been arguing is that social opacity is intrinsically bound up with the values of freedom and self-realization, and these are the ideals which make ignorance and delusion the misfortunes that they are. Our goal cannot, therefore, be to make our social or even individual lives fully transparent, but to overcome those sources of error or ignorance which render us *prisoners* of our delusions. This task requires theoretical knowledge that can give us some understanding of our selves and our situations. But, as I argued above, there are critical limits to what social theory can accomplish. Even when it is successful in enlightening us in some ways, it may mislead us in others. Further, by becoming incorporated into social practices and expectations, theory can contribute to changes that neither theorists nor social actors could possibly anticipate and so be itself a further source of opacity. Much the same is true at the level of the individual. Moreover, the best of our theories are necessarily limited, conjectural, and subject to testing and revision, and so our undestanding of self and of our situation is always incomplete. Self-understanding is not a state that one can achieve, living thereafter in perfect self-clarity, at one with one's activities, capable of pure, unmediated spontaneity. The very fact that one's relationships to others and, in a certain sense, to oneself, must be mediated through theory means that we must live with an element of externality, of otherness or alienation. This is compounded by the limits necessarily attendant on the best of our theories. To believe that one can escape these limits is to live under the greatest illusion.

4. Conclusion

I have not said a great deal about the nature of social science, beyond stressing its general or theoretical character, and that it is cultivated largely by specialists. I have argued not only that there is no prospect for the withering away of social science, but that social science knowledge ought to play an important, indeed a central, role in political choice. In the short space remaining I cannot begin to characterize all the different ways in which social and political science might contribute to political choice, but I would like to call attention to one crucially important contribution, a contribution suggested by the discussion of the disjunction between appearance and reality in social life.

Situations in which such disjunctions arise are always problematic, especially when the practices or institutions involved tend to give rise to false or illusory beliefs. At the most obvious level, policies formulated in ignorance, or predicated upon false beliefs, may fail to achieve the results their authors intended. At a deeper level, ignorance of, or false beliefs about, society call the legitimacy of the social order into question. At the very least, their existence raises the question of whether the society is "well-ordered," whether it is known to be based upon and to satisfy publicly recognized and accepted principles of justice. I stress again that they *raise* such questions — they do not by themselves answer them. As I argued in section two, the mere existence of a discrepancy between appearance and reality does not demonstrate that the social order depends upon that discrepancy. The fundamental question is whether or not social actors have good grounds to accept the practice in question even if it tends to give rise to false beliefs. A crucial role for social science is to provide answers to that question.

Unfortunately, questions of this sort are very difficult to answer, because any answer would necessarily have to rest upon the truth of certain counterfactual statements. Specifically, one would have to be able to exhibit the range of possible institutional or social practices relevant to the matter in dispute, showing that the adoption of some alternate arrangement would be preferable to the existing arrangements or, alternatively, that no other possible arrangement would be preferable. In the example I used in section two, I argued that the Marxian critique of the commodification of labor under capitalism could be defeated if we were to accept and generalize the analysis that Konrad and Szelenyi give of the socialist alternative. But, as the mere statement of that example reveals, making such judgments is enormously difficult. In this case, for example, not only would we have to decide that their account of state socialism is essentially correct, at least in this regard, but that the alternative of an administrative system for allocating labor vs. a labor market exhausts the range of options.

At the present time, it is probably true that the social sciences do not have theories that are powerful enough to enable us to answer questions such as these with any confidence. It may, of course, turn out that we never will be able to do so. But the importance of these issues suggests that we should make an effort to do so, particularly by focusing more of our research and theory on what might be called questions of institutional design. For if the kinds of judgments that must figure in questions of political choice involve the comparison of alternative institutional structures, then social science can contribute to political choice by developing the kinds of theories that make such comparisons possible.[5]

Notes

I would like to thank Brian Fay and Nancy Schwartz for their very helpful comments on an earlier version of this essay.

1. This stress on rationality as a means of overcoming the disjunction of reality and appearance is characteristic of an important strand in political theorizing, uniting such disparate figures as Plato, Hegel, and Marx. One could imagine other ways in which freedom and even something like "transparency" could be conceptualized. One might, for example, have a conception of the self that would make its freedom depend not on knowledge, but on intuition, inspiration, authenticity of feeling, "blood knowledge," or some other nonrational or irrational faculty. In such a view, the role of "transparency" might be taken, for example, by the emotional quality of one's relationship to the group or its leader. While I will be concerned with the limits of reason, I will not consider these possible alternative understandings of freedom and their relationships to reason.

2. Many theorists for whom the distinction between reality and appearance is central do not suppose that this opposition can be fully overcome. Connolly, who offers a deep and suggestive account of modern liberal-democratic societies from this perspective, qualifies the ideal of transparency. In a footnote he writes, "I should note that I do not hold that the self can become fully transparent to the agent or that we can anticipate a society in which all dimensions of life are transparent to the participants" (1981, 204–205).

3. For an example of the kind of analysis that is required to address these issues, see Wollheim's excellent study, *The Thread of Life*, especially chs. 5, 6, and 8.

4. See Taylor 1979a, pp. 140–66 for an excellent discussion of these issues.

5. For an example of social theory that focuses on the problem of institutional design, see Carens (1981).

References

Anderson, Charles W. 1984. "Political Philosophy, Practical Reason and Policy Analysis." Paper presented to the 1984 meeting of the American Political Science Association.

Berlin, Isaiah. 1969. "Two Concepts of Liberty," reprinted in his *Four Essays on Liberty*. London: Oxford University Press.

Carens, Joseph H. 1981. *Equality, Moral Incentives, and the Market*. Chicago: University of Chicago Press.

Cohen, G.A. 1972. "Karl Marx and the Withering Away of Social Science." *Philosophy and Public Affairs* 1, 2, Winter.

Connolly, William E. 1981. *Appearance and Reality in Politics*. Cambridge: Cambridge University Press.

Duncan, Greg J. et al. 1984. *Years of Poverty, Years of Plenty*. Ann Arbor, Mich.: Institute for Social Research.

Engels, Friedrich. 1892. *Socialism: Utopian and Scientific*. Reprinted in *The Marx-Engels Reader*, 2d ed., edited by Robert C. Tucker. New York: Norton, 1978.

Konrad, George, and Ivan Szelenyi. 1979. *The Intellectuals on the Road to Class Power*. New York: Harcourt Brace Jovanovich.

Marx, Karl. 1887. *Capital*. vol. 1. New York: International Publishers, 1967 ed.

Plamenatz, John. 1975. *Karl Marx's Philosophy of Man*. Oxford: Oxford University Press.

Rawls, John. 1980. "Kantian Constructivism in Moral Theory: The Dewey Lectures 1980." *Journal of Philosophy*, 77, Sept.

Ryan, Alan, ed. 1979. *The Idea of Freedom*. Oxford: Oxford University Press.

Stouffer, Samuel A. et. al. 1949. *The American Soldier*, vol 1. Princeton: Princeton University Press.

Taylor, Charles. 1979a. *Hegel and Modern Society*. Cambridge: Cambridge University Press.

———. 1979b. "What's Wrong with Negative Liberty." In Ryan 1979.

Wollheim, Richard. 1984. *The Thread of Life*. Cambridge, Mass.: Harvard University Press.

Contributors

TERENCE BALL, the editor of this volume, is Professor of Political Science at the University of Minnesota. He is the author of, most recently, *Transforming Political Discourse*, editor of *Political Theory and Praxis*, co-editor of *After Marx* and *Political Innovation and Conceptual Change*, and a frequent contributor to professional journals.

FRED DALLMAYR is Dee Professor of Political Science at the University of Notre Dame. He is the author of several books, including *Twilight of Subjectivity, Language and Politics*, and, most recently, *Polis and Praxis*, in addition to numerous articles on political philosophy.

JAMES FARR is Associate Professor of Political Science at the University of Minnesota. He is co-editor of *After Marx* and has published articles on political theory and philosophy of the social sciences in *Inquiry; Philosophy of the Social Sciences; Political Theory, History and Theory; The Journal of Politics;* and elsewhere.

KATHY E. FERGUSON is Associate Professor of Political Science at the University of Hawaii. She is the author of *Self, Society and Womankind* and *The Feminist Case Against Bureaucracy*, along with numerous published articles.

MICHAEL T. GIBBONS is Assistant Professor of Political Science at the University of South Florida. He has contributed articles on political theory and philosophy of the social sciences to *Polity* and other journals.

RUSSELL HARDIN is Professor of Political Science and Philosophy at the University of Chicago. He is the Editor of *Ethics*, author of *Collective Choice* and of numerous articles on ethics and rational choice theory.

CONTRIBUTORS

JEFFREY C. ISAAC is Associate Professor of Political Science at Indiana University. His articles on critical philosophy of the social sciences have appeared in *Sociology, Polity,* and other journals. His *Power and Marxist Theory: A Realist View* was published in 1987.

J. DONALD MOON is Professor of Political Science at Wesleyan University. His articles on political inquiry, philosophy of the social sciences, and political theory have appeaared in *The Handbook of Political Science, Political Theory, The Journal of Politics*, and elsewhere.

STEPHEN K. WHITE is Professor of Political Science at Virginia Polytechnic Institute and State University. His articles on Habermas and critical theory have appeared in *American Political Science Review, The Review of Politics, Polity,* and other journals.

Index